Visual Effects Cinematography

Visual Effects Cinematography

Zoran Perisic

Focal Press

Boston • Oxford • Auckland • Johannesburg • Melbourne • New Delhi

Focal Press is an imprint of Butterworth–Heinemann.
Copyright © 2000 by Butterworth–Heinemann

ᐊ A member of the Reed Elsevier group

∞ Recognizing the importance of preserving what has been written,
Butterworth–Heinemann prints its books on acid-free paper whenever
possible.

 Butterworth–Heinemann supports the efforts of American
Forests and the Global ReLeaf program in its campaign for
the betterment of trees, forests, and our environment.

Stills from the film *GUNBUS*. Courtesy of J&M Entertainment Limited.

Library of Congress Cataloging-in-Publication Data

Perisic, Zoran.
    Visual effects cinematography / Zoran Perisic.
        p. cm.
    ISBN 0-240-80351-5 (paperback : alk. paper)
        1. Cinematography--Special effects.   I. Title.

    TR858.P474 1999
    778.5'345--dc21   99-042963

British Library Cataloguing-in-Publication Data
A catalogue record for this book is available from the British Library.

The publisher offers special discounts on bulk orders of this book.
For information, please contact:
Manager of Special Sales
Butterworth–Heinemann
225 Wildwood Avenue
Woburn, MA 01801-2041
Tel: 781-904-2500
Fax: 781-904-2620

For information on all Focal Press publications available, contact our
World Wide Web home page at: http://www.focalpress.com

10 9 8 7 6 5 4 3 2 1

Printed in the United States of America

For Chloe Anne

Table of Contents

Foreword

When I started out in the visual effect field there were hardly any books available on the subject by "hands on" practitioners of the craft. The established leaders in this field believed in keeping the secrets to themselves and, in some cases, even from their closest associates. Early on in my career I had the good fortune of working on Stanley Kubrick's *2001–A Space Odyssey*, where experimentation was not only welcomed, but positively encouraged. As a result, a high proportion of the young camera technicians of the "class of *2001*" have gone on to achieve considerable success in the visual effects field as Directors of Photography or VFX Supervisors and several have been awarded Oscars for their work.

To a newcomer in the field today, visual effects in blockbuster movies can appear overwhelmingly complex and difficult to comprehend. However, all effects shots can be analyzed in isolation and broken down to reveal the elements making up the composite. Armed with the knowledge and understanding of the visual effect tools now available to the filmmaker, it becomes relatively easy to figure out how a particular effect was accomplished.

All new techniques build on existing ones and add to the arsenal available to the filmmaker. In order to find the most efficient solution to any particular visual effects problem, it is essential to have an understanding of all possible alternatives. I hope that not only newcomers to the visual effects field but also those already working in one particular area or who encounter visual effects from time to time in their production capacity will benefit from reading this book. It is also hoped that the nontechnical people, particularly the studio "suits," will benefit from reading at least Part 1 of this book.

"Those who are enamored of practice without science are like sailors who board a ship without rudder and compass, never having any certainty as to whither they go."

—*Leonardo da Vinci*

Visual Effects Cinematography epitomizes this perhaps better that any other art form.

There are two basic areas of special visual effects: **PHYSICAL EFFECTS** (explosions, special mechanical rigs, support system, stunts, etc.) and **PHOTO-GRAPHIC** or more precisely **CINEMATOGRAPHIC FX** (i.e., anything involving the recording and manipulation of an image)—also referred to as Optical Effects (opticals) or Visual Effects. It is this latter category that is the subject of this book.

Zoran Perisic
September 1999, Los Angeles

Acknowledgments

I would like to thank my friends Greg McMurry and Bruce Logan for taking the time to read the manuscript and to discuss various aspects of visual effects production and for their many helpful suggestions.

PART I

The Creative Approach

This section deals with the various options available to the filmmaker in selecting the most effective approach to a variety of visual effects problems.

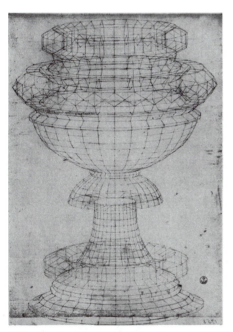

"The Chalice" by Paolo Uccello, circa 1450

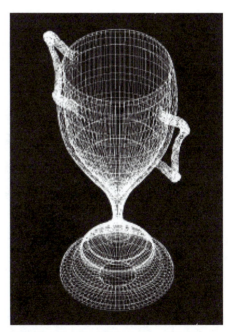

"The Trophy Cup" by Acumodels, circa 1999 (www.acuris.com)

> *The thing that has been is that which shall be . . . and there is nothing new under the sun.*

Acquisition of knowledge is a truly humbling experience.

Understanding Visual Effects

Visual effects can be divided into four basic categories, each of which will be introduced in this chapter:

1. Models and Miniatures
2. Matte Paintings and Stills
3. Live-Action FX
4. Animation — Cell or Computer-Generated

Each category consists of several elements. A visual effects shot may incorporate one or more elements from these categories. (See Figure 1.1.)

MODELS AND MINIATURES

The following provides brief descriptions of the elements in this category.

a) Mechanical or Animatronic Models: For example, a model airplane against real sky or terrain; or an animatronic puppet in a real setting. Commonly used for airplane crashes and explosions.

b) Mechanical and/or Animatronic models photographed in front of neutral backgrounds for compositing with various types of background elements at a later date or by direct-compositing methods such as process projection.

c) Miniature sets: For example, a moon landscape. Commonly used for alien, inaccessible, or unavailable locations and sets; explosions, floods, collapsing buildings, fires; and so on.

d) Background plates of Models, Miniature sets, or a combination of the two, which are later composited with a foreground element that may be live action, animatronics, or a model.

VFX Categories and Their Elements

1. Models and Miniatures
    a) Mechanical or animatronic models against real backgrounds
    b) Mechanical and/or animatronic models against neutral backgrounds
    c) Miniature sets
    d) Background plates of models and/or miniature sets
2. Matte Paintings and Stills
    a) Full paintings or stills
    b) Partial paintings or stills
    c) Background plates of paintings or stills
3. Live-Action FX
    a) Background plates—live action
    b) Actors against real backgrounds
    c) Actors against neutral backgrounds
    d) Live animatronic characters
4. Animation—Cell or Computer-Generated
    a) Captions and animated overlays
    b) Animated characters
    c) Background plates—animated
    d) Animated and rotoscoped mattes

Figure 1.1   Graphic flowchart

MATTE PAINTINGS AND STILLS

The following provides brief descriptions of the elements in this category.

a) Full paintings or stills where the entire frame consists of a matte painting or a photograph, such as cityscapes (particularly futuristic), landscapes, and complex interiors.

b) Partial paintings or stills, where only a section of the frame is made up of a painted element or photograph. For example, a cityscape above a live-action element that may be either a set or a location, or a sky painting above a miniature set. Removal of wire and other supports, such as TV aerials, and so on, also comes into this category. There is a choice of techniques for compositing these partial matte paintings (or stills) with other elements. (See Chapter 3, "Visual Effects Compositing.")

c) Background plates: A full frame painting or a photographic still can be used as a background for compositing with foreground elements. Large format stills (5" x 4" and 10" x 8") are often shot for use as background plates for compositing with foreground elements at a later date. A background plate can also be produced in two or more steps whereby a still or a painting is composited with another element such as a model or a miniature to produce a composite background plate, which is then used for compositing with the live-action element.

There are several techniques for compositing these elements. (See Chapter 3, "Visual Effects Compositing.")

LIVE-ACTION FX

The following provides brief descriptions of the elements in this category.

Background Plates

Live-action background shots filmed for later compositing with principal actors are commonly referred to as background plates. They include, for example, tracking shots through city traffic to be composited later with principal actors riding in cars; flying shots; dangerous stunts such as explosions; and so forth.

There are obvious advantages to shooting background plates in remote or dangerous locations and compositing them later with the principal actors photographed on a studio stage. A more subtle advantage involves photographic considerations. For example, when shooting at night in a dimly lit environment at wide-open aperture, the resultant shallow depth of field (focus) does not offer much scope for creative lighting. It is also easier to coordinate foreground action and lighting effects with the background if the background plate has already been shot. In addition, it may be necessary to shoot the background at a different frame rate for the purposes of speeding up or slowing down the action. At the compositing stage, the camera speed can be varied again with the actors in order to achieve a desired effect, such as a man in the foreground moving in slow motion while the action in the background is speeded up.

Actors against Real Backgrounds

When photographing dangerous stunts such as collapsing buildings or pyrotechnic explosions, the illusion of danger will be enhanced if the principal actor is clearly recognizable in the shot instead of a stunt double. Visual effects can be used to create this illusion without endangering the actor, as in Figure 1.2.

This type of shot requires either a locked-off camera or a matching-motion control move. (See Chapter 10, "Motion Control Camera and FX.") An effective way of adding movement to a shot of this type without resorting to full motion control is to shoot both passes on a large format film (e.g., VistaVision) and then pan across the composite in the standard format. (See Chapter 3, "Visual Effects Compositing.")

Figure 1.2 An actor takes cover behind a tree trunk as the car explodes behind him. The action with the actor is shot first. Soon after, the car explodes, but without the actor in the shot. These two elements are then composited by a simple split-screen method with the matte line running along the outline of the tree trunk.

Actors against Neutral Backgrounds

Actors are often photographed in front of neutral backgrounds for compositing with various types of foreground or background elements at a later date. This is the travelling matte approach to compositing. It is a two-step process in which the actor is photographed in front of a screen of a neutral color such as blue or green. A high-contrast silhouette of the actor is then extracted from the original negative and used to hold back a clear area on the background plate so that the image of the actor can be inserted into it during the compositing process; this is called the color-difference method. In certain circumstances, a matte can be extracted successfully from a clear white or a black background using the contrast-difference method.

The compositing can be done either optically or digitally. (See Chapter 3, "Visual Effect Compositing.") An actor can also be photographed in front of a suitable screen onto which the background picture is projected resulting in a "one step" composite. This is called the process projection method. (See Chapter 11, "Process Projection.")

Live Animatronic Characters

These are usually actors in creature costumes with partially or fully articulated features. The photographic requirements involving these "live" animatronics is much the same as with regular actors, except that these types of shots often need additional "cleaning up" in order to remove unwanted objects such as supports, wires, cables, and so forth.

They can be shot against real backgrounds or against neutral backgrounds for later compositing with various types of background and/or foreground elements. This latter approach is particularly useful where the animatronic character has to be scaled up or down from normal size.

ANIMATION — CELL OR COMPUTER-GENERATED

The following provides a brief description of the elements in this category.

Captions and Animated Overlays

A caption superimposed over a live-action scene is perhaps the most basic and certainly the most underrated of visual effects, yet it is an effect that in its most sophisticated form uses all the skills and technology usually associated with the more "flashy" examples. For example, a caption with gold lettering would not look golden if superimposed over a blue sky because the colors on film negative mix in the same way as on a palette. Therefore, a "holdout matte" is necessary to keep the colors from mixing. If the caption is to move around the screen, the "holdout matte" becomes a "travelling matte" — just as in any other effects shot employing this particular compositing technique.

Animated overlays such as sparkles, shimmers, glowing effects, and others also fall into this underrated but very important category. (See Chapter 9, "The Animation Rostrum Camera and FX.") Captions and animated overlays created on a computer have an advantage of being able to generate their own mattes and can be composited with the background plate digitally. However, the cost of transferring the background plate from film to digital media, and then transferring the composite back to film negative, should be taken into account when less costly alternatives are available. (See Chapter 8, "Optical Printers and FX.")

Animated and Computer-Generated Characters or Objects

An animated character or object in a live-action scene can originate either as:

1. cell animation,
2. computer generated image (CGI), or
3. three-dimensional puppet.

The animation element is composited with the live-action background plate either digitally or optically. Three-dimensional puppets can also be composited by process projection.

Cell animation is generally used for stylized, cartoon-type characters (*Pete's Dragon*), and CGI covers the full range, from cartoon-type characters (*Toy Story*) to photorealistic images (the dinosaurs in *Jurassic Park*).

Animated and Rotoscoped Mattes

A less obvious use of both traditional cell animation and digital animation is in generating mattes for various effects from animated "wipes" that obscure portions of the image of the outgoing scene and replace them with selected portions of the incoming scene, to more complex "morphing" effects where one image transform into another.

Rotoscoping is a technique whereby an outline is traced of a chosen image for each frame of action. A matte is then derived from this and used to obscure part of the frame that needs replacing; a countermatte made from the original matte is then prepared so that the replacement image can be inserted in the corresponding position of the frame without an overlap.

Background Plates

When a shot requires the compositing of a live-action character in an animated background, a background plate is prepared as a separate element. This may range from a simple background painting (cell-animation style) to full animation, including cartoon characters that interact with the live-action character (e.g., *Mary Poppins* and *Who Framed Roger Rabbit?*).

Background plates produced as Computer Generated Images (CGI) can range from stylized to photorealistic. Potentially one can construct a virtual image set and then select the appropriate camera angles and moves within that set to produce a background plate.

This is an excellent approach when a stylized "computer" look is required for the backgrounds. However, there are considerable limitations when it comes to totally photorealistic sets due to the enormous amount of information that needs to be stored in digital form. Limiting the size of the virtual set or the extent of camera moves can help to reduce the computer storage and memory requirements. Another option is to select a section at a time of the virtual set and output the computer-generated image to a large format still (5" x 4" or 10" x 8"). This allows for the creation of a very detailed, high-quality photorealistic image that can then be composited with the live-action element as process projection.

A "moving" background plate generated as a CGI can be composited with the live-action element in two ways:

a) The live-action element is transferred to digital media and, since the background is in digital form already, the two are composited digitally.
b) Alternatively, the CGI background plate can be transferred to film (preferably to a large format like VistaVision) and composited as process projection.

2

Mattes and Methods of Generating Them

WHAT ARE MATTES?

By far the largest part of visual effects work involves combining two or more elements into the same picture. This is accomplished by masking off one area of the frame while exposing another and then reversing the procedure for the second element. For example, a typical split-screen effect is created with the split line running vertically down the middle of the frame: the left-hand side of the frame has image A and the right-hand side has image B. Image B may be entirely different from image A, or both images may be depicting a different action from the same shot (see Figure 1.2, an illustration of an explosion in the background with an actor in the foreground). This technique is also used when an actor is required to play more than one character in the same frame.

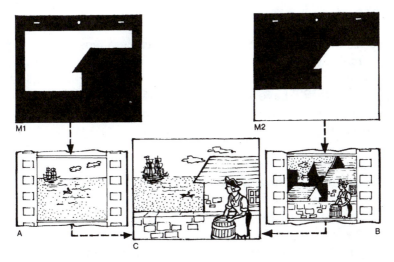

Figure 2.1 Split-screen matting. M1-matte used with scene A; M2-countermatte used with scene B. C is the composite of scenes A and B. The sharpness of the line joining the A and B elements defines the matte as a "soft edge" of a "sharp-edge" matte.

The shape of the matte and countermatte varies according to the specific shot. The matte line may take the form of a geometric shape, or it may follow the contours of a specific feature within the image, such as the edge of a building, the horizon line, and so on. Mattes and countermattes are complementary to each other whatever their shape. A holdout matte in the shape of a circle is commonly referred to as a "male matte" and its countermatte as a "female matte."

There are two basic type of mattes, "fixed mattes" and "travelling mattes."

Fixed Mattes (Static)	Travelling Mattes (Moving)
External (in front of lens)	Physical mattes
Internal (behind lens)	Photographic mattes

Figure 2.2   Types of mattes

FIXED MATTES

A static or fixed matte is mostly associated with "in-camera" techniques of visual FX compositing. They consist of the following categories:

1. External
2. Internal
3. Glass shots
4. Mirror shots
5. Self-matting miniatures

External Mattes

These are physical masks placed in front of the camera lens. They are usually of a simple geometric shape cut out of black card and placed in the filter holder on the lens hood or on a solid frame some distance in front of the lens. If the cutout is in focus the matte will have a "sharp-edge" look, and if it is out of focus it will have a "soft-edge" look. The degree of softness of the edge of this type of matte and countermatte is determined by these factors:

1. Focal length of the lens
2. Primary focus setting of the lens
3. Distance of the mask from the lens
4. F-stop (aperture setting)

External mattes are inherently more suitable for a soft-edge effect. A "hard-edge" effect requires the mask to be positioned within the "depth of field" focus range of the lens at the chosen f-stop. This inevitably means that it is placed at some distance from the lens. The edge of the mask can be brought into sharper focus with the use of a lens with a wider angle or by stopping down the lens iris and so increasing the depth of field. Matching the line-up of the matte and countermatte is of critical importance but so are the other factors: focus, f-stop, and relative distance from lens.

A useful variation on this technique is to shoot several takes of the same scene under identical conditions and only process one take, holding the rest in cold storage. Each take must have a frame mark (an outline of the frame in the camera gate) at its head (or tail) to ensure correct line-up when the film is loaded into the camera again for the second run through the camera at a later date. The negative of the processed take is projected through the camera so that a countermatte can be aligned correctly to the original. It is also important that all the other factors involved in shooting the first element are replicated. A first-generation composite can be produced in this way combining two or more elements on the original negative.

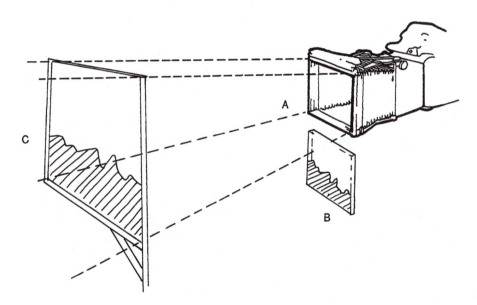

Figure 2.3 A matte box can be used to carry masks attached to clear glass (B). A mask placed farther away from the lens can produce a "sharp-edge" matte (C).

Internal Mattes

A physical mask can be placed inside the camera between the lens and the film plane. Certain cameras have a "behind-the-lens" filter slot that can be used to carry a mask and countermask.

The sharpness of this type of mask is much harder to judge without shooting a test since it cannot be seen through the viewfinder. It is affected by two factors: the distance to the film plane and the f-stop, since the f-stop determines the depth of the "back focus" of the lens in the same way as it determines the "depth of field" focus range in front of the lens but obviously over a much smaller distance. It is quite difficult to achieve a perfect line-up between a matte and a countermatte with this approach.

Some specialized cameras also have an effects attachment with movable masking blades that provide a vertical or horizontal matte and countermatte at any point of the frame.

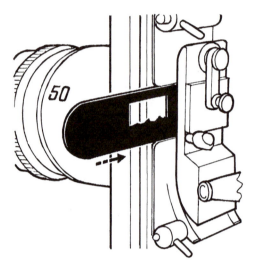

Figure 2.4 Mask inserted in the camera gate.

Glass Shots

A matte painting (or a photographic cutout) is placed on a large sheet of glass mounted in a support frame and placed at a distance from the camera. The live-action part of the scene is visible through the clear portions of the glass; the painting (or photo cutout) acts as its own matte, holding out the areas of the scene that will be replaced by it. The illumination on the painting is matched to that of the background scene and a first-generation composite is achieved.

As with the standard external matte and countermatte approach, careful consideration must be given to the perspective in the preparation of the painting so that the matte line is undetectable. The blending of the painting with the real background is affected by the sharpness of focus, which in turn is determined by the following:

1. Primary focus setting of the lens
2. F-stop (lens aperture setting)
3. Distance of matte painting from the lens

Care must be taken in staging the background action so that the actors do not disappear behind the matte line—unless of course this is intentional, as in the case of going behind a building.

This approach also offers the possibility of camera moves over the composite image during the take. The camera is mounted on a "nodal head" that is specifically designed for this purpose (see Figure 5.17). In order to avoid a perspective shift between the glass painting and the background scene, the camera lens must remain on its nodal point during the panning and tilting operation.

1

2

Figure 2.5   (1) Glass with additional features painted on it, placed between the camera and the exterior scene. (2) Composite scene of glass shot.

A nodal pan may be compared to the movement of the eye across a scene, whereas a regular pan may be compared to the movement of the head to scan the same scene. If you register the position of an object in the foreground in relation to some other object in the background and then scan the entire scene with your eye as far as you can see, you will notice that there is no shift between the two points. However, when you do the same exercise of noting a foreground object then scan the scene by moving your head, the shift becomes immediately apparent.

This is an extremely effective visual FX technique for producing first-generation composites in one pass. The only drawback is that it requires some advance planning and a decision regarding the camera position several days prior to the shoot in order to prepare the glass shot.

A note of caution on the choice of glass: a standard sheet of glass without any obvious distortions may be adequate in most cases. However, this type of glass produces a certain amount of color distortion that affects the live-action scene, adding a green bias to it. The ideal glass for this purpose is the "water white" type.

Mirror Shots

Mirror shots make it possible to combine a live-action element and a painting (or a photograph) by using direct photography in one pass. It also allows actors to appear to go behind a foreground object. Camera moves are possible with the use of a nodal head (panning, tilting, and limited zooms).

Mirror shots require the use of a front-silvered mirror that has the reflecting surface applied to the front of the glass by a vacuum-coating process. Ordinary mirrors of the domestic variety have the reflective coating applied on the rear surface of the glass so that the light has to go through the glass before reaching the reflective surface; this produces a secondary reflection from the first surface that appears as a faint ghost image.

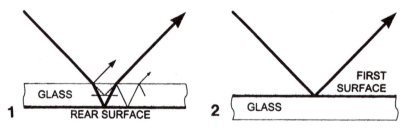

Figure 2.6 (1) Reflection from a regular mirror. (Note ghosting effect of additional reflections.) (2) Reflection from a front-silvered mirror.

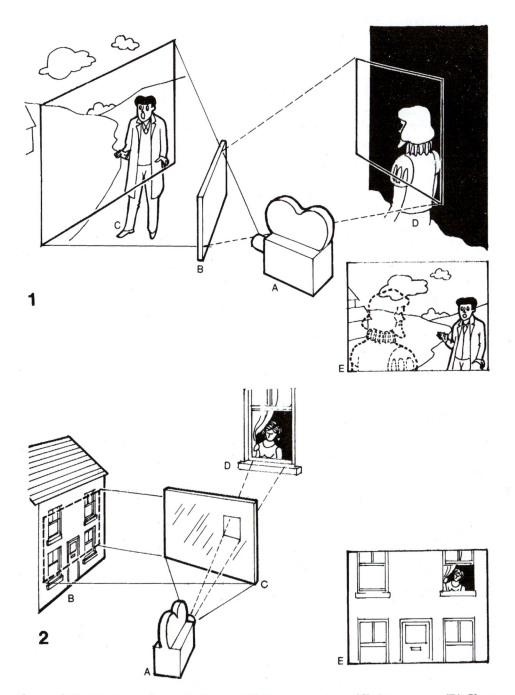

Figure 2.7 (1) Ghost effect. (A) Camera. (B) Two-way mirror. (C) Actor on set. (D) Ghost actor in front of black backing. (E) Composite. (2) Mirror matting. (A) Camera. (B) Miniature. (C) Front-silvered mirror with clear section. (D) Live-action set. (E) Composite.

The edge of a mirror placed in front of the camera lens and partially obscuring the scene acts as both a matte and a countermatte. The secondary image reflected in the mirror is positioned to the side, above, or below the field of view of the primary image. This image should be prepared with reversed geometry (mirror image) in order to appear correctly when reflected in the mirror.

A variation on this is to place the mirror so that it obscures the entire field of view of the lens. Then, by carefully scraping off the mirror coating in a chosen area, the insert scene is visible through the clear glass. A countermask (male matte) may be needed in certain circumstances in front of the reflected image to prevent "ghosting" due to partial reflections in the clear glass. If the scene reflected in the mirror is a photograph or a painting, the countermatte may be in the form of an area painted black on the artwork.

A custom mirror can be made with a clear area and a reflective area on the same piece of glass by masking off the chosen area before the silvering process. There is also a technique by which a silver coating can be sprayed directly onto the glass. The results are not as good or as durable as with the vacuum coating process, but this method has two distinct advantages: (1) the masking and the silvering can be done in situ, and (2) much larger areas of glass can be used.

Self-Matting Miniatures

A miniature strategically placed in front of the camera lens can create the illusion of extending a set. For example, a miniature building placed close to the edge of the frame can be used to mask off an unwanted area of a street set and at the same time can make the set appear larger than it really is. In addition, the actors can go behind the building as if it were a real, full-size set piece. By lighting the miniature set to match the background and ensuring for an adequate depth of field, a realistic appearance is achieved. Often a deliberate soft focus on the foreground miniature can also add to the illusion. When the miniature has to be in sharp focus but the depth of field at the working f-stop of the lens cannot reach back far enough, a split diopter attachment can be used to bring the selected area into focus.

This type (see Figures 5.13a and b) of self-matting miniature is commonly referred to as a "hanging miniature." One of the most frequent uses for a hanging miniature is to add a ceiling to a large interior set. The miniature of the ceiling is "hung" in a strategic position in front of the lens so that it blends with the background set. The obvious advantage of this approach is that it eliminates the cost of constructing a full-size ceiling. The less obvious one is that it helps to hide the lamps that are positioned along the top of the set and used to light the scene. Panning and tilting camera moves are possible with self-matting miniatures when the camera is mounted on a nodal head.

TRAVELLING MATTES

In those cases where an object being composited into a background image moves around in the frame, the mask (or the matte) of that object has to move in exactly the same way. Mattes and countermattes of this type are referred to as "travelling mattes."

Physical Travelling Mattes

The simplest example of this type of travelling matte is a front-silvered mirror mounted on tracks and moved across the frame at an angle. This self-contained travelling matte progressively obscures one image while simultaneously replacing it with another.

For stop-motion work, a travelling matte can be used consisting of a series of cutout masks made from black paper or card and mounted on register pins. These cutouts are then placed in sequence for one (or more) frame at a time to progressively obscure an image.

Motion-control equipment can also be used with a physical matte to composite two or more elements on the original negative. Alternatively, the matte and the countermatte elements can be processed and composited later, allowing greater flexibility in matching the action within frames. The precise repeatability of mechanical moves made possible by motion-control equipment allows for a number of variations:

1. The matte may be fixed while the camera moves, effectively revealing or obscuring the scene. The same identical move is later repeated when shooting the other element with a countermatte in place.
2. The matte may be moved by motion control while the camera remains static. The move is then repeated with a countermatte in place.
3. Both the camera and the matte/countermatte may be moved by motion control.

Most of the time the elements are of the same scale, but this is not always so: for example, one element may be a full-scale live-action set and the other a scaled-down miniature representing the extension of that set. In those cases where there is a difference in scale, the motion control moves can be adjusted to reflect the correct scale relationship between the moves.

Photographic Travelling Mattes

The more advanced forms of travelling mattes involve some form of photographic or digital imaging process. There are six basic methods for generating these types of travelling mattes, as shown in Figure 2.8.

GRAPHIC METHOD
Animated (cell- or computer-generated)
Rotoscoped

MOTION-CONTROL METHOD
Front light/Back light
Ultraviolet

SELF-MATTING METHOD
Process projection
Aerial image

CONTRAST-DIFFERENCE METHOD
Black
White

COLOR-DIFFERENCE METHOD
Blue screen
Green screen

MULTIFILM METHOD
Infrared
Ultraviolet
Sodium-vapor

Figure 2.8   Methods of generating (photographic) travelling mattes.

GRAPHIC METHOD FOR GENERATING TRAVELLING MATTES

Animated (Cell- or Computer-Generated)

A Travelling matte can consist of a series of hand-drawn cells tracing out progressive changes of a particular shape. These are normally photographed on high-contrast film to ensure maximum contrast and density in the black area. A countermatte is prepared by copying the original matte and reversing the black and white. Another alternative is to shoot the original matte animation twice, then to process one take as a "reversal" while the other is processed as a negative.

A travelling matte can also be produced from a single graphic illustration by panning across it with the camera, zooming, rotating, and so forth. A graphic shape can be produced and animated on the computer, or it can originate as a graphic drawing that is scanned into the digital media and then manipulated as required.

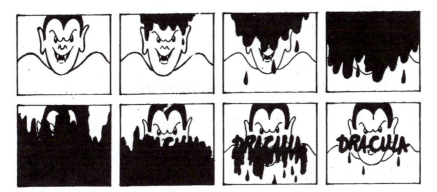

Figure 2.9a Animated travelling matte acting as a transition wipe between scenes and finally metamorphosing into a title.

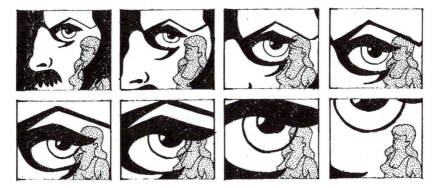

Figure 2.9b A travelling matte, produced by a camera move across a graphic illustration of a man's face, acts as a transition to the incoming scene with the girl.

Rotoscoped Mattes

A travelling matte can follow precise outlines of a live-action subject from frame to frame. This is achieved by rotoscoping, that is, by projecting the negative or the interpositive of the live-action element through the camera in precise registration and tracing out the appropriate outline. The artwork produced in this way has to be registered by means of an animation peg bar or a similar device on punched cells or black paper (see Figure 9.3). Creating special effects such as adding falling debris in the foreground of a live action scene can be done by rotoscoping as relatively few frames are involved. It is also possible to rotoscope the outlines of a spaceship particularly when it is going to be composited with a background consisting of only stars; any imperfections in the matte outline are masked by the blackness of the background. A good example of the effectiveness of rotoscoping can be seen in Stanley Kubrick's *2001—A Space Odyssey*, a milestone in special effects movies. All shots of the spaceship, the pods as well as the astronauts float-ing in space, were done using this approach.

The artwork produced with rotoscoped mattes can be used in two ways:

1. The matte artwork can be photographed frame by frame on high-con-trast stock to produce a male and female matte on film which is then used to composite the corresponding elements.
2. The matte artwork can also be used directly in compositing the elements using bi-pack, aerial image, or back-projection methods (see Figures 7.4 and 9.10).

A rotoscoped matte can also be produced digitally by placing marker points along the outlines of the image and connecting them to form a continuous line. By linking the outline to the subject it is possible to track the subject as it moves within the frame.

MOTION-CONTROL METHOD FOR GENERATING TRAVELLING MATTES

Repeating all camera moves to an extremely high degree of accuracy with the use of motion-control equipment makes it possible to produce travelling mattes of a model or miniature by running two matching passes.

Front Light/Back Light

On the first run the model is photographed against a black background and lit conventionally (front light). This negative is then printed on an interpositive stock to produce a self-matting positive (an image of the model on a black back-ground). This is the "beauty pass." For the second run (the "matte pass"), the model is photographed against a white background (backlight) as a silhouette. When this negative is printed onto a high-contrast stock, the result is a male trav-elling matte (black on a clear background).

Painting the Model

An alternative way to do the second pass is to paint the model white, light it evenly, and photograph it against the same black background. If this is done using high-contrast stock, then the original negative can be used as a male matte.

Monochromatic Emulsion

Certain black-and-white film emulsions are only sensitive to one specific color and will only record that color. For example high-contrast film stocks are gen-

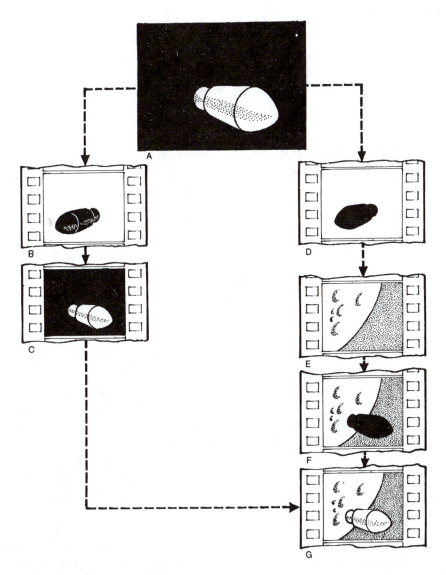

Figure 2.10 (A) Original scene. (B) Original negative. (C) Self-matting positive. (D) High-contrast negative shot on a second pass after the rocket had been painted white (note incompatible geometry). (E) Background positive. (F) Background positive printed through high-contrast matte (D). (G) Final composite when self-matting positive is added.

erally color-blind to everything else but the blue. If the model is painted blue for the second pass, a black-and-white high-contrast emulsion would see it as white. This approach is only practical when the basic color of the model falls within the range of a monochromatic emulsion and actual repainting of the model can be avoided.

Ultraviolet Coating

If the model is coated with a thin layer of ultraviolet paint, it would not be noticeable in the first run when the model is lit conventionally. On the second run the model is lit by ultraviolet light only and photographed against the same black background resulting in a black image on clear background—a male matte.

SELF-MATTING METHOD FOR GENERATING TRAVELLING MATTES

Process Projection

In process projection the subject being composited is effectively self-matting; in other words, it forms its own matte. The great advantage of this method is that the composite picture can be seen through the camera and displayed on video monitors by means of a video assist. This makes it ideal for checking perspective alignments and interaction (coordination) between foreground and background elements, and most importantly, interactive lighting and color/density balance between the background plate and the foreground subject. A large format is preferred for background plates because this gives the highest quality in direct 1:1 image reproduction as well as a certain amount of room for panning and tilting within the frame when required. The preferred approach is to use VistaVision format for the backgrounds when shooting on 35mm and 35mm format for backgrounds when shooting on 16mm. Quite often a smaller format can be used for projection when the image is an insert that does not occupy a large portion of the composite frame.

The projectors used for process work employ pin-registration mechanisms like those of a camera. The projector and camera are interlocked frame-to-frame and run in synchronization with each other during the take. This is accomplished in two ways:

1. *By means of an electronic box controlling crystal sync motors.* A sensor placed on the shaft of the projector motor at a specific point in the frame cycle is matched up to a sensor on the camera motor that indicates the corresponding position of the camera frame cycle. The two motors run separately until they reach full speed, then the camera motor is held back slightly until it is in phase with the projector motor. An indicator light on the control panel lights up when the two motors are running in sync. If for any reason synchronization is lost during the take, the indicator light starts to flash or goes off altogether.

   Several preset speeds are available with this method, but the speed cannot be varied during the take. With some controllers, two cameras can be run in sync with one projector.

2. *By means of selsyn motors.* These motors are of a special design, enabling them to stay in complete interlock throughout the speed range. A typical

configuration may be as follows: A master selsyn motor is driven by a regular synchronous motor. A "slave" selsyn motor drives the projector and another "slave" selsyn motor drives the camera. Additional slave motors can be added as well as additional masters, so that an infinite number of projectors and cameras can be run in perfect synchronization. A great advantage of this approach is that the camera/projector speed can be varied as desired from 1 fps (frames per second) to 32 fps without affecting the synchronization. It can also be used in stop-motion process projection.

A variant on this is the use of stepper motors, but this approach requires that synchronization is set before every take. Stepper motors are more convenient for stop-motion work than live action.

A standard studio camera can be used for process projection. However, cameras with pellicle type viewing instead of the mirror shutter make it possible to see the composite picture during the take and not only during rehearsal.

There are two basic types of process projection: rear projection and front projection. Both types are used for live-action as well stop-motion cinematography.

Rear Projection

The subject is placed in front of a translucent screen and lit to match the background plate, which is projected from the opposite side of the screen. There are several types of rear projection screens with different transmission-to-absorption ratios. Some of them are more tolerant to ambient light than others. It is therefore important to weigh up all the relevant factors when choosing the rear projection screen.

Longer focal length lenses and denser screens are preferred in rear projection because of the "hot spot" problem. Hot spots mean long overall distances from the projector to the camera, a considerable loss of brightness, and, therefore, a smaller projected area. Xenon arc lamps are generally used for rear projection, although their color characteristics are not ideal.

Panning and tilting are accomplished by means of a conventional camera head. A useful setup for car shots is to mount the camera on a small crane or gimbal and float it around during the take.

For car shots a second projector is often used to provide the reflection in the windshield or the side windows. This secondary projector should be slaved to the primary one that is projecting the background scene. When this is not possible, the second projector is installed with a three-bladed shutter and run "wild." Although this approach generally produces acceptable results, it is not ideal, and there is no guaranteed consistency between the exposure of the reflection plate and that of the background plate.

Front Projection

In front projection the subject (actor) is placed in front of the screen and lit to match the background plate, which is projected from the front so that the shadow of the subject falls onto the screen. It is this shadow of the subject that acts as an instant matte.

In order to avoid seeing the shadow, the camera and projector have to be lined up so that the cone of light emanating from the projector lens matches the cone of light entering the camera lens. This is accomplished by mounting the camera and projector so that the axis of their lenses are at 90-degree angles to each other, and by placing a half-silvered mirror (a two-way mirror) at the point of intersection. The two-way mirror enables the projector and camera lenses to occupy an identical position optically, so that the entrance pupils of both lenses coincide. Any misalignment results in the camera lens seeing the shadow of the subject.

This technique obviously requires a special screen that has the property of being able to reflect the projected light beams back along their optical path. The screen is made up of tiny glass spheres, each of which acts as a retroreflector (see Figure 2.11b). The result is that virtually all the light that reaches the screen is redirected back towards the source (the projector) and picked up by the camera lens. The brightness of this reflected image is more that 500 times greater than the one reflected from a white card. Consequently, if the actor in front of the screen is dressed in white clothes, the contrast between the light being reflected from the screen and from his clothes would result in a totally black silhouette of the actor. By lighting the actor to match the projected plate, a perfect match can be achieved between the two. Any spill light falling on the screen is also taken care of by the directional reflectivity of the screen. The front-projection screen is manufactured by 3M Company and is available in lengths of fifty feet by two feet, or in four-foot-wide rolls on a self-adhesive backing.

The advantage of front projection is that a much smaller light source is required; therefore the projector need not be much bigger than the standard camera, resulting in a compact overall package. It is possible to use tungsten halogen light bulbs—the same type of light source used to illuminate the foreground action—and this in turn means that the color balance can be matched perfectly. Since the projector and camera are on the same side of the screen, there is no need for the long working distances required in rear projection (see Figure 2.11a).

Panning and tilting within the shot are accomplished by means of a nodal head. In addition, other possibilities open up, such as panning off the mirror. The projector camera package can be mounted on a crane and moved around not only for easier positioning but also for creating specific effects by moving during the shot (see Figure 11.20).

Aerial Image

This technique involves rephotographing an image that only exists "in the air" (see Figure 2.12) by projecting an image onto a large condenser lens (or a pair of lenses) instead of onto a back-projection screen. The "aerial image" can be seen by placing a sheet of semitransparent paper onto the condenser lens surface (on the side of the camera). The camera lens is focused at this same point. Artwork

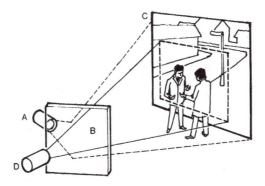

Figure 2.11a Front Projection. (A) Projector. (B) Beam-splitter. (C) Front-projection screen. (D) Camera.

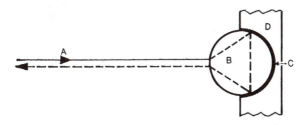

Figure 2.11b Spherical bead. (A) Light ray. (B)"Window" of sphere. (C) Reflective coating on the outside of sphere. (D) Plastic backing.

placed at this focus point and illuminated conventionally will be seen through the camera as a composite image with the projected background. Because of the relatively small sizes of the condenser lenses, this approach is best suited to animation work in which animated characters appear in live-action scenes.

The animation artwork can be prepared either as cutouts or as conventional painting on cell. The painting needs to be opaque in order to prevent the projected image from coming through, and the clear part of the cell needs to be very clean. Limited panning, tilting, and zooming on the projected image is possible while the animation artwork is manipulated by movable peg bars. (See Chapter 9, "The Animation Rostrum Camera and FX.")

CONTRAST-DIFFERENCE METHOD FOR GENERATING TRAVELLING MATTES

The difference in contrast between the background and foreground subject can be used to derive a satisfactory travelling matte in certain circumstances. The lighting of the subject plays a crucial role in this approach and thus is not suitable for every situation.

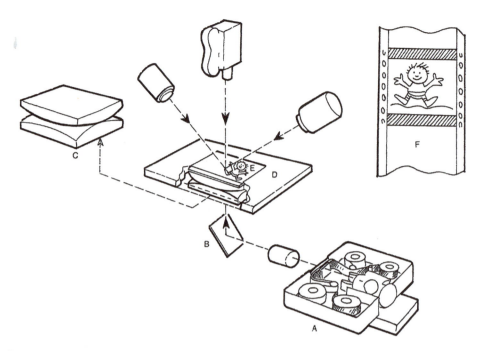

Figure 2.12   Aerial-image back projection. (A) Projector with bi-pack magazines. (B) Front-silvered mirror. (C) Condensers. (D) Animation table. (E) Focus plane. (F) Composite image.

The actual process of deriving a matte from a neutral white or black background can be either digital (using a computer), optical (using printers), or a combination of the two. Most of the detailed descriptions below deal with the optical approach, but precisely the same approach is used by computer software to perform these tasks digitally.

In order to understand what is going on inside the computer during digital compositing, it is important to understand all the visual elements and processes involved, since the computer programs were written to reproduce these processes electronically. Compositing considerations start with planning and photographing the constituent elements—and not when these are handed over to a postproduction facility

Neutral Black Backgrounds

A travelling matte and countermatte can be derived from a neutral black background provided that the subject has been lit in the high-key style: that is, flat with hardly any shadows, or a minimum contrast ratio between highlights and shadows. (The deepest shadow area should be at least one f-stop lighter than the background.)

By printing the color negative onto a black-and-white high-contrast stock, a high-contrast positive—the female matte—may be derived in one pass; the opposite male matte is then made by printing the female matte. For final compositing with the background only the male matte is required, since the color interpositive (made from the original negative) will be self-matting. However, the density of the black on a color interpositive stock is not always sufficient, and in those circumstances the female matte is used. Alternatively, a positive, made on color-print stock, may be used since it has a greater contrast ratio.

If a satisfactory female matte cannot be produced in one step, as above, then additional steps will be needed to clean it up. The high-contrast positive—the female matte—will have some dark patches inside the clear matte area; these can be eliminated by rotoscoping and tracing out the unwanted areas, painting them white, and adding this element as a "burn in" during the copying stage to produce a male matte. This "clean up" procedure is relatively easier in digital form because specific shapes can be identified and tracked automatically.

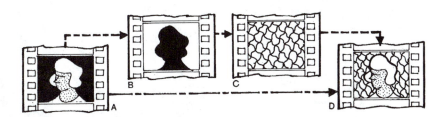

Figure 2.13 (A) Self-matting positive (subject lit flatly). (B) High-contrast matte. (C) Positive of background scene. (D) Composite.

Neutral White Backgrounds

If the subject is photographed against a neutral white background, then the contrast between the background and the foreground must meet specific requirements: the white background should be at least one f-stop brighter that the highlights of the subject.

A high-contrast print from the original color negative will produce a satisfactory female matte in most cases. The male matte is derived by printing the high-contrast female matte onto high-contrast stock. In those cases where the female matte is not completely clear, a "clean-up" matte has to be prepared by rotoscoping and painting out the unwanted areas within the matte outline, as in the case of neutral black backgrounds. A digitally prepared matte of this type can be cleaned up more easily.

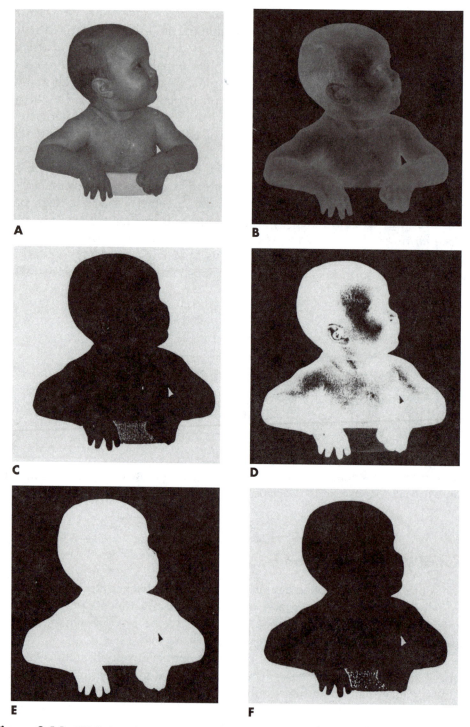

Figure 2.14 (A) Original scene. (B) Color negative. (C) High-contrast print from the original negative that was processed conventionally, with a clear background and a positive image, to produce a male matte. (D) High-contrast print from the original color negative that was processed as "reversal," with a black background and negative image, to produce female matte. (E and F) Cleaned up mattes.

Another approach to matting with neutral white backgrounds is to use "reversal processing" for the high-contrast print that is made from the original negative and thus obtain a female matte (black background) in one go. The male matte can be obtained by processing the high-contrast stock in the conventional way, by producing a positive image on a clear background. The advantage of this approach is that both male and female mattes have identical geometries (i.e., they do not need to be flopped left to right).

A photographic approach to the "cleaning up" procedure would be to print both male and female mattes onto the same high-contrast negative in consecutive passes. Since one matte carries the positive image of the subject and the other the negative, by printing one over the other the residual unwanted elements inside the matte are "burnt out."

Filming against white background always presents more problems than filming against black because it is not easy to light a fairly large area evenly. However, using front-projection equipment and projecting white light can get around this problem very efficiently. When working with models, an identical second pass could be done without the projector light, effectively producing a self-matting positive. Another variation is to reproduce the front-light back-light approach by taking two frames for each move: take the first frame with the white background (projector light on and studio light off), and the second with the projector light off and the studio lights on. The negative is then step-printed skipping (missing out) every other frame to produce a self-matting positive and a male matte.

COLOR-DIFFERENCE METHOD FOR GENERATING TRAVELLING MATTES

A travelling matte can be derived from a background of neutral color, usually blue, red, or green. The criteria for choosing a specific background color have as much to do with the subject matter as with the specific technique used.

The best way to understand the color-difference approach for generating travelling mattes is to consider the makeup of a typical film emulsion of a color negative stock. It consists of three layers, each of which is sensitive to a primary color: blue, green, and red. The sensitivity curves of these layers overlap in order to produce an overall sensitivity of the emulsion within the visible spectrum between 380 and 770 nanometers. Each color layer has a peak at a specific frequency. By selecting an appropriate cutoff filter, this peak frequency can be isolated to produce maximum exposure on the chosen layer without affecting the other two.

To ensure that a good separation is achieved between the color layers on the negative, test exposures are made and density readings of the blue, green, and red layers are compared. The greater the difference in density between the layer of the background color and the other two layers, the easier it will be to pull off a clean matte.

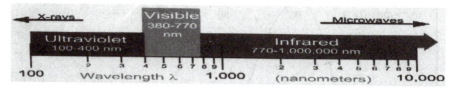

Figure 2.15a   Light is just a portion of the electromagnetic spectrum between the ultraviolet and the infrared range. The wavelength of the "visible" spectrum is between 380 and 770 nm (nanometers).

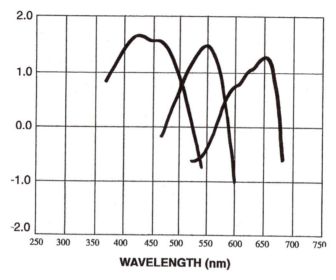

Figure 2.15b   Spectral sensitivity curves of a typical color negative film are matched to cover the spectral range of the visible spectrum. Note that a narrow band of blue light, from 420 to 450 nanometers, will produce maximum exposure density on the blue layer of the film emulsion without affecting the green and red layers ("blue screen"). For "green screen" work the optimum wavelength is 550 nanometers.

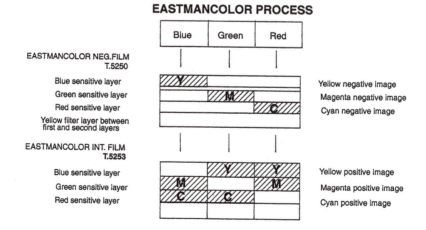

Figure 2.15c   Cross-section of Eastman color-negative film emulsion.

Color Backgrounds

Blue is the color most commonly used as the background for generating travelling mattes, for either optical or digital compositing. The main reason for choosing blue is that the absence of a narrow band in the dark blue range of the spectrum (420–450 nm) which is used to abstract the matte is less likely to make a noticeable difference to the photographed image than the absence of a similar band width in the red range, particularly when the scene involves flesh tones. Red, however, can be equally effective in certain circumstances, but it is the green that has become popular for digital work.

The "color backing" is painted on canvas or a solid surface and lit evenly from the front. It is also available as a fabric with a velvet surface which helps to diffuse the light. Alternatively, the screens are made from a translucent material of the appropriate color and transilluminated (lit from behind). Another alternative is to use the front-projection approach and project the chosen color onto a front-projection screen.

The actor is placed in front of the color background and illuminated by white light. The balance between the background and foreground can be checked by looking at the scene through color-separation filters. When looking at a blue backing through the blue filter, the balance between foreground and background should be equal. However, the blue backing should appear totally black through the red filter. Lighting adjustments should be made until this balance is struck.

The necessity for many different generations in the production of the mattes results in unsteadiness in the picture and a variation in matte sizes, producing a halo effect around the matted figure where the mismatch has occurred. Translucent objects, nets, loose hair, glass, and other elements tend either to be lost altogether or to produce strange "fringing" problems due to overlaps between the matte and counter-matte. Naturally, the background color cannot be used in the costumes or props in the foreground without resorting to additional matting procedures.

Digital compositing can correct for many of these problems, but the final result is determined by the photographic quality of the original element, or how good the density difference is between the background layer and the other layers on the original negative.

One of the problems that is not readily recognizable is that the color backing itself acts as a giant light source, backlighting the subject and producing a color fringe around the edges and color contamination in the shadow areas. This presents particular problems with night scenes or backlit and crosslit low-key scenes. An additional clean-up procedure is required to eliminate the unwanted wraparound contamination, whether the compositing is done digitally or optically.

The problems of contamination can be avoided when the background color is front-projected. It is also easier to control the frequency of the light output—

restricting it to a very narrow band in any chosen part of the spectrum—with the use of cutoff filters.

As a general rule of thumb, front-projected blue/green or red is better suited for scenes requiring more subtle lighting, such as a night scene with backlight and crosslight, or heavy contrast. Front-lit color screens are better for flat, frontal lighting.

A Simple "Blue Screen" Approach

A master color positive made from the original color negative is printed onto black-and-white panchromatic stock, through a blue filter, to produce a negative image on a black background. The same master positive is printed again through a red filter to produce a black-and-white negative image on a clear background (the red filter absorbs the blue of the background, resulting in no exposure in that area). By printing this last matte onto a high-contrast stock, we get a positive image on a black background. The extra printing involved can be eliminated by processing the exposed red matte as a reversal. Thus, both a positive and a negative image are produced on a black background. These are printed onto the same piece of high-contrast stock, in succession, to produce a male matte. A female countermatte has to be made from the male matte to block out the blue background on the master color positive during the final compositing.

Alternatively, the black-and-white film record made through a blue filter, which produces a negative image on a black background, can be processed as a reversal, or copied again to produce a positive image on a clear background. A female matte can be obtained by sandwiching the blue-filtered record in bi-pack emulsion-to-emulsion with the red-filtered record (which also has a clear background but a negative image) and rephotographing it on high-contrast stock. (See Chapter 8, "Optical Printers and FX.")

Color Difference: Blue-Screen System

The color difference blue-screen system is a more complex method for deriving travelling mattes but produces better results than the simple system described above. It utilizes the color separation approach for duplicating the original negative instead of the interpositive/internegative method. The original negative is printed through the three-color separation filters (blue/red/green) on three separate strips of black-and-white panchromatic stock and then reassembled through the same filters onto a color negative stock to produce a duplicate negative. The photographic approach for shooting the blue-screen element is basically the same as in the earlier example. The subject is placed in front of a screen (front-lit blue, backlit blue, or front-pro-

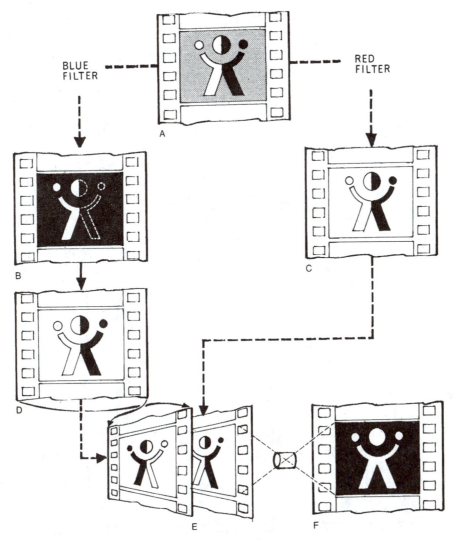

Figure 2.16 (A) Master positive. (B) Black-and-white panchromatic print through blue filter. (C) Black-and-white panchromatic print through red filter. (D) Duplicate of B. (E) Bi-pack "sandwich" of C and D. (F) Full female matte.

jected blue) and lit conventionally by incandescent light. Occasionally, a variation on this is used in which a small amount of yellow filtration is added to the lights to counter the effect of blue spill and increase the separation; this is later compensated for in compositing.

A color negative of this scene is copied onto black-and-white panchromatic stock through the color separation filters: blue, red, and green to produce three black-and-white records that correspond to the yellow, cyan, and magenta content of the negative. This produces black backgrounds on the red and green separation positives, and a clear background on the blue one.

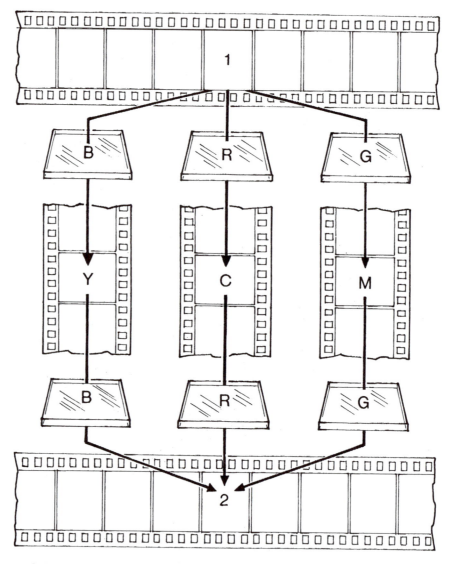

Figure 2.17   Color Separation. The original negative (1) is printed separately on three pieces of black-and-white panchromatic film through three color-separation filters (blue, red, and green). This produces separate records of the yellow, cyan, and magenta elements of the negative. Printing through the same three separation filters onto color negative stock produces a duplicate color negative (2).

The key to this system is to produce a synthetic blue separation positive with the same density value as the original but with a black background instead of a clear one. The first step is to make a "color-difference" matte. This matte is, in effect, the density difference between the blue and green separation positives and is obtained by printing the original color negative and the green separation positive in bi-pack. A matte obtained this way is then printed in bi-pack with the green separation master. Further cover masks are normally also required before the final compositing can be done.

For digital compositing the blue-screen element is shot in exactly the same way. The negative is then scanned into digital media and the travelling matte is abstracted electronically. The background element is also scanned into the digital media and composited with the blue-screen element.

Color Difference: Green-Screen System

With the advent of digital compositing, green has come to be used as a background for travelling matte work. It is commonly referred to as "digital green." The green-screen system utilizes a narrow band of light at the peak of the spectral sensitivity curve of the green layer of the negative—around 550 nanometers. A good density on the green layer will produce maximum separation on the negative from the red and blue layers. This density difference is then used to generate a matte electronically.

The reason for choosing green for digital compositing also has to do with the fact that electronic media in general has a narrower and more compressed spectral range than the film negative. A blue-screen background utilizing the light close to the extreme end of the visible spectrum (420 nanometers) photographs well on film, but when it comes to scanning it into a digital format it is on the very edge of the electronic range.

Front-Lit Green Screen

These screens are commonly available as large sheets of fabric dyed a green color. They can be used on locations lit by available light. For studio work the green screen is illuminated by incandescent lamps with additional green filtration on the light source. However, a mercury arc lamp with a sharp peak from 540 to 550 nanometers provides a narrow band of light that, with some additional filtration, can be ideal for this application (see Figure 3.18, part 3).

A backlit green screen utilizes a translucent screen with suitable green filtration on the light source. A fluorescent light source is particularly suitable for this application (see Figure 3.18, part 4). A front-projected green screen utilizes front-projection equipment with a specially designed lamphouse that provides illumination with the narrow band to match the spectral sensitivity curve of the negative stock. (See Chapter 11, "Process Projection.")

MULTIFILM METHOD FOR GENERATING TRAVELLING MATTES

A matte can be shot at the same time as the original negative by using a specially designed camera with two identical film movements. One of the film gates is in line with the lens axis and receives the image directly; the second one is set at 90 degrees to the lens axis and receives the image via a beam-splitter. The main advantage of this system is that any color can be used in the foreground as the matte is recorded on a separate strip of film. There is also much less risk of contamination from the background illumination. There are three basic systems using this approach, and they are known by the light source by which the matte image is produced: infrared, ultraviolet, and sodium vapor.

Infrared Process

In the infrared process black nylon velvet is used as the background; it reflects the invisible infrared light while absorbing the light in the visible spectrum. Alternatively, a translucent screen illuminated with a light source with an infrared filter can be used. The subject is lit by normal incandescent lighting.

   Once the background is set up, one of the camera gates is loaded with infrared film, the other with color film. The subject in front of the screen is lit by normal white light from which the infrared radiation is absorbed by dichroic filters. Another dichroic filter in the beam-splitter ensures that all infrared radiation from the background is directed to the infrared film and that only visible light reaches the color film loaded in the other gate.

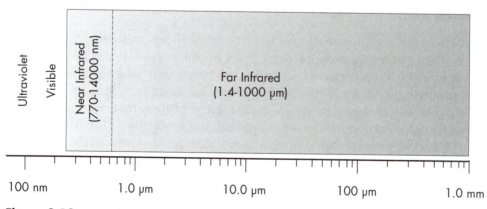

Figure 2.18   The infrared spectrum

Since it has longer wavelengths (above 770 nm) than the light in the visible part of the spectrum, the infrared radiation focuses farther back from the lens and produces a slightly larger image. A matte produced by this method has to be reduced optically before it can be used.

Ultraviolet Process

Fluorescent lamps are used to illuminate a translucent screen from behind, providing the necessary ultraviolet radiation for the background. Ultraviolet-sensitive black-and-white stock is used to record the matte, and the beam-splitter is coated with a Corning filter medium to reflect the ultraviolet radiation to it. An ultraviolet absorbing filter is placed over the lights to eliminate the unwanted radiation from the foreground action. As in the case of the infrared process, the color image is self-matting (in the positive mode); a female matte (clear in the area of the subject and black in the surrounding area) is produced at the same time.

The ultraviolet light, having a shorter wavelength, focuses closer (nearer) than the light in the visible part of the spectrum, resulting in a smaller image. The matte has to be optically enlarged.

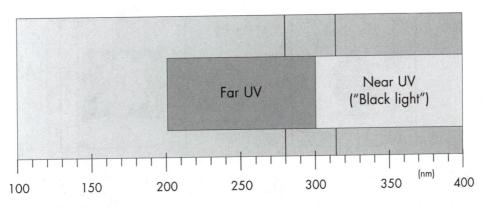

Figure 2.19 Ultraviolet spectrum

Sodium Vapor Process

This method produces a matte that is identical in image size to the color record. It uses monochromatic yellow light produced by sodium-vapor lamps. Incandescent lamps are used for the illumination of the foreground, with additional filtration to extract the narrow band of yellow from the spectrum. In practice, additional blue filtration is needed to maintain the color temperature of the foreground lights at 3,200 Kelvin.

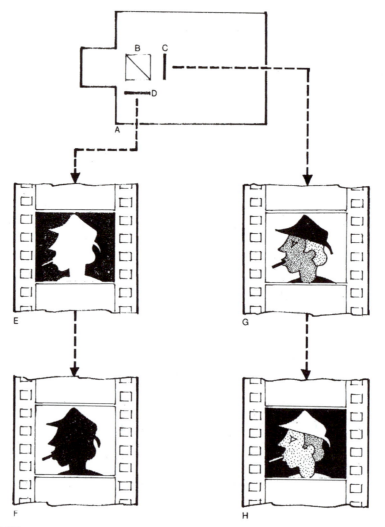

Figure 2.20 Multifilm travelling matte system. (A) Two-strip camera with beam-splitter prism (B). (C) Film gate in line with lens axis. (D) Film gate at 90 degrees to lens axis. (E) Original negative travelling matte. (F) High-contrast positive print from E producing a male matte. (G) Color negative. (H) Self-matting positive from color negative (G) can be married with any prefilmed background with the help of the male matte (F).

Additional filtration inside the camera ensures complete separation. A monochromatic (narrow band) yellow filter in the beam-splitter as well as in front of the mechanism or gate that is recording the matte image ensures that only the light from the background reaches the black-and-white panchromatic stock. A didynium filter in front of the camera gate loaded with color stock prevents the background light from reaching the image.

3

Visual Effects Compositing

KEY PHOTOGRAPHIC CONSIDERATIONS FOR A GOOD COMPOSITE IMAGE

The relative accessibility of digital compositing techniques can lead to an obsession with creating a seamless join between various elements at the expense of all other considerations that go into making a good composite. The results often look like photo-collage rather than a believable, integrated, composite image. These problems are due in large part to the tendency to shoot the foreground elements first because of production pressures, and then look for "suitable" backgrounds later. This has given a boost to the old scourge of good visual effects: "Just shoot it and we'll fix it in post!"

The most common compositing error involves changing or adding a background to a previously shot foreground element where the background is treated merely as wallpaper. This may be fine for a pop video in the collage style, because that is exactly what the background is meant to be—wallpaper. However, if the background and foreground elements are meant to form a believable, integrated image, then a lot more than a seamless join is needed to create and sustain the illusion.

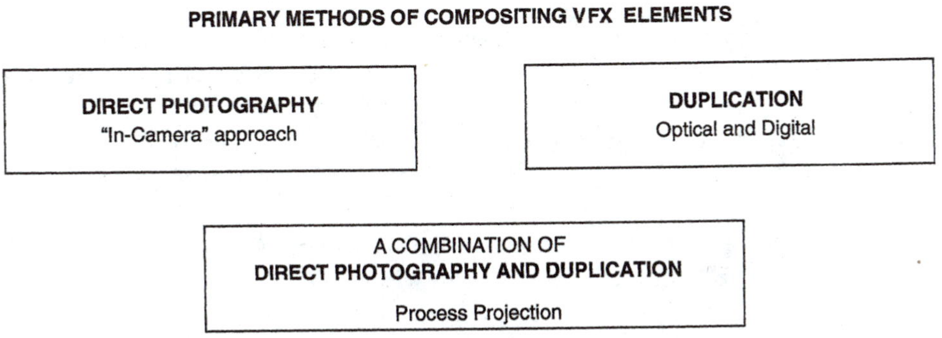

PRIMARY METHODS OF COMPOSITING VFX ELEMENTS

DIRECT PHOTOGRAPHY	DUPLICATION
"In-Camera" approach	Optical and Digital

A COMBINATION OF DIRECT PHOTOGRAPHY AND DUPLICATION
Process Projection

Figure 3.1 Primary Methods of Compositing Visual FX Elements

A bad visual FX composite can consist of several elements that are perfectly good on their own but do not match when they are joined together. Such a composite is like an orchestra playing a well-known piece of music with each group of instruments playing in a different key. The tune may be recognizable, but the overall effect will be less than pleasing to the ear. The eye is just as discriminating as the ear, and just as there are rules for musical composition and arranging, so there are rules for visual composition and execution. Just as in music, the visual rules have evolved and been refined over the centuries. It is on the shoulders of the giants who have labored in the fields of painting, sculpture, and architecture that we now stand as we explore the same world with the aid of new technologies.

In the case of visual effects compositing, the key considerations are perspective and lighting.

PERSPECTIVE

> *Perspective is the rein and rudder of painting.*
> — LEONARDO DA VINCI

Perspective is something we usually take for granted, but in fact it was not until the early Renaissance in the fifteenth century that perspective was discovered in Florence. Its subsequent application has had a profound effect on Western art. Perspective is probably the single most important consideration in creating believable composites and is of supreme importance in all aspects of visual effects. It is also the most common error.

Photography and cinematography are natural extensions of the art of painting. In a painting, the picture surface is a window through which the subject painted can be seen; the cinema screen is a window through which a live scene can be seen. In both cases, three-dimensional reality is "translated" into a two-dimensional representation of that reality. This is accomplished with the use of perspective.

True linear perspective is based on the way the eye sees. It follows clear mathematical laws and is closely related to optics, the study of the laws of sight.

Although the field of vision of the human eye is around 90 degrees, the binocular field of vision—the overlap area of the two eyes—is just over 60 degrees. The field of vision encompassed by linear perspective is approximately 60 degrees.

In photographic terms, the choice of format will determine the focal lengths of the lens that will best match the 60 degrees horizontal angle of true linear perspective. In 35mm film format (1.85:1 aspect ratio), this is a lens of 18mm focal length, and in VistaVision format the focal length is 33mm.

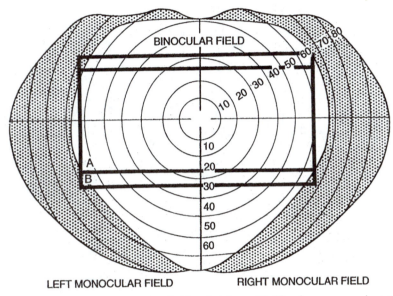

Figure 3.2 Monocular and binocular fields of vision with film frames superimposed on 60 degrees horizontal of the binocular field. (A) 35mm anamorphic frame (2.35:1 aspect ratio). (B) 35mm frame (1.85:1 aspect ratio).

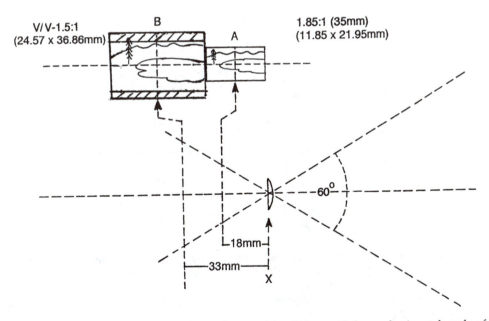

Figure 3.3 A lens of 18mm focal length at position X has a 60-degree horizontal angle of coverage on 35mm film format in 1.85:1 aspect ratio. A lens of 33mm focal length at the same position has the same horizontal angle of view on VistaVision format at the same aspect ratio.

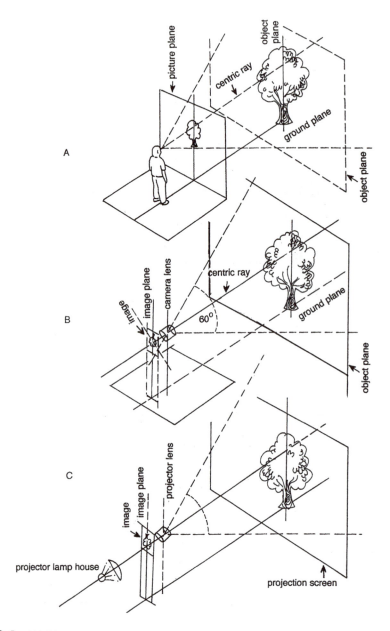

Figure 3.4   (A) Linear perspective is based on the fixed viewpoint of one eye. The picture plane in front of the observer is like a glass window intercepting the perspective lines of the object plane. The rays of light reflected from the object can be plotted to form a scale image.

(B) A camera lens placed in the position of the observer produces a flat, two-dimensional image that corresponds to the plane of the distant object.

(C) When the film image is projected onto a cinema screen, the screen itself becomes the "glass window" of the picture plane intercepting the perspective lines of the distant object. When the screen size is equal to the size of the object plane and viewed from the "lens" position, a true perspective reproduction is possible.

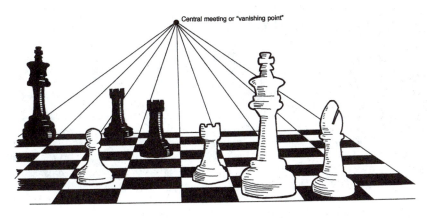

Figure 3.5a The white king appears much larger than the black one at the far side of the board. (Redrawn from *Perspective* by Alison Cole, Covent Garden, London: Dorling-Kindersly, 1992.)

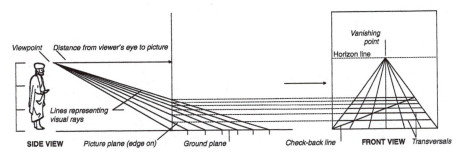

Figure 3.5b Alberti's system of linear perspective. (Redrawn from *Perspective*.)

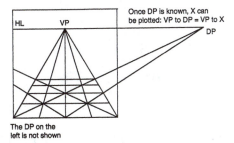

Figure 3.5c Calculating the distance point is of great help when combining scaled model sets with full-size ones. (Redrawn from *Perspective*.)

The size of the cinema screen and the relative viewing position are of vital importance in creating the illusion of a "window on reality." The best viewing position would be a point on the center line from where the imaginary lines extended to the sides of the screen form a 60-degree angle. A scene

 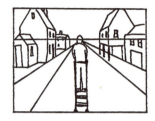 

Figure 3.6 Perspective viewpoints. (REDRAWN FROM *PERSPECTIVE.*)

(Left) Normal viewpoint–Camera at eye level of a spectator standing on the ground; horizon line is at eye level (lens height). Tilting the camera up and down changes the position of the horizon line relative to the frame center line but does not alter the viewpoint.

(Middle) High viewpoint–Camera on a crane. The horizon line is still at the eye level (lens height) but more of the ground plane is visible. The angle formed by the lines of the pavement converging at the vanishing point gets smaller as the viewpoint height increases.

(Right) Low viewpoint–The angle formed by the lines of pavement increases dramatically as the camera position is lowered; at ground level this angle would be zero, as the pavement lines merge with the horizon line.

photographed with a lens matching the standard linear perspective and viewed from the ideal position would appear as in nature—and any foreground objects placed in front of the screen would blend in with the perspective of the projected scene. This can be particularly effective for special venue presentations such as amusement parks, incorporating foreground live action and projected backgrounds.

Ideally, the size of the screen should be determined by the chosen size of the "window" it is representing. This is extremely important in three-dimensional cinematography in particular.

Practical Applications of Perspective Viewpoints to Car Shots

If the viewing angle on the background plate does not match the viewing angle used for the composite shot of actors in a car, the car will appear to float high above the road or it will appear too low—as if sliding along on its chassis without wheels. In order to avoid this problem, both the background plate and the compositing element should be shot from matching viewpoints.

The perspective problems in car shots are usually compounded by a mismatch in the lens angles between the background plate and the live element. This does not mean that identical lens angles have to be used on the background and foreground at all times. When the scene requires a camera move inside the composite, then the lens used during the rephotographing stage will have to be of a longer focal length; provided that the viewpoints match, the illusion will be maintained.

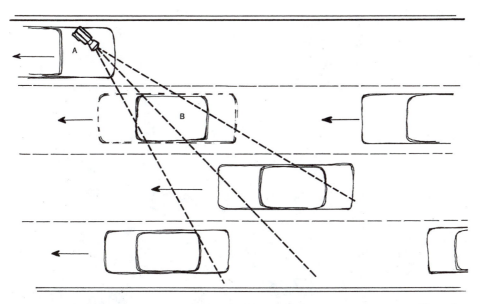

Figure 3.7 The correct camera position for a background plate of a car travelling along a freeway is in the adjoining lane. (A) The active lane is occupied by the "phantom" car (B).

Using extreme wide angles on the background plate is not a good solution, because the matching viewpoint can be inaccessible. Shooting in all directions from a camera car is also not a good idea, as illustrated in Figure 3.7.

Perspective Considerations When Inserting Live Action into a Model

The simplest solution to perspective issues when inserting live action into a model is to use the same lens for the live-action element as for the model element, but to move back to the correct scale distance. The depth of field is matched by the primary focus setting and iris.

If a camera move is required over the composite image, then the elements are shot on a larger format, such as VistaVision or 65mm, and scanned into the final format. The alternative method is to use motion control with appropriate scaling of tracking and craning moves.

"Virtual Frame" Approach

The easiest way to work out the correct lens angle and elevation for an insert element is to visualize the final composite as a virtual frame. Assuming that this virtual frame was shot on a lens with a horizontal angle of 60 degrees (standard linear perspective), then the frame is divided along the horizontal and vertical

Figure 3.8a   Vertical picture with two distinctive perspectives. In the top part of the picture we are looking up at a castle on top of a hill, and in the bottom of the picture we are looking down at a rocky seashore below. (The castle may be a miniature, a matte painting, or the real thing, but it is in a different location.)

Figure 3.8b Both elements are shot as static setups on a VistaVision frame with the camera turned on its side. Each element occupies the appropriate portion of the VistaVision frame. A realistic "tilt-down" camera move from the castle to the rocky seashore below is accomplished by scanning the image the right way up during the compositing of the two elements.

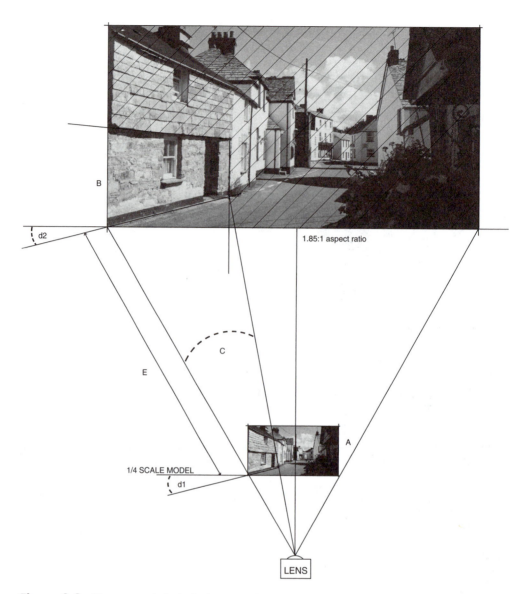

Figure 3.9 The correct (relative) viewpoint between two elements at a different scale, using the same focal length lens. (A) Model set 1/4 scale. (B) Full-scale set. (C) Lens angle of full-scale set matches the insert area of the model set. (d1 and d2) Matching perspective angles. (E) Relative scale distance.

lines away from the frame center into 10-degree increments. This can be done on a storyboard of the proposed composite or on a still of the master frame, if available. By looking up the appropriate section where the insert is to be placed, you can read off the horizontal and vertical lens angles required; then, by checking these on the lens angle chart, the focal length of the appropriate lens is estab-

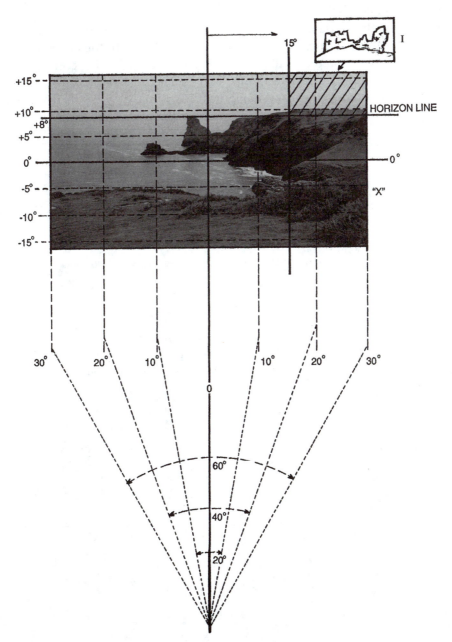

Figure 3.10a Virtual frame approach. Master frame "X" was shot with a 60-degree horizontal angle of view. The insert of the castle (I) is to be composited at the top right-hand corner of the frame. From the grids indicating the horizontal and vertical angle division of the frame, we see that the horizontal angle of the insert (I) is 15 degrees. Referring to the table below, we find that a 80mm lens (on 35mm film with 1.85:1 aspect ratio) has a 15-degree horizontal angle of view.

Note that the bottom frame line of the insert (I) lies on the horizon line of the frame (X). The vertical angle of an 80mm lens is just over 8 degrees, so we can calculate that the camera lens angle for the insert (I) should be 4 degrees up.

lished. The tilt angle at which the camera lens is pointing is obtained by adding or subtracting the angle indicated by the center of the insert frame from the tilt angle of the master frame. The insert can then be shot with the appropriate lens at the correct elevation on a full frame; it is later reduced to the correct size and position in the frame during the compositing stage.

The perspective of the insert in Figure 3.10a would adequately match that of the master frame "X" for most situations, but there will still be a discrepancy

Transmitted or Projected Image	0.380"	0.463"	0.825"	1.676"	1.485"	1.912"	0.286"	0.251"	0.446"	0.594"	0.700"	0.991"	0.870"
Angle (°)	16 mm	Super-16 1.85:1 AR	35 mm 1.85:1 AR	35 mm ANA	35 mm VISTA	65 mm	16 mm	Super-16 1.85:1 AR	35 mm 1.85:1 AR	35 mm TV TRANS	35 mm TV ANA	35 mm VISTA	65mm
0.5	1106	1348	2401	4878	4322	5565	832	731	1298	1729	2037	2884	2532
0.7	790	963	1715	3484	3087	3975	595	522	927	1235	1455	2060	1809
1	553	674	1201	2439	2161	2782	416	365	649	864	1019	1442	1266
1.5	369	449	800	1626	1441	1855	277	244	433	576	679	961	844
2	276	337	600	1219	1081	1391	208	183	325	432	509	721	633
2.5	221	269	480	975	864	1113	166	146	260	346	407	577	506
3	184	225	400	813	720	927	139	122	216	288	339	481	422
3.5	158	192	343	697	617	795	119	104	185	247	291	412	362
4	138	168	300	610	540	695	104	91	162	216	255	360	316
4.5	123	150	267	542	480	618	92	81	144	192	226	320	281
5	111	135	240	488	432	556	83	73	130	173	204	288	253
6	92	112	200	406	360	463	69	61	108	144	170	240	211
7	79	96	171	348	308	397	59	52	93	123	145	206	181
8	69	84	150	304	270	347	52	46	81	108	127	180	158
9	61	75	133	270	240	309	46	41	72	96	113	160	140
10	55	67	120	243	216	278	42	36	65	86	102	144	126
15	37	45	80	162	143	184	28	24	43	57	68	96	84
20	27	33	59	121	107	138	21	18	32	43	50	71	63
25	22	27	47	96	85	110	16	14	26	34	40	57	50
30	18	22	39	79	70	91	14	12	21	28	33	47	41
35	15	19	33	68	60	77	12	10	18	24	28	40	35
40	13	16	29	58	52	67	10	9	16	21	24	35	30
45	12	14	25	51	46	59	9	8	14	18	21	30	27
50	10	13	22	46	40	52	8	7	12	16	19	27	24
55	9	11	20	41	36	47	7	6	11	15	17	24	21
60	8	10	18	37	33	42	6	6	10	13	15	22	19
65	8	9	16	33	30	38	6	5	9	12	14	20	17
70	7	8	15	30	27	35	5	5	8	11	13	18	16
75	6	8	14	28	25	32	5	4	7	10	12	16	14
80	6	7	12	25	22	29	4	4	7	9	11	15	13
85	5	6	11	23	21	26	4	3	6	8	10	14	12
90	5	6	10	21	19	24	4	3	6	8	9	13	11
95	4	5	10	20	17	22	3	3	5	7	8	12	10
100	4	5	9	18	16	20	3	3	5	6	7	11	9

Figure 3.10b   Horizontal and vertical angles versus effective focal length.

because the angle of the focal plane and the perspective line cutting across the screen do not match that of frame "X." This also affects the focus, even if the depth of field of the insert is set up to match that of frame "X." This can be corrected with the use of a "pitching lens," but care must be taken to ensure that the correct horizontal angle required for the insert is maintained.

The Ideal "Virtual Frame" Setup

Large Format Field Camera Approach

The best way to achieve a perfect perspective match when shooting insert elements is to use a combination of a large-format field camera (with all the advantages of perspective adjustments that such a camera offers) and the basic body of a movie camera such as the Mitchell Standard.

Large-format ground glass is marked with the appropriate format of the final composite frame, with additional markings added to indicate the horizontal and vertical angles along the center lines. The horizontal-field-of-view angle of the large format lens matches the horizontal angle of the lens used for the master frame "X" or other elements.

In order to ensure a perfect visual lineup, a blow up of the master frame "X" can be made as a large-format transparency that is then placed on the ground glass (in register). A white card placed in front of the taking large format lens provides illumination for the transparency while obscuring the "unwanted" part of the scene. The lens is set up to image the insert element on the ground glass in the correct position and at the correct scale. The film camera slides into position to capture the insert frame only.

Several elements can be photographed in this way and composited together to create a single image with a totally integrated perspective. These elements do not have to be within the 60-degree horizontal angle of the standard linear perspective. The virtual frame can represent a wide or narrow field of view depending on the choice of lens; the angle markings on the ground glass will therefore be different for each focal length.

Virtual Frame: The "Nodal Point" Approach

By repositioning the lens on the nodal point for each segment, the entire area of the virtual frame can be covered with static setups regardless of the physical size of the space covered by the virtual frame. A camera "pan and tilt" move within the virtual frame area can be introduced later in the compositing stage.

An extreme example of this would be to shoot a series of setups that would produce a pan of 180 degrees or even 360 degrees when composited. The number of segments will depend on the horizontal angle of the lens used. In the case of a 60-degree angle of view, the camera would be panned 60 degrees for the second insert and another 60 degrees for the subsequent one. It is advisable to have a certain amount of overlap between the adjoining

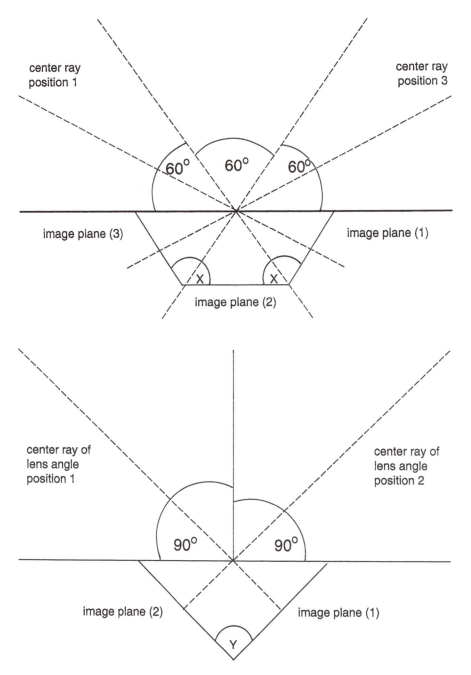

Figure 3.11   Plan view of a 180-degree pan with 3 x 60-degree and 2 x 90-degree segments. Compare angles at the join point of 3 x 60-degree (x) and 2 x 90-degree (y) segments. Objects at the overlap points will suffer from an element of distortion that is compounded by the corner distortions of wide-angle lenses. Segments with narrower horizontal angles (i.e., longer focal length lenses) produce less acute corner distortions.

images. Shooting on full aperture and using 1.85:1 markings would give the extra overlap area. This approach is very useful in cases where it is not practical to use motion control.

A background plate of different static segments can be produced using the virtual frame approach; the segments are then composited into one continuous pan. The compositing of the plate elements in Figure 3.11 can be done either digitally or optically, and the final composite with foreground action can be done either as process (front projection/rear projection) or as travelling matte (blue screen/green screen).

Using the virtual frame approach we can envisage a 180-degree pan starting with an African dawn through high noon over the Sahara and ending on a sunset over a modern metropolis. The lighting can be transformed gradually from one lighting setup to another as the scene progresses using a dimmer console. The added bonus in process projection is that the final composite can be seen on a video-assist monitor as it is being photographed, so that any subtle changes in lighting or action can be incorporated. This example also illustrates the importance of why the background plates should be done first and the actor shot against this reference.

Perspective and the "Moving Stills" Projector

A "moving stills" projector is a front-projection stills unit utilizing the virtual image principle in reverse.

As the camera pans and tilts across the composite image (foreground and background), sensors on the gear-head feed this information to the computer, which then sends a signal to the motors to move the transparency along the horizontal and vertical axis by a corresponding amount and in real-time. The result is that the camera lens always sees the appropriate part of the background in whatever direction it points. (See Chapter 11, "Process Projection.")

The Choice of Lenses

The choice of the projection lens is governed by the field of view covered by the 2.25-inch area of the transparency. This in turn will depend on the focal length of the large-format lens used in the photography of the background still.

In practical terms, if the horizontal field of view of the large-format lens on a 10-inch transparency was 60 degrees, the corresponding angle for the 2.25-inch area of that still will be 13.5 degrees; on a 5-inch transparency, the corresponding angle will be 27 degrees. The camera lens with a matching horizontal angle of view on the chosen format to the projection lens will reproduce a perfect match in the perspective of the foreground set and the background.

The camera lens can be a longer focal length if required (with a narrower field of view), with the result that a smaller part of the projected image (as well as the foreground) will be photographed. This allows for a certain amount of zooming on the composite image.

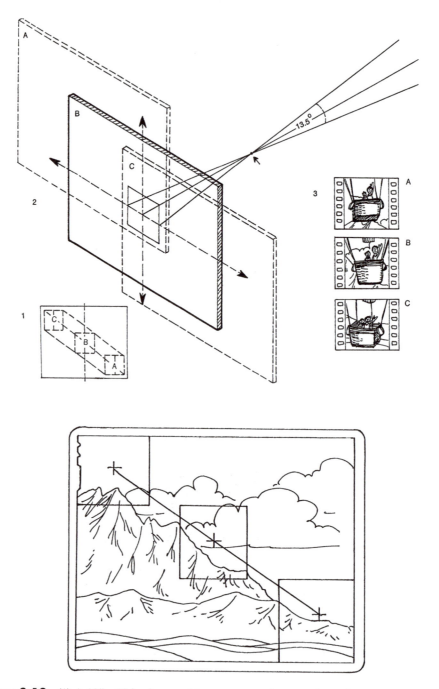

Figure 3.12 (1) A 10″ × 8″ background transparency shot on a large-format camera with a wide-angle lens (60-degree horizontal and 48-degree vertical angle of view). (2) As the transparency moves from position (A) to position (C) the projection lens (P) projects only the part of the transparency directly in line with it (2 1/4-inch square). The horizontal projection angle of 13.5 degrees is proportional to the angle of view of the full image. (3) Composite image. Camera pans up and to the left as it follows the basket of an ascending balloon.

Using the moving-stills projector, a large-format transparency taken by a panoramic camera can be projected onto a curved front-projection screen behind the actor to produce a 360-degree panning shot. The foreground sets will maintain true linear perspective with the background. Instead of building a full-size circular screen (with all the lighting restriction that that entails), only a section of the screen needs to be built and moved around on a circular track.

Anamorphic Lenses and Perspective

An anamorphic lens is a composite lens with two different focal lengths: one affects the horizontal image plane and the other the vertical. It is like having two

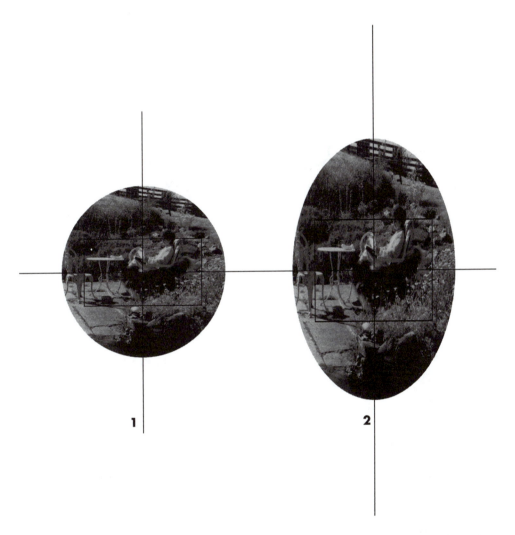

Figure 3.13a A spherical lens forms a circular image (1) and an anamorphic or 'Scope lens forms an elliptical image (2).

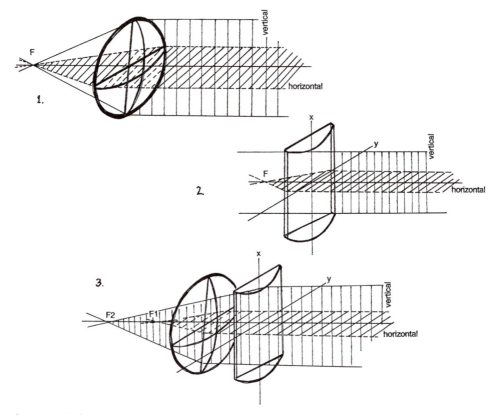

Figure 3.13b   (1) A single-element spherical lens of positive power is modeled on a segment of a sphere. It affects focus in both horizontal and vertical planes equally. (2) A single-element cylindrical lens of positive power is modeled on a segment of a cylinder. It affects the focus in one plane only. (3) When a spherical lens element is combined with a cylindrical element it results in different focal points for the horizontal (F1) and vertical planes (F2).

lenses whose images are superimposed over each other at the focal plane; in order for these images to fit the same format, one image is either compressed or "squeezed" horizontally, or stretched vertically.

The best approach for establishing the correct angle of view for an anamorphic lens in the horizontal and vertical planes is to ignore the fact that one is dealing with a squeezed image and think of the two focal lengths and their respective angles of view. It is not always necessary to use anamorphic lenses when shooting the elements for a squeezed composite image. The elements can be shot with spherical lenses and the squeeze introduced in the compositing stage.

Figure 3.13c   Squeeze and aspect ratio. The standard optical squeeze ratio in current use is 2:1 (Panavision and Technovision) on a 35mm format with an aspect ratio of 2.4:1. (1) Anamorphic image on a film frame (aspect ratio 1.20:1). (2) "Unsqueezed" anamorphic frame, aspect ratio 2.4:1 (2.35:1).

An anamorphic lens consists of a multielement spherical unit combined with cylindrical elements. The two groups have a common focal plane but different nodal points for the horizontal and vertical planes.

Foreshortening

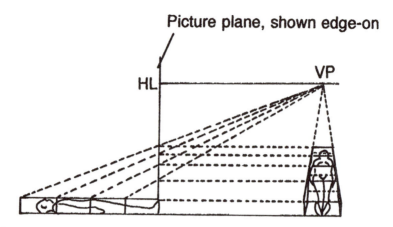

Figure 3.14 The effects of perspective. Foreshortening can be used deliberately to produce "forced perspective" backgrounds. (Redrawn from *Perspective* by Alison Cole: Doring-Kindersly, 1992.)

Perspective and 3-D Cinematography

Linear perspective is two dimensional; it is based on the fixed viewpoint of one eye. However, natural vision is based on the viewpoint of two eyes, that is, it is three-dimensional. Consequently, an understanding of linear perspective is even more necessary in three-dimensional cinematography.

It is necessary to forget some of the approaches developed and accepted in two-dimensional cinematography and look at the problems of three-dimensional cinematography with both eyes — literally. The size of the projection screen, the viewing position and distance to the screen, the focal length of the lenses and their interocular distance all have a more drastic effect on a three-dimensional picture than on a flat, two-dimensional one. (Incidentally, seeing things as a flat, two-dimensional representation is not something we are born with but something we all have to learn as demonstrated in tests with people who had been blind from birth and gained their sight as adults. People in primitive tribes who have not encountered photographs before cannot recognize the two-dimensional representation of a familiar face or object.)

Atmospheric Perspective

One thing that can destroy the illusion of an exterior model set is the lack of that gradual softening of the features as they recede into the distance, that is, atmospheric perspective. The effect of atmospheric perspective can be created by enclosing the miniature set inside a plastic tent and pumping fog into it until a specific density is achieved. A selective use of fog filters and a subtle manipulation of color within the scene can add to the effect of atmospheric perspective and enhance the overall illusion of reality.

Curvilinear Perspective

Curvilinear perspective was developed by Leonardo da Vinci and is based on the fact that the human field of vision is circular. Curvilinear perspective is particularly appropriate for understanding and dealing with wide-angle fields of view.

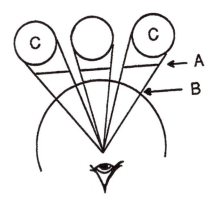

Figure 3.15 The outer columns appear wider than the central one when looked at in terms of linear perspective A. However they are identical when considered in terms of curvilinear perspective B. (REDRAWN FROM *PERSPECTIVE*.)

LIGHTING

If perspective is the mother, then lighting is the father of a good visual FX composite. The two work hand in glove to create the illusion of reality.

It is often the lighting of a studio set representing an exterior scene that gives it away as unreal, particularly when it is composited with a real exterior element. In order to sustain the illusion that the entire scene was shot on location, the lighting of the element shot in the studio has to match that of the one shot on location. This is not as easy as it sounds. The most obvious mismatches occur in the direction of the key light, which in a typical exterior setting is meant to emulate the sun. It shows up in the direction and density of the shadows.

The "one-light source" effect of the sun is difficult to reproduce in a studio environment with artificial illumination. The main reason for this is that sunlight is made up of collimated rays: the light rays are parallel to each other over the entire area lit by the sun. Even the largest artificial light sources, on the other hand, produce a light output that is essentially conical in shape: the light rays diverge as they travel from the light source.

Focussing lamps with good optics such as theatrical spotlights can come close to imitating sunlight, but the area of coverage is small. At true collimation the size of the beam equals the diameter of the lens. Another approach is to use groups of pre-focused spotlight lamps mounted closely together on a common framework. Even with the best of these lamps it is hard to achieve a true "one-source-one-shadow" result.

When compositing two or more elements photographed at very different locations or studios, it is often possible to overlook the obvious—the shadows. Yet the shadows are of crucial importance to the composite picture if it is to look convincing. A mismatch in the direction and density of the shadows destroys the illusion even if the perspective is matched perfectly, making the composite picture appear as a collage.

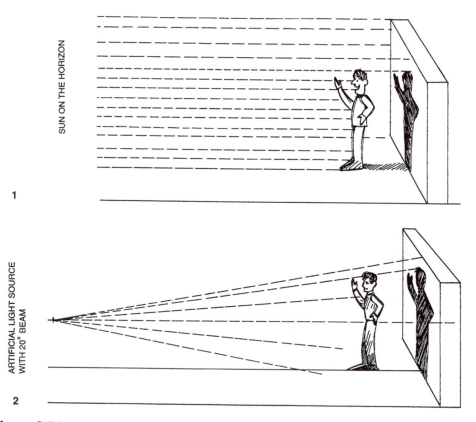

Figure 3.16 (1) Because the sun's rays are parallel to each other, the shadows produced by sunlight are the same size as the subject when the shadow plane is perpendicular to the axis of the rays. (2) An artificial light source produces a shadow that is bigger than the subject.

Hard Shadows and Miniature Sets

The importance of parallel light illumination is even more apparent when dealing with miniature sets, particularly when they need to match actual exterior locations. Wherever possible, the best solution is to take the miniature set outside and use direct sunlight. The problem of moving shadows is dealt with by mounting the miniature set on a moveable framework so that it can be rotated and angled as required to produce the desired shadow angle.

Not only the direction but also the quality (or density) of the shadows has to match. The contrast ratio between the highlights and shadows of the various elements of the composite image should correspond to each other, if they are to give the appearance of being lit by one and the same light source. The density of the shadows is controlled by the use of low-contrast filters or by reflecting sunlight off strategically positioned white sheets.

The effect of speckled lighting, such as is found under trees, is relatively easier to achieve, since the overlap areas of the multiple light sources emulating sunlight are less likely to be noticeable than in the case of direct hard shadows.

Diffused lighting is obviously easiest to reproduce, although even then there is a clear direction from which the light is emanating. A "skylight" effect is accomplished with the use of groups of soft lights or spotlights with additional diffusion (see Figure 11.30).

The sunlight has a special property of being "polarized" when reflected from certain surfaces at specific angles. This too can be imitated with the use of polarization filters (see Figure 5.11).

Interactive Lighting

It is the changes in the lighting of the foreground element in response to the changes in the lighting conditions on the background plate that make a good composite shot even better. These lighting changes can be subtle, such as wisps of clouds passing overhead or the shadows of a tree branch swaying, or more obvious, such as the effects of street lighting at night or when the actor steps out of an area of direct sunlight into a shadow of an object on the background plate.

When it comes to matching the shadows it is worth remembering that the color temperature of the average summer shade is 8,000 Kelvin as opposed to 6,500 Kelvin for the average summer daylight.

The Nature of Light

Visible light (optical) radiation covers a range from 380 to 770 nanometers in wavelength. It occupies a narrow band on the electromagnetic spectrum, ranging from x-rays with wavelengths of a billionth of a meter to radio waves with wavelengths of a meter or more.

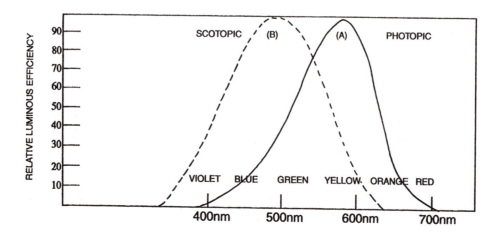

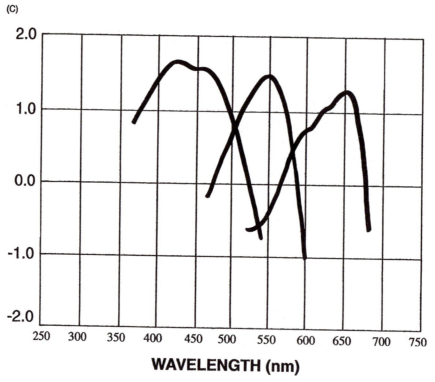

WAVELENGTH (nm)

Figure 3.17 Due to the fact that there are two sets of receptors in the retina (rods and cones) the sensitivity of the human eye can be plotted as two separate curves. (A) The photopic curve represents the responsiveness of the retina at higher levels of illumination (color vision). (B) The scotopic curve represents the responsiveness of the retina at low levels of luminosity (black-and-white vision). (C) Compare the spectral sensitivity curve of a typical color negative film to the sensitivity curves of the eye.

The sensitivity of color film emulsions does not correspond exactly to the sensitivity of the eye. Film is less sensitive and simply does not register certain wavelengths that the human eye does, yet it is more sensitive to other wavelengths that are beyond the range of the human eye.

Matching the Color of Light

Even when the perspective is correct and a perfect match of shadows and highlights has been achieved, the composite shot may still appear odd if there is a

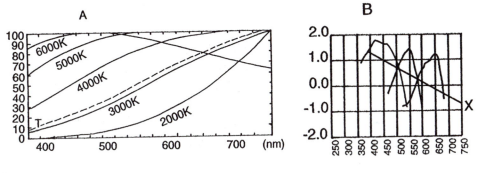

1.

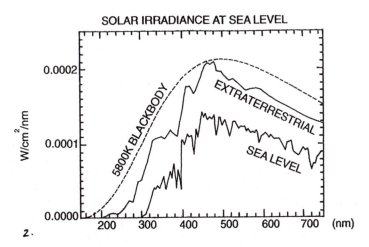

2.

Figure 3.18   1. (A) Spectral sensitivity curve of a tungsten filament lamp (T) follows closely the blackbody* radiation curve at 3,200 Kelvin.** (B) The spectral sensitivity curve of the color negative film (X) is almost a mirror image of the blackbody radiation curve.

2. Spectral sensitivity curve of sunlight closely follows a blackbody radiation curve at 5,800 Kelvin.

* "BLACK BODY" RADIATOR IS AN IDEAL LIGHT SOURCE BECAUSE ITS SPECTRAL RADIATION PROPERTIES ARE SOLELY DEPENDENT ON THE TEMPERATURE TO WHICH IT IS RAISED. IT IS USED FOR COMPARING AND DEFINING THE COLOR CONTENT OF OTHER LIGHT SOURCES WITH A SIMILAR CURVE IN THE VISIBLE PART OF THE SPECTRUM.

** DEGREES KELVIN (K) = DEGREES CELCIUS (C) PLUS 273 DEGREES.

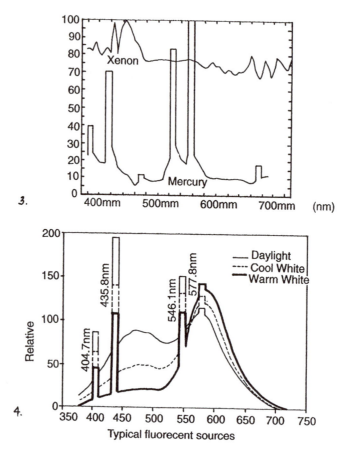

Figure 3.18 (continued) 3. Spectral sensitivity curve of Xenon and Mercury arc lamps. 4. Spectral energy distribution of typical fluorescent sources.

discrepancy in color balance between the various elements. Often it is not until all the elements are composited together that the mismatch in color becomes apparent.

A considerable amount of color correction can be done in the lab, but it cannot correct for an imbalance between the foreground and background elements. It is not possible to correct the one without making the other much worse.

The key factor governing color reproduction is the color temperature of the light used to expose the film. Different types of light sources have different spectral characteristics. Compare the spectral power distribution curves of sunlight and some of the commonly used artificial light sources with the spectral sensitivity curve of typical color negative stock.

It is important to maintain a careful match between the light sources; mixing light sources with different spectral energy distribution can lead to unexpected results even when the overall color temperature appears to match.

Color Temperature

In order to ensure the correct reproduction of color it is essential that the color temperature of the light source should match the specifications of the film emulsion. This is represented in degrees Kelvin (K). Most color-negative movie stock is balanced for tungsten light at 3,200 degrees Kelvin — this being the color temperature of the most commonly used studio lamps (tungsten halogen). However, there are a number of emulsions available that are balanced for daylight (5,600 degrees K). The actual color temperature of daylight varies according to the geographic location, the time of year, and the time of day. For absolute accuracy, color temperature readings should be taken at regular intervals, particularly early in the morning and late in the day.

A color temperature meter is used to check the color temperature of the light source. It indicates the degree of color correction required. This is accomplished with the use of color-correction filters.

When a color-correction filter is used on the camera lens it affects the color balance of the whole scene, but when it is used on the light source it changes the color temperature of the light source only. The filters are made of gelatin or acetate and are available in varying densities in additive form (red, green, and blue) and subtractive form (cyan, magenta, and yellow).

In addition to the full range of additive and subtractive color correction filters, composite filters are also available. These are specifically designed for producing an overall shift in the color temperature in steps of 100 degrees Kelvin. These are the

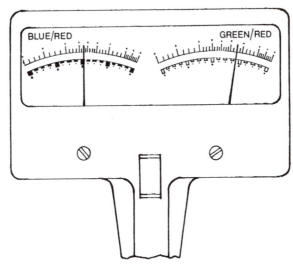

Figure 3.19 Color temperature meters have a photocell and two filters, usually red and blue. Some models use three filters (red, blue, and green) and are more accurate. Relative proportions of red and blue (or red, blue, and green) light are indicated on a precalibrated scale and can be converted to Kelvin (degrees). Some models give a direct reading in Kelvin as well as a recommended filter for a specific type of color emulsion.

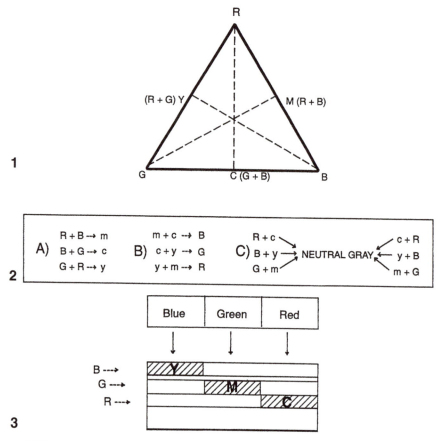

Figure 3.20   (1) Triangle of additive primaries at the corners (blue, red, and green), and the corresponding subtractive primaries on the opposite sides (yellow, cyan, and magenta). (2) Additive and subtractive charts. (A) Combining two additives makes one subtractive. (B) Combining two subtractives makes one additive. (C) Using the complementary (opposite) colors produces neutral grey. (3) Cross-section of a color-negative emulsion: blue-sensitive layer produces a yellow negative image; green-sensitive layer produces a magenta negative image; red-sensitive layer produces a cyan negative image.

Wratten 82 and 80 series (bluish in appearance), which shift the color temperature towards the blue end of the spectrum, and the Wratten 81 and 85 series (orange), that shift the color temperature towards the red end of the spectrum.

Voltage Supply and Color Temperature.

A variation in voltage supply produces changes in the color temperature of the light source, therefore it is advisable to keep an eye on the voltage fluctuations of the studio supply. A dedicated generator is the best bet for consistent results. When a light source is operated on a higher-than-rated voltage, the

A	B
82 = cc10C + cc5M*	81 = cc5Y
82A = cc15C + cc5M	81A = cc5Y + cc2M
82B = cc20C + cc7M	81B = cc10Y + cc2M
82C = cc25C + cc7M	81C = cc15Y + cc5M

*Wratten filter number 82 is equal to (or has the same effect as) standard correction filters (c.c.) 10 cyan plus 5 magenta (combined).

Figure 3.21 Composite filters produce a shift in color temperature: A-Blue shift; B-Red shift.

color temperature shifts towards the blue end of the spectrum. This is very useful for manipulating the color balance. A relatively small increase in voltage results in a considerable increase in light output and a sharp drop in the rated life of the lamp.

In Figure 3.22a, an increase of less then 10% in voltage of a lamp rated for 120V results in a 100 K shift in color temperature. This is equivalent to using color correction filters: 10 cyan and 5 magenta, which would require an exposure compensation of 1/3 f-stop. Instead, the output is up by 1/3 f-stop, resulting in an effective difference of a 2/3 f-stop between the direct filtration approach and the voltage increase.

When the lamp is run at a lower-than-rated voltage 3.22b, the color-temperature shifts towards the red end of the spectrum with a corresponding drop in light output and a dramatic increase in the life of the lamp.

1. @ 120V: light output 100%; color temperature 3,200 K; lamp life 100%.
2. @ 130V: light output 130%; color temperature 3,300 K; lamp life 35%.
3. @ 140V: light output 160%; color temperature 3,450 K; lamp life 15%.

Figure 3.22a Percentage of rated operating voltage.

1. @ 120V: light output 100%; color temperature 3,200 K.
2. @ 110V: light output 75%; color temperature 3,100 K; lamp life 300%.

Figure 3.22b Incandescent lamp rated for 120V (General Electric Calculator).

The color temperature of a lamp can also change towards the end of its life. A regular check of color temperature readings of the lamps as well as of the supply voltage is a wise precaution.

Variation in exposure and film processing are additional factors that affect the accuracy of color reproduction.

A color chart and a grey scale shot at the head of each take will help to maintain quality control between the elements that will be used to make a composite image. It is important that the color chart and the grey scale are shot under the same conditions as each separate element.

Quality Control

A grey scale and a color chart are essential aids in maintaining a consistent reference between the compositing elements. They also play an important part in maintaining a standard reference through all the compositing stages as well as transfers in and out of electronic media.

The Grey Scale

An ideal test scene would contain the full range of neutral color tones from white to black. But as such a scene is not easy to come by, a suitably stepped grey scale is used as a standard reference. The grey scale ranges from black with 2% reflectivity to white with 93% reflectivity, with the middle grey at 18% reflectivity.

A correctly exposed, processed, and printed negative will result in a black-and-white grey scale without a color cast and with both ends of the scale (black and white) looking normal.

Color Chart

A color chart in conjunction with a grey scale is used to determine the appropriate color correction and establish a basic standard filtration for the lights. A color temperature meter will give a good indication of the degree of color correction required; but a wedge test, processed normally and printed at middle light, is the best way to determine the exposure and color correction, particularly when two or more compositing elements are involved.

Color compensating filters absorb the light proportionally to their strength (or density), so a color correction "wedge" has to be linked with exposure. A series of exposures is made with each color-compensating filter, usually at 1/4 f-stop intervals and covering a range of 1 f-stop on either side of the calculated mean exposure. This is repeated for each successive filter.

Processing

Film processing plays a crucial role in obtaining consistent results. Before embarking on a project with an unfamiliar lab (or a new film stock), it is advisable to shoot a grey scale and color chart test and print it at middle light. In black and white, the middle light is 13, and in color printing it is 25 across (i.e., 25-25-25), which indicates equal amounts of blue, red, and green colors. Due to several other factors affecting the development and printing of the film negative, it is advisable to get the middle range printing lights from the particular laboratory doing the processing. These can also be affected by the particular batch of negative film stock requiring overall correction; the same may apply to the printing stock used by the lab. In certain circumstances a lighter or denser print "look"

GREY SCALE

2%	4%	10%	18%	38%	60%	93%

COLOR CHART

Red	Green	Blue	Yellow	Cyan	Magenta

Figure 3.23 (Top) Grey scale, a series of neutral color patches of progressively greater density. (Bottom) Color chart.

may be preferred, and a different set of printer lights can be chosen to represent the mean exposure.

A grey scale may have a color cast when printed at 25-25-25. The need to print it on 28-24-23, for example, to get rid of the cast does not indicate that the negative was incorrectly exposed (the average is still 25).

4

Visual FX Preproduction and Planning

It's the old problem of the chicken or the egg. Which should come first, script breakdown of FX elements (components), the conceptual design, storyboarding, or "costing" (budgeting)? In an ideal world the order would be:

1. Conceptual design
2. Storyboarding
3. Script breakdown of shots requiring FX
   Grouping of shots by type of effect required
   Choosing the best approach for each group of FX shots
4. Scheduling
5. Budgeting

In the real world, however, all of the above are done in a haphazard manner, and more often than not in reverse order.

CONCEPTUAL DESIGN

Ideally, conceptual design would be the first stage of preproduction on a visual FX project. This is normally undertaken by the production designer or an outside illustrator who works either from the screenplay or from the input of a producer, production designer, or even the film's director if he or she is on board at the time. The conceptual stage may involve the design of some exotic creatures, machines, or elaborate sets and costumes. The conceptual artist should be free of any constraints relating to the physical production. It will be up to someone else to figure out how to translate his or her creation into a real image on celluloid. Often illustrators who have no prior experience of film production produce the best conceptual art.

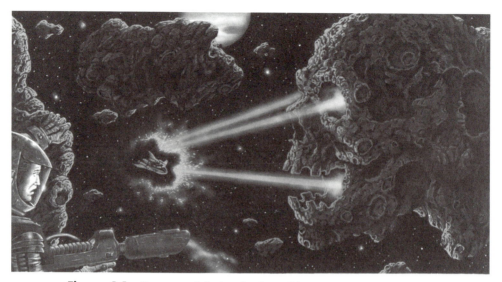

Figure 4.1 Conceptual design for *Space Pirates*. COURTESY OF ZOPTIC S.F/X.

The main purpose at this stage is to establish two key factors:

1. what the subject is going to look like, and
2. what the relative scale of the subject is (i.e., how much larger or smaller than life-size).

The initial design is then elaborated and enhanced until it is finally approved as "the look" for that specific subject or set.

STORYBOARDING

Storyboards are a series of drawings indicating key setups (frames) in a sequence. They are based on the conceptual design and incorporate the look of the sets, location, and any other elements (such as animatronic and other exotic creations) that may be required. At this stage, it is often the case that neither the sets nor the locations exist, so they may have to be created in large part as models and miniatures. However, the "look" established in the conceptual design stage and the camera angles indicated on the storyboards will serve as a blueprint and common reference for everyone involved.

During the storyboarding stage it is not really necessary to be concerned with how the effects for specific shots will be accomplished or what technique will be required. In fact, the director and the production designer do not need to know anything about visual FX techniques as long as they have a clear idea of what they want to see on the screen and can convey this to the storyboard artist.

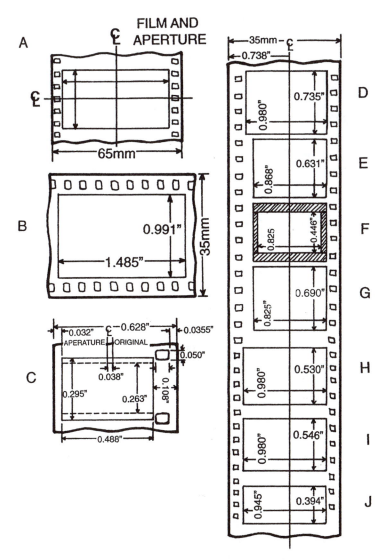

Figure 4.2a   It is important to establish the film format and aspect ratio to be used. (A) 65 mm. (B) VistaVision or double format. (C) Super 16mm. (D) 35mm full aperture (silent). (E) Academy aperture (1.33:1). (F) Wide screen (1.85:1). (G) Wide screen anamorphic (2.40:1) — 0.825″ × 0.690″. (H) Super 1.85 (1.85:1) — 0.980″ × 0.530″. (I) Three Perf (1.78:1) — 0.980″ × 0.546″. (J) Two Perf (2.40:1) — 0.945″ × 0.394″.

The resultant roughs should be approved by the director and amended where necessary before they are "locked" and rendered as finished boards.

Storyboarding is often done even when the scenes do not require any visual FX but involve complex action that needs to be thought through and laid out clearly so that everyone involved, from the editor to the stunt coordinator, knows exactly what is intended.

Figure 4.2b   Single storyboard from *Space Pirates*. Courtesy of Zoptic S.F/X.

The visual effects supervisor may be working directly with the storyboard artist or serving as a liaison between the director, production designer, and the storyboard artist. In any case, it is his or her job to get as much detailed information from the director and the production designer as possible and ensure that it is reflected in the storyboards.

As the storyboarding progresses and other elements start coming into the picture, it often becomes necessary to modify the original concept. This obviously has a domino effect on other elements and has to be incorporated into the overall plan.

Ideally, any locations required for the production should be locked in before the storyboarding stage begins in order to establish how many shots can be filmed in a real location and how many will require FX elements such as matte painting or models and so on. Once this has been established, the photographs of the actual locations can then be incorporated into the storyboarding process. Decisions can be made regarding the design and sizes of those elements that have to be built, and a rough idea of the costs can then be extrapolated. In real life there is a tendency for the visual FX supervisors to skew the effects solutions towards the particular techniques that they have firsthand experience of or have readily available at the FX company with which he or she works or has a close relationship.

Electronic Storyboarding

Computer software is available that can speed up the storyboarding process. It provides generic characters in typical settings that can, in some cases, be modi-

Figure 4.3 Storyboard sequence from *The Phoenix and the Magic Carpet*. (COURTESY OF MAGIC CARPET FILMS.)

fied to suit particular requirements. Additional images can be imported and manipulated within the program.

Perhaps the most interesting way of using the electronic approach to storyboarding is with architectural CAD (Computer Aided Design) software programs. The user can input the actual dimensions of a set or model and view it as a three-dimensional representation from any chosen angle and elevation with the correct perspective. This can speed up the storyboarding process when working with a storyboard artist because it makes it so much easier to be specific about the camera angle. The artist can add the characters at the correct scale and perspective either electronically or by drawing them over a printout.

The CAD approach can replace the need for a physical model mockup, which is a fairly standard approach, particularly when large-scale sets are

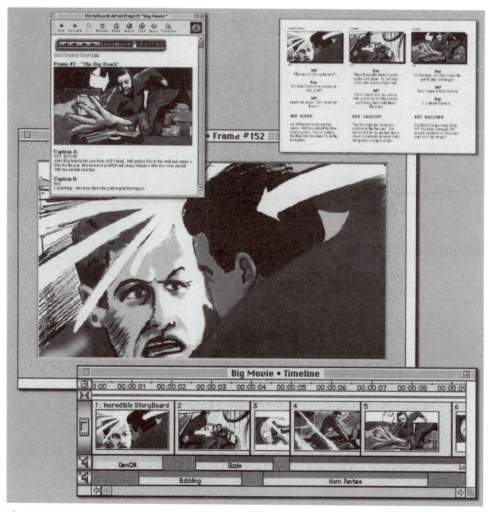

Figure 4.4   This example of an electronic storyboard was produced by *Storyboard Quick* software.

involved. However, some directors find it easier to visualize camera angles within a real physical model as opposed to the virtual set.

A major advantage of an electronic previsualization approach is that the chosen camera positions can be transferred to the real set at the corresponding scale. This is particularly useful when the shot involves compositing two or more elements. The set could end up being constructed in miniature instead of full size and the actors would then need to be composited into it at the corresponding scale and perspective.

Animatics

Some storyboarding software offers the facility of creating fairly crude animation of action and camera moves within a scene. This is a useful tool when it is difficult to convey a complex action in static frames. However, it is very time-consuming and costly to produce a good animatic.

VISUAL FX SCRIPT BREAKDOWN

Once the storyboarding stage is completed it becomes clear which sequences require visual FX. These are then noted down together with the appropriate scene number and a brief description of the action within the scene. Often the scene has to be broken down into individual shots in order to identify the visual effects requirement more accurately. The FX shots are then grouped into various categories in much the same way as is done in the general breakdown for actors. By analyzing the shot count in each of these categories it becomes possible to make a firm choice of the most appropriate visual FX technique for each category.

There are two types of visual FX script breakdowns in principle:

1. a rough early version, and
2. the final detailed version from which a shooting schedule can be prepared.

The Rough-and-Ready Approach

A rough, early breakdown is often done even before the conceptual design and storyboarding stage as a kind of a stab in the dark to give the producer a ball park figure for visual FX. It is not the best way to estimate the cost, but unfortunately it is a very common practice. Most of the time the visual effects supervisor has to make certain assumptions, since there is usually no director involved at this stage. The script itself is likely to go through several rewrites before the filming begins—if it ever gets that far.

At this stage, the script does not normally have scene numbers indicated, and it is best to go by page numbers. However, since there are likely to be several FX shots on the same page, a system has to be adopted to differentiate one shot from another. One way is to number each shot with the page number given first, then the shot number, starting with shot one for every new page: such as,

TITLE — S. F/X BREAKDOWN — Sequence "A"

Shot No.	Page No.	EXT/INT	SCENE	DAY/NIGH	ACTION	MAIN Prod.	F.P.	B.P.	MOD Prod.	Plts.	L & Opt.	CGI Gr.	PLAT Air.	S 1	2	3	4
1	11	EXT	HANGER # 1	S/set	Fiske's plane blasts out of the hanger		(X)		X			(X)	X		1		
2	11	E/I	F-16 COCKPIT	S/set	Fiske cranks the jet to full burner		(X)	X	X				X		1		
3	11	EXT	RUNWAY-GEORGE A.F.B.	S/set	F-15 leaps off the ground (wheels tuck in)			X	X			(X)	X	1	1		
4	11	E/I	F-16 COCKPIT	S/set	Fiske snaps the jet into vertical climb.		(X)	X	X					1	1		
5	11	EXT	HANGER # 2	S/set	Blaney's plane blasts out		(X)		X			(X)	X			2	
6	11	E/I	F-16 COCKPIT	S/set	Blaney cranks his jet		(X)	X	X				X			2 B	
7	11	E/I	F-16 COCKPIT	S/set	Fiske climbs to 30,000 ft.		(X)	X					X	F			
8	11	EXT	SKY	S/set	Fiske's plane levelling off				X				X	F	1		
9	11	INT	F-16 COCKPIT	S/set	Fiske scans the skies. Reports.		(X)	X					X	F			
10	12	EXT	SKAY ABOVE OCEAN	S/set	F's P.O.V of JUMBO jet.				X				X				
11	12	EXT	SKAY ABOVE OCEAN	S/set	Fiske's plane flashes past jumbo.				X				X	1			
12	12	EXT	SKAY ABOVE OCEAN	S/set	Fiske's plane initiating a barrel roll				X				X	1			
13	12	INT	F-16 COCKPIT	S/set	Fiske does a barrel roll; talks to base.		(X)	X					X	F			
14	12	EXT	SKAY ABOVE OCEAN	S/set	Fiske's F-15 flies parallel with JAL.				X				X	1			
15	12	EXT	SKAY ABOVE OCEAN	S/set	Blaney's plane appears;passes close.				X				X			2	
16	12	INT	F-16 COCKPIT	S/set	Fiske reacts to Blaney's close pass		(X)	X	(X)	(2)			X	F (2)			
17	13	INT	F-16 COCKPIT	S/set	Blaney responds to Fiske's call		(X)	X					X		B		
18	13	EXT	SKAY ABOVE OCEAN	S/set	Fiske pulls into vertical climb				X				X	1	1		
19	13	INT	F-16 COCKPIT	S/set	Blaney looks around; can't see Fiske.		(X)	X					X		B		
20	13	EXT	SKAY ABOVE OCEAN	S/set	Blaney's plane heads for home.				X				X			2	
21	13	INT	F-16 COCKPIT	S/set	Fiske is alone with his thoughts		(X)	X					X	F			
22	13	EXT	SKAY ABOVE OCEAN	S/set	Fiske's plane pulls away from camera				X				X	1			

TITLE — LIVE ACTION FX — Sequence "A"

Shot No.	Page No.	EXT/INT	SCENE	DAY/NIGH	ACTION	MAIN Prod.	F.P.	B.P.	MOD Prod.	Plts.	L & Opt.	CGI Gr.	PLAT Air.	S 1	2	3	4
2	11	E/I	F-16 COCKPIT	S/set	Fiske cranks the jet to full burner	1	(X)	X				X		F			
4	11	E/I	F-16 COCKPIT	S/set	Fiske snaps the jet into vertical climb.	1	(X)	X						F			
7	11	E/I	F-16 COCKPIT	S/set	Fiske climbs to 30,000 ft.	1	(X)	X					X	F			
9	11	INT	F-16 COCKPIT	S/set	Fiske scans the skies. Reports.	1	(X)	X					X	F			
13	12	INT	F-16 COCKPIT	S/set	Fiske does a barrel roll; talks to base.	1	(X)	X					X	F			
16	12	INT	F-16 COCKPIT	S/set	Fiske reacts to Blaney's close pass	1	(X)	X	(X)	(2)			X	F (2)			
21	13	INT	F-16 COCKPIT	S/set	Fiske is alone with his thoughts	1	(X)	X					X	F			
6	11	E/I	F-16 COCKPIT	S/set	Blaney cranks his jet	2	(X)	X				X			B		
17	13	INT	F-16 COCKPIT	S/set	Blaney responds to Fiske's call	2	(X)	X					X		B		
19	13	INT	F-16 COCKPIT	S/set	Blaney looks around; can't see Fiske.	2	(X)	X					X		B		

TITLE — MODEL FX — Sequence "A"

Shot No.	Page No.	EXT/INT	SCENE	DAY/NIGH	ACTION	MAIN Prod.	F.P.	B.P.	MOD Prod.	Plts.	L & Opt.	CGI Gr.	PLAT Air.	S 1	2	3	4
1	11	EXT	HANGER # 1	S/set	Fiske's plane blasts out of the hanger		(X)		X			(X)	X		1		
12	12	EXT	SKAY ABOVE OCEAN	S/set	Fiske's plane initiating a barrel roll				X				X	1	1		
18	13	EXT	SKAY ABOVE OCEAN	S/set	Fiske pulls into vertical climb				X				X	1	1		
14	12	EXT	SKAY ABOVE OCEAN	S/set	Fiske's F-15 flies parallel with JAL.				X				X	1	1		
11	12	EXT	SKAY ABOVE OCEAN	S/set	Fiske's plane flashes past jumbo.				X				X	1	1		
8	11	EXT	SKY	S/set	Fiske's plane levelling off				X				X	1	1		
3	11	EXT	RUNWAY-GEORGE A.F.B.	S/set	F-15 leaps off the ground (wheels tuck in)				X			(X)	X	1	1		
22	13	EXT	SKAY ABOVE OCEAN	S/set	Fiske's plane pulls away from camera				X				X	1	1		
15	12	EXT	SKAY ABOVE OCEAN	S/set	Blaney's plane appears;passes close.				X				X			2	
20	13	EXT	SKAY ABOVE OCEAN	S/set	Blaney's plane heads for home.				X				X			2	
5	11	EXT	HANGER # 2	S/set	Blaney's plane blasts out		(X)		X			(X)	X			2	
10	12	EXT	SKAY ABOVE OCEAN	S/set	F's P.O.V of JUMBO jet.				X				X				3

Figure 4.5 A typical visual FX breakdown form (rough).

p24/3 or p24 S3. Another method is to indicate the shot numbers sequentially from the first page, then the page number, as in shot 34/p6 (or S34/p6). The problem with this method is that it is more difficult to add or delete shot numbers without resorting to suffixes like a, b, c, or x, y, z.

Other key elements in the script breakdown are the SCENE TITLE and a brief description of the ACTION within the shot.

A rough estimate of the visual FX costs done in this way often kills the project at an early stage. Yet virtually all initial bids by the visual FX houses are prepared on this basis, and it is no wonder that disagreements arise and costs start to escalate once the picture goes into production. Someone, however, has to come up with a breakdown that will serve as a blueprint for the next stages of preproduction and give a reasonably accurate projection of the costs, and an experienced visual FX supervisor is in a better position to do this than anyone else.

The Detailed Approach

A detailed visual FX breakdown is done after the storyboarding stage and is often an evolution of the original rough-and-ready breakdown. By this point the picture is in full preproduction, and it is important to lock down as many elements as possible. Any changes that occur from this point on will have a domino effect and must be accounted for in the shooting schedule. For example, it may become apparent that a miniature can be replaced by a matte painting, in which case it would be dropped out of one group and added to another.

Once a detailed visual FX breakdown is prepared, the shots can be grouped into various categories and subcategories as per the specific requirements both in terms of technology and subject matter. Very often the same shot may require several elements, and these have to be indicated and taken into account. There may also be alternative ways of tackling a particular effect and these too should be noted down. It is now time to lock in the technical approach that will best accomplish the effects in each category.

In the final visual FX breakdown the shot number follows the scene number (e.g., 9.02 refers to scene 9, shot 2). A separate column also indicates the appropriate storyboard number.

There are breakdown and scheduling programs available that make it easier to manipulate data. Alternatively, you can create your own custom form with a spreadsheet program like Lotus 123.

THE SHOOTING SCHEDULE

A visual FX shooting schedule is prepared from the detailed breakdown, taking into consideration the order of priorities so that all the elements can be ready on time. This is of the utmost importance if serious problems are to be avoided down

"SPACE PIRATES"

DETAILED BREAKDOWN

Sequence "K"

Shot No.	Sc. No.	EXT•INT	SCENE	Story Board No.	SET No.	ACTION	MAIN Prod.	MAIN F.P.	MAIN T.V.	2nd. Unit	MOD L Prod.	MOD L F.P.	Plts.	Opt.	DAVID 1	BIGMAN 2	HENRREE 3	ANTON 4	DINGO 5
376	127.05	INT	"SHOOTING STAR"/CONTROL CABIN	K 2	16	ANTON APPEARS ON THE MONITOR	PL								1			(4)	
377	127.06	INT	"SHOOTING STAR"/CONTROL CABIN	N.S.B.	16	REVERSE ON DAVID; THREATENS TO DESTROY ANTON'S SHIP		x	x				x		1	2		(4)	
378	127.07	INT	"SHOOTING STAR"/CONTROL CABIN	N.S.B.	16	CLOSE ON BIGMAN; FINGER HOVERS OVER FIRING BUTTON		x					x		1	2		(4)	
379	127.08	INT	"SHOOTING STAR"/CONTROL CABIN	N.S.B.	16	CLOSE ON DAVID		x					x		1	2		(4)	
380	127.09	INT	"SHOOTING STAR"/CONTROL CABIN	K 3	16	C.U. VIDEO MONITOR; PULL BACK TO SEE BIGMAN CREEPING OUT		x	x				x		1			(4)	
381	127.10	EXT	"SHOOTING STAR"/CONTROL CABIN	N.S.B.	16	CLOSE ON DAVID	PL								1			(4)	
382	127.11	INT	"SHOOTING STAR"/CONTROL CABIN	N.S.B.	16	CLOSE T.V. MONITOR, IT GOES BLANK	PL					PL			1			(4)	
383	127.12	INT	"SHOOTING STAR"/CONTROL CABIN	N.S.B.	16	DAVID LOOKS AROUND THE CABIN; BIGMAN HAS GONE		x				PL	x		1	2		(4)	
384	128.00	EXT	SPACE/ASTEROID BELT	K 4	28	BIGMAN FLOATS TOWARDS ANTON'S SHIP, HIDING BEHIND A ROCK		x	x				x		1	2		(4)	
385	129.01	INT	"SHOOTING STAR"/CONTROL CABIN	AS K 2	16	CLOSE T.V. MONITOR ; ANTON APPEARS	PL					PL			1			(4)	
386	129.02	INT	"SHOOTING STAR"/CONTROL CABIN	N.S.B.	16	CLOSE ON DAVID						PL			1			(4)	
387	129.03	INT	ANTON'S SHIP / CONTROL CABIN	K 5	10	ANTON TELLS DAVID (ON T.V. SCREEN) OF HIS SURPRISE	PL	x	x			PL	x		1			(4)	
388	129.04	INT	"SHOOTING STAR"/CONTROL CABIN	K 6	16	DAVID LOOKS TO THE SIDE AT THE SKULL ASTEROID		x				PL	x		1			(4)	
389	130.01	E/I	SPACE/ASTEROID BELT/"S.STAR" COCKPIT	N.S.B.	16	DAVID'S P.O.V. OF SKULL ASTEROID TURNING TO FACE THE SHIP				1		PL			(1)			(4)	
390	131.01	INT	"SHOOTING STAR"/CONTROL CABIN	N.S.B.	16	ANTON (ON T.V. SCREEN) GIVES ORDER	PL	x	x				x		1			(4)	
391	131.02	INT	"SHOOTING STAR"/CONTROL CABIN	K 7	16	DAVID REACTS TO THE LAZER BEAMS FROM THE SKULL ASTEROID		x					x		1			(4)	
392	131.03	EXT	SPACE/ASTEROID BELT	K 7	28	SKULL ASTEROID DOMINATES THE SCENE ; BIGMAN REACTS (F.G.)						PL		x		2			
393	131.04	INT	"SHOOTING STAR"/CONTROL CABIN	N.S.B.	16	DAVID TRIES TO PRESERVE AS MUCH ENERGY AS POSSIBLE		x				PL	x		1				
394	131.05	INT	"SHOOTING STAR"/CONTROL CABIN	N.S.B.	16	CLOSE ON ENERGY DEPLETION DIAL		x				PL	x		1				
395	132.00	INT	SPACE/ASTEROID BELT	N.S.B.	MDL	THE DEAD, DARK SHOOTING STAR HANGS IN CONE OF LIGHT				x		V/V		x					
396	133.01	EXT	ANTON'S SHIP / AIRLOCKS	N.S.B.	10 X	SATISFIED, ANTON CALLS FOR THE BOARDING PARTY TO PREPARE						PL						4	
397	133.02	INT	SPACE/ASTEROID BELT	N.S.B.	10	BOARDING PARTY REACT TO ANTON'S ORDER		x				PL	x		1				
398	134.00	INT	SHOOTING STAR"/CONTROL CABIN	N.S.B.	16	DAVID CHECKS HIS JET-PACK AND OXYGEN TANKS		x				PL	x					4	

Figure 4.6   The visual FX script breakdown is very much like the general script breakdown, except that it is much more detailed and involves every single cut in the scene that has any type of visual FX.

Figure 4.6 *(continued)*

the line. An obvious example is that a background element (the plate) should be scheduled to be shot sometime before the foreground element involving actors. This way the cinematographer can match the lighting on the foreground subject with that of the background plate, particularly when interactive lighting to ensure that the light changes on the foreground subject match the lighting conditions of the background scene.

This rule applies regardless of the technique used for compositing the two elements, such as whether it's the process approach (front or rear projection) or the travelling matte approach (blue or green screen). Unfortunately, there is always a temptation in the case of the travelling matte approach to shoot the actor first. In such cases the best a cinematographer can do is provide basic illumination — and hope that someone down the line in "post" (postproduction) will find an appropriate background that matches the lighting, lens angle, and perspective.

The production manager needs as much information as possible, including a clear order of priority for shooting the effects elements for inclusion in the final schedule. Both of these have to allow for other key factors, such as the availability of actors, locations, sets, FX crew and equipment, and so forth.

On larger productions a unit manager is appointed to handle the needs of the visual FX team and serve as a liaison with the main unit. In addition, second unit directors or visual FX directors are appointed to direct separate units dealing with a particular aspect of visual FX, such as models and miniatures; stunts; aerial; location backgrounds; process projection; and so on. Second unit directors are often Directors of Photography (DPs) and/or visual FX supervisors with specific experience in one or more visual effects fields.

On some productions an overall visual FX supervisor is appointed to oversee the farming out of effects shots to outside vendors. The best approach is for the production to set up one or more visual FX units under the direction of second unit directors and/or FX supervisors who are directly responsible to the film's director and producer. This is not as common an approach in Hollywood as one might expect. However, the most prolific and successful producer/directors in this field have either set up their own FX facilities (or are closely involved with one) in order to service their production needs and also handle work for other productions: Lucas, Spielberg, and Cameron, for example. The majority of studio producers appear to favor the insurance factor of farming out the responsibility for visual effects production to someone else. On an effect-laden movie this approach seems totally absurd.

HOW LONG IS A PIECE OF STRING? THE ROUGH-AND-READY APPROACH TO FX BUDGETING

The usual line a visual effects supervisor hears from a producer is, "I just need a rough idea of the FX costs — I won't hold you to it." What that really means is, "Give me an idea of what you think it will cost, and I'll come back to you later — if I find the money — and ask you to do it for less."

PRODUCTION TITLE:

A/C Code	DESCRIPTION	Page No.	TOTALS
	Production Staff		
	Extra Talent		
	Art Direction		
	Set Construction		
	Set Striking		
	Set Operations		
	Physical Effects		
	Set Dressing, Oper. & Strike		
	Property, Oper. & Strike		
	Wardrobe		
	Animatronic		
	Makeup & Hairdressing		
	Elect., Rig, Oper., & Strike		
	Camera Operations		
	Sound Operations		
	Transportation		
	Location		
	Film & Laboratory		
	Stage Facilities		
	Process Projection		
	C.G.I. compositing		
	Opticals		
	Animation		
	Models & Miniatures		
	Tests		
	Fringe Benefits		
	Insurence		
	TOTAL:		
	Contingency		
	Overheads		
	Mark up		
	TOTAL:		

Figure 4.7 Top sheet of a typical VFX budget form.

In order to be able to make an educated guess of the budget for the visual FX component of a movie, it is essential to have an idea of the size and scale of this undertaking; in other words, the number and type of visual FX shots.

The best way to arrive at a shot count for each of the various types of effects (categories) is to do as detailed a breakdown as possible under the circumstances. By noting down the assumed parameters at this stage, it will be possible to update the breakdown later when the chosen parameters are either confirmed or superceded by others.

From these shot counts a summary can be prepared for each category that indicates the total number of models, miniatures, background plates, and other elements. The next step is to decide on the most appropriate and cost-effective technique to be used. Then, on the basis of the average cost per shot from previous experience, one can estimate the cost for each group of effects. One can also have a pretty good guess at how long it is going to take to do all the shots if they are done in a particular order.

VFX Production Schedule

major Studio
dragonqueen
Prod #: FI-300-251098

Unit B schedule

BA 5.01

f **hero attacking dragon**

dragon smokes hero with fire breath. Princess enters the starship, dragon slowly follows her. Cam pans right to left

greenscreen - mc

dragon breathes fire.   hero turns to skeleton, smoke rises.   princess goes to starship, dragon

---

End of Day - Monday, October 26, 1998

RE 1.01

b **Princess screaming**

princess screaming for help, dragon attacks her

Princess
greenscreen - mc
Dreamscape Imagery Inc.

BA 5.01

d **princess**

dragon smokes hero with fire breath. Princess enters the starship, dragon slowly follows her. Cam pans right to left

Princess
greenscreen - mc

dragon breathes fire.   hero turns to skeleton, smoke rises.   princess goes to starship, dragon

---

End of Day - Tuesday, October 27, 1998

BA 5.01

l **starship on ground**

dragon smokes hero with fire breath. Princess enters the starship, dragon slowly follows her. Cam pans right to left

model starship
motion control

dragon breathes fire.   hero turns to skeleton, smoke rises.   princess goes to starship, dragon

---

End of Day - Thursday, October 29, 1998

BA 5.02

b **starship flying right to left**

princess flying with starship around dragon, fires and pulverises him

CG starship
CGI
Dreamscape Imagery Inc.

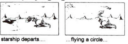

starship departs....   ...flying a circle...   ...shoots and pulverises dragon...   ...dragon skeleton is left, starship leaves.

End of Day - Wednesday, November 04, 1998

Figure 4.8   Production schedule

PART 2

Visual Effects Tools: The Nuts and Bolts of VFX Production

THE GENESIS OF VISUAL EFFECTS

In the beginning there was an apparatus, and it was called a camera . . . and this was good for visual effects.

The camera consumed film that was processed in the land of Lab and printed on another apparatus called the printer, which had a bi-pack magazine . . . and this too was good for visual effects.

The camera begat a bi-pack magazine of its own . . . and this was even better for visual effects.

In time the printer begat a projector and was named an optical printer . . . and this was good news for visual effects.

Then the camera (with its bi-pack magazine) grew a support column so that it could look down upon and have dominion over the flat world of artwork, and it became an animation stand.

And it came to pass that the animation stand became motorized, and soon after, computerized . . . and this was good for visual effects.

Meanwhile the optical printer became fruitful and multiplied . . . and this was good for visual effects. Then it came to pass that one of the offspring became attached to the animation stand and this blessed union begat an aerial image projector.

Then a miracle happened: the animation stand grew extra arms, raised itself on wheels, and developed a synthetic brain to control its many movements . . . and it was called motion control . . . which was good for visual effects.

And lo, another miracle happened: the optical printer split in half and begat process projection . . . and it was good for visual effects.

And lo, another miracle happened: the optical printer became attached to the digital camera and begat a digital scanner . . . and this was good for visual effects.

5

In-Camera FX

*In the beginning there was an apparatus,
and it was called a camera . . . and this was
good for visual effects.*

A great deal of visual effects work can be accomplished with conventional cameras and equipment. In fact, there is not a clear dividing line between standard production cinematography and special visual effects. Most of the "in-camera" effects can be achieved by other means, but these other means require the original negative to be duplicated, whereas in-camera effects are always first-generation. This is a very important consideration, even when the same scene may have to be duplicated later on, in order to add some other effects element.

THE BASIC FX CAMERA

Virtually any production camera can serve as an effects camera in most cases. The most important requirements are good optics (lenses) and good film registration (steadiness). A variable shutter is a major asset for visual effects work. Some of the best effects cameras are old Mitchell Standards with various degrees of custom modification, including pellicle-reflex (a very thin two-way mirror). Mitchell S35R is a very popular effects camera of the reflex type. Relatively newer designs are made specifically for animation work and/or digital scanning, such as Oxberry and Nielson-Hordell.

Registration

All movie cameras employ some method of registering the film frame in the camera gate while it is being exposed. In some cases, this is done by the intermittent claw movement alone. However, for "in-camera" effects, only cameras with the highest standard of registration are really good enough. These cameras employ registration pins that engage the film perforations during the exposure and disengage again before the pull-down claw moves it forward for the next exposure.

Without good registration the film tends to "weave" when it is projected. This is not usually noticeable for normal shooting, but when another element is added to the same negative (such as a "supered" caption), the weave is exaggerated because the two elements move against each other. If the same camera is used for both passes engaging the same perforations, an identical weave will be produced on both runs through the camera, which makes it less noticeable.

Fixed-Pin Registration

Fixed registration pins are attached to the gate aperture plate. The transport mechanism is designed to advance a frame of film and place it over the pins. At the end of the exposure the intermittent movement lifts the film up from the registration pins and pulls down the next frame. This is the Bell and Howell registration system, which is used on many high-precision cameras specially designed for visual effects work. It is also known as the clapper gate or the shuttle gate. It is most suitable for stop-motion work (and continuous running at slower speeds) and is widely used on animation cameras, optical printers, as well as digital scanners and recorders.

Moving-Pin Registration

Moving-pin registration employs two pins that move down to engage the film perforations at the start of the exposure and move up again at the end of the exposure so that the next frame can be brought into position by the pull-down claw. One of the pins is slightly undersized in the lateral profile to allow for possible film shrinkage and expansion due to temperature changes. This is the Mitchell type mechanism.

Steady Test

The steadiness of a camera depends on the efficiency of its registration mechanism. This can be tested by photographing a grid made up of white lines on a black background that extends beyond the frame area. On projection, the film should be racked up so that the frame line is clearly visible. Any unsteadiness will be indicated by a relative movement of the vertical white lines at the bottom of one frame and those at the top of the next. Steadiness for multiple passes through the camera is checked by photographing the grid twice; for the second run the grid is moved diagonally to give sufficient separation between the two images. On projection the two images of the grid move against each other if the camera is unsteady.

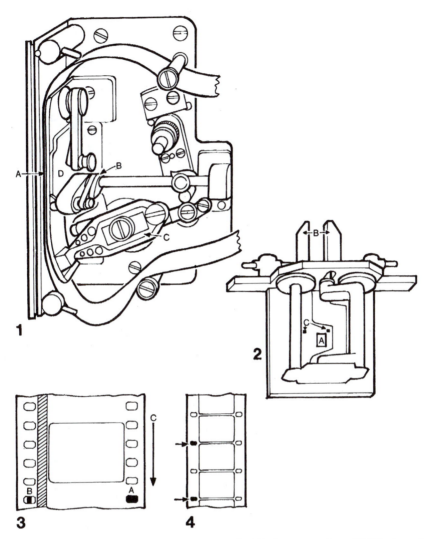

Figure 5.1 (1) Moving-pin registration (Mitchell). (A) Aperture plate. (B) Moving pins. (C) Pull-down claw. (D) Pressure plate. (2) Fixed-pin registration (Bell and Howell). (A) 16mm aperture. (B) Shuttle mechanism driven by a cam. (C) Fixed pins. (3) 35mm film. (A) Position of full fitting registration pin relative to frame area. (B) Vertical fitting pin. (C) Direction of travel. (4) 16mm film. Register pins are located along one side only.

Film Pitch

Other factors contributing to unsteadiness can be film shrinkage, damaged or inaccurate perforations, or inaccurate setting of the camera's intermittent claw movement for the particular "pitch" of the film stock used. Film pitch is the distance between the leading edges of two adjoining perforations. Essentially there are two types, short pitch and long pitch, just as there are two types of perforations, positive and negative. Camera films are normally punched with negative, "short" pitch perforations. Some cameras have the facility for making fine adjustments in the pull-down mechanism to accommodate small changes in the perforation pitch of different batches of film stock. When the pitch setting is wrong, the film makes a "picking" (clicking) noise as it goes through the camera gate.

The film stock is perforated on long runs in batches that are indicated on the film can. The perforations are not always identical from batch to batch, but they can be relied to be identical within the same batch because they have been done on the same machine. A trained mechanic can check the perforations to establish their accuracy over a given length and choose the best set to use. These are numbered relative to a recurring circular hole punched on the negative as 1st, 2nd, 3rd, or 4th downstream. When loading the camera the camera assistant has to ensure that the chosen perforations are engaged by the camera pins (see Figure 6.1).

REVERSE-ACTION EFFECT

The effect of a person jumping out of the water and landing on a diving board can be accomplished by simply running the film in reverse through the camera during the take. The film in the camera now runs from bottom to top, instead of top to bottom. When the film is run in the projector conventionally, top to bottom, the action will be seen in reverse.

Most cameras have the facility for shooting in reverse, and those that do not have this facility can often be easily adapted. The camera mechanism itself is just as capable of running backwards as forwards, but the film has to be taken up properly when running in reverse. DC motors can be made to run backwards by simply reversing the polarity. Synchronous three-phase motors can be made to run in reverse by changing over any two of the three phases on the power supply.

The reverse action effect can also be accomplished by turning the camera upside down and running the film forwards, as usual. The film is now running from bottom to top in relation to the scene, therefore when it is turned the right way up and projected conventionally, the action will be seen in reverse.

There are two main disadvantages with this method. Firstly, the registration pins engage the film perforations at the top of the frame instead of the bottom (or vice versa) because the picture within the frame area is upside-down. This only presents a problem if the same scene is to be duplicated so that other elements can be added to it, as it could make the image unsteady. The simple remedy for this is to ensure that the same perforations are used during the next stages in the preparation of the effects elements.

The second disadvantage of shooting with the camera upside-down is that the soundtrack position is reversed. Of course this problem does not arise in 16mm shooting as long as the negative that is used is perforated on both sides (double perforation); otherwise, the negative of this scene cannot be cut into the rest of the film. In 35mm format it is best to shoot on full aperture, provided the area is covered by the lens. Some cameras have a facility to move the lens over to full aperture center. When framing, it must be remembered that the effective Academy format area (see Chapter 3, "Visual Effects Compositing") is now shifted to the opposite side of the full aperture. In some cases it is possible to turn the ground glass in the viewfinder around so that the Academy area is indicated correctly. Alternatively, a ground glass can be prepared especially for this purpose.

Reverse action can be used very effectively for dramatic as well as the obvious comedic effects. An example is to bring a crushed flower to life again; each petal is revived individually and joined onto the stem. The effect is enhanced when other action within the frame area appears perfectly normal; in reality, actors have to walk backwards and perform all other actions in reverse during the shot.

A good example of the use of this technique in a dramatic context can be found in Jean Cocteau's classic film *Beauty and the Beast*. In one scene the camera tracks with the actor as he walks toward a bonfire, reaches into the flames, and pulls out a piece of paper.

STOP MOTION

Virtually all professional cameras have accessories to facilitate single-frame shooting. In most cases this means the substitution of the standard "live" motor for a stop-frame one. In addition to this, it is also possible to have an automatic time-lapse device (an intervalometer) that activates the stop-motion motor at preset intervals. This is particularly useful when shooting a plant flowering, or in similar situations where the desired change takes place over a very long period of time. The main consideration is that the stop-motion motor always stops when the camera shutter is in the closed position.

A stop-motion motor can be run in "continuous" as well as "frame-by-frame" mode during the same shot at speeds of up to 120 fpm (frames per minute)—with an effective exposure of 1/4 sec with a 180-degree shutter opening. Higher running speeds result in a difference in exposure time between the two modes of operation and are used in "continuous" mode only or for winding the film onto the desired frame and rewinding it for an additional pass.

Stop motion is particularly effective in adding life to inanimate objects. As each brick of a wall is laid in position a single frame is taken. At a predetermined point the film can be advanced by, say, 100 frames, and the same stage in the building of the wall is recorded also at this point. As each brick is laid from then on it is photographed on successive frames as well as on frames before and after the 100-frame point. This frame acts as the key point, representing the "low" when the film is run normally. After this point the wall appears to carry on building. The result is that on projection the wall appears to build itself, "hesitates": at one point, then goes back and continues to build.

Another example of a stop-motion effect is to photograph an action from a chosen zero point both forwards and in reverse. In this way the same action is recorded both in reverse and forward modes. The two sections are then fully interchangeable. A cloth can be torn and mended by either visible or invisible means; objects can be twisted or bent out of recognition and then spring back to their normal shapes; and so on. In this case the sequence for filming is:

expose; wind forward 199 frames;

expose; wind back 198 frames;

expose; wind forward 197 frames;

expose; etc.

Shooting in stop-frame mode and in reverse, chemicals or paint are applied gradually over the photograph or a painting of the fresco to bleach or otherwise degrade the image. The live-action element is shot by matching it up to a line-up clip of the fresco. (Alternatively, the fresco can be painted to match the live

Figure 5.2 (1) A plant grows visibly. (2) A brick wall builds itself, then goes down again before it continues to build up once more. (3) Rubbing out certain parts of the picture as others are added on can produce subtle transformations. (4) A zoom into a brick wall before or after live action can be used to animate hand-drawn titles, by changing over to stop-motion shooting with the appropriate compensation for the exposure difference.

action). The two elements are then joined by a long dissolve or by sectional substitution. (See Chapter 3, "Visual Effects Compositing").

Stop motion can be used to provide some really zany backgrounds to equally zany foreground actions that can be added later. Combined with a judicious use of reverse action, it can also be very amusing in itself.

Stop Motion and Live Characters

Although stop motion is normally used to photograph inanimate objects, it is quite possible to use it for shooting live action. Characters can be treated in the same way as puppets except that they can make their own moves between frames. People can appear to slide along as if propelled by some unseen force, sometimes leaving a furrow in sand as they move. A figure can be made to slither along the floor in a snakelike motion, or appear to squeeze in or out of caves, rock crevices, holes in tree trunks, and so on—all as though driven by some supernatural force! Fast, zany movements of this kind are easy to accomplish by simply running the camera at a slow speed (undercranking) and shooting continuously. However, really smooth, stunning effects require a frame-by-frame approach and an understanding of the principles of animation on the part of both the operator and the performer. Naturally, there should be no other "normal" movement in the background for this type of shot.

Figure 5.3 A live-action figure can appear to shoot out from a hole in the ground.

Undercranking and Overcranking

When the camera motor is running slower than the standard speed (24 fps), the action will be speeded up when the scene is projected at normal speed, and vice versa. Camera motors used for visual effects work are commonly of the variable-speed type and can run at a range of speeds from one frame per second to the standard live-action speed and beyond. For higher speeds, it is advisable to use special high-speed motors; maximum speeds are achieved by specially designed high-speed cameras.

Variation of the camera speed alters the effective exposure time; this is usually compensated for by either adjusting the lens iris setting (the f-stop), closing down the shutter where a variable shutter is fitted, or using neutral density filters. Every time the camera speed is doubled, the exposure time is effectively cut in half, resulting in 1 f-stop exposure. When the camera speed is reduced, the effective exposure time is increased proportionally. At 12 fps, the result is an increase in exposure of 1 f-stop; at 6 fps the difference is 2 f-stops.

When running at slower camera speeds, the exposure can be compensated for by closing down the variable shutter. If the standard shutter opening is 180 degrees at 24 fps, then, at half that speed (12 fps), the shutter should be set at 90 degrees to maintain the same effective exposure time. At 6 fps the shutter is closed down to 45 degrees and at 3 fps the shutter is set at 22.5 degrees. The effective exposure time remains at the same value as it would be at 24 fps, that is, 1/50 second.

A variable shutter can be closed down not only to compensate for exposure but also to achieve a specific effect. Shooting at high speed with a shutter set at 10 degrees creates crisp clear images that have a surreal feel to them.

It produces a unique dramatic effect which is perhaps best illustrated in the Academy Award winning film *Chariots of Fire*. The films cinematographer David Watkin describes this approach in his autobiography:

> *Something that may be counted upon in a film about athletes is that the director will, sooner or later, want to shoot bits of the action in slow motion. This is a customary resort and I'd a fancy to do that stuff another way. The exposure time in the cinema is 1/48 of a second. If you took a still photo of a racing car at that shutter speed the resulting image would be a blur; at 1/800 on the other hand it would be quite clearly defined. You can do the same thing in a film camera by closing the normal 180-degree shutter down to 10 degrees (at any rate one used to be able, most modern cameras in the way of progress have not the facility any more). The best illustration of what happens is a fountain of water, because when every drop is separated in outline it looks completely different. With someone running it would mean that their hair and limbs would be better resolved, nothing as noticeable as the falling water, rather the audience senses something unsusual without knowing what it is a much more attractive possibility. When explaining the idea to Hugh I said the only snag was that it needed always to be fairly clear behind them (like a horizon or the sea's edge) otherwise the background would strobe.*

'But that is exactly how they did all their running—along the beach at Broadstairs.'

> [*Why is there only one word for THE-*
> *SAURUS?*, David Watkin (p242).]

Varying the Motor Speed During a Take

When a scene is required to start with the camera running at standard speed and then slow down gradually during the take so that a specific action appears to speed up, the effective exposure must remain constant throughout. This is done by closing down the camera shutter or the lens iris simultaneously with the change in the speed of the camera motor. In those circumstances where the changes in speed are gradual and protracted, the operation can be carried out

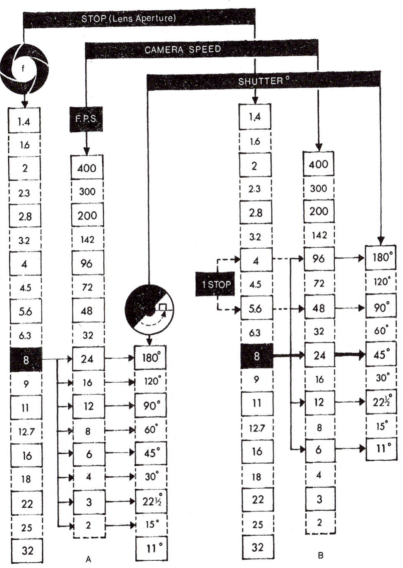

Figure 5.4   (A) If the lens aperture is kept constant (e.g., f 8, as the camera motor is slowed down from 24 fps to 2 fps), the shutter will be reduced progressively from 180 degrees to 15 degrees in order to maintain constant exposure. This scale can also work in reverse in those cases where the shutter remains fixed and the compensation is done by stopping down the lens iris; the appropriate f-stop is indicated in the top column. (B) If the camera motor is to be speeded up during the shot from 24 fps to 96 fps, then the camera shutter must be set to at least 45 at the start, in order to be able to compensate two full stops.

manually. Alternatively, a servo system linked to the camera motor can be employed to provide automatic compensation on either the shutter or the lens iris. Altering the iris setting (f-stop) alters the depth of field and should be avoided when such changes are likely to make an appreciable difference to the photographed image—unless, of course, this is intentional. The change in the depth of field of the camera lens can be exploited deliberately to produce stunning effects in certain circumstances. On the other hand, varying the shutter opening does not affect the lens performance, and the f-stop remains unaltered throughout the operation.

In-Camera Fades

If the camera is equipped with a variable shutter it is a relatively simple operation to produce fades. A fade-in is done by gradually opening the shutter from the fully closed to the fully open position during the shooting. A fade-out is produced by the same operation in reverse. The shutter mechanism can be motorized so that the entire operation can be done by remote control. Most of the fades for a film can be done this way at the time of the shooting, in the camera, instead of at the postproduction stage. Of course, it is easier to sit back and look at the print of a scene and choose the precise frame where the fade should start and end, and very often this approach is absolutely essential. However, in such a case the fade can only be accomplished by the duplication of the entire scene or by A and B roll printing (see Chapter 6, "Laboratory Effects").

Dissolves (Mixes)

It is a common misconception to assume that a dissolve from one scene into the next is produced by overlaying a fade-out and a fade-in of the same duration. If this were done there would be a noticeable drop in exposure in the middle of the transition. The fact is that a fade-in/out and a dissolve-in/out follow entirely different curves. During a dissolve the exposure of the negative must remain constant. Consequently, the exposure loss with each progressive step of the dissolve-out phase of the outgoing scene has to be made up in corresponding proportions during the dissolve-in phase of the incoming scene.

The test of a perfect mix is to do a mix-out and mix-in over the same shot at the same point; the result should be invisible, as though there was no mix involved. The problem with the in-camera mixes is that although many live-action cameras are equipped with variable shutters, very few of them have been adapted to perform the task of mixing successfully. Apart from a selection of dissolve lengths, such a device must include a positive method for activating the mix either by presetting or by manual operation. The start of the mix-out and mix-in must be overlapped accurately. Of course, this is much more easily accomplished when shooting at stop-frame than live-action speeds.

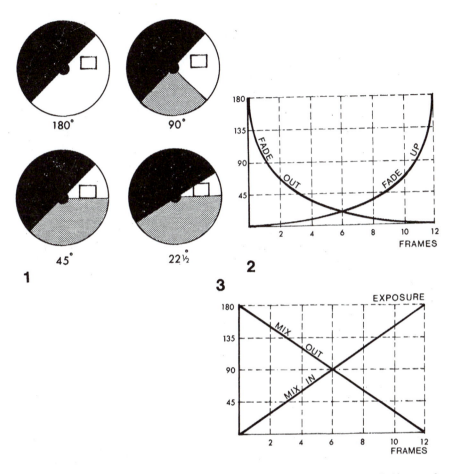

Figure 5.5 (1) Variable shutter: 180 degrees = normal exposure; 90 degrees = half normal exposure (add 1 stop); 46 degrees = quarter normal exposure (add 2 stops); 22 1/2 degrees = eighth normal exposure (add three stops). (2) A fade-up and fade-out curve superimposed. (3) Graph showing mix- (dissolve) in and mix-out. When mixing, the shutter angles must add up to the same (usually 180 degrees) for each frame.

Using the "In-Camera" Dissolves

In-camera dissolves are best suited to stop-motion work, although it is possible to adapt a variable shutter and program it to execute dissolves at live-action speed. The ideal effect that can be done this way is one in which characters or objects materialize in a scene in mid-action (or disappear into thin air just as unexpectedly), such as a dancer appearing in the shot at the height of a leap. Other effects can be added to the same negative on a second run through the same camera, or later on a rostrum camera or an optical printer, with the help of a dip-test.

Dissolves are most often used to link different scenes that may have been shot at different times and on locations many miles apart. This is one of the main reasons why "in-camera" mixes are not as popular as might be expected. Although it is possible to shoot a scene with a mix-out allowing enough stock for the next scene and then canning it up until the next scene can be shot, this is rarely attempted in practice. There is also the question of timing, which is more easily determined in the postproduction stage.

Superimpositions, overlays, and double exposures (see Chapter 6, "Laboratory Effects") can often be introduced and/or made to disappear with the aid of a mix or a fade.

SUPERIMPOSITIONS

A white caption superimposed over a live scene is perhaps the most common visual effect of all, and it is hard to believe that such an apparently simple, harmless thing could be the cause of so much aggravation among the postproduction people. (The colored "supers" have been known to cause near heart failures to the uninitiated.) But like any other visual effect, this plain, simple effort requires both planning and patience (the two Ps of visual effects).

If the white caption is to be "supered" on a live-action scene after the scene has been processed, it is necessary to duplicate that entire scene in order to produce a composite negative that has both the scene and the superimposed caption on it. If, on the other hand, the white "super" is added to the original negative before it is processed, then this in-camera effect produces a first-generation composite image of the highest quality, and the need for duplication is avoided.

This obviously necessitates two runs through the camera, but it is quite immaterial which element is photographed first. The white super on a black background is overexposed by one f-stop relative to the exposure "norm" that is calculated from the incident light reading of the artwork. If the exposure for the live scene has been calculated in the same way, then the elements will be well matched. It is important to ensure that the black of the caption background does not photograph at all and that no other stray light reaches the lens, as this will degrade the image. The caption artwork is best prepared photographically on a high-contrast sheet film (Kodalith). This is then backlit so that only the clear lettering is visible; the dense black of the surrounding area ensures that no stray light reaches the lens.

Alternatively, if the captions are hand-painted or transfer-lettered, it is best to use a glossy black background (paper or card). A matte black surface is not suitable for this purpose because it reflects too much light when the caption is overexposed. With this front-lit approach it is essential to use polarized lighting to ensure that the background does not reproduce over the already exposed frame area.

The overexposure of the white area ensures that the supered caption is "burnt" in over the background image, producing a dense black image on the negative. (Gross overexposure, however, makes the edges of the caption appear fuzzy.)

The normal procedure for this kind of operation is to make a sync mark at the head of the shot. The camera frame counter should be zeroed with the sync frame in the gate. If the background shot was done in stop-motion mode, then the precise frame where the super is to start can be read off from the frame-counter at the appropriate point. At live-action speeds when the super is to appear at a specific point some way into the scene, a stopwatch is used to measure the time from when the camera started running to that particular point in the action. Alternatively, someone could be given the task of keeping an eye on the footage counter. In either case, the precise position for the super can be determined to within ten frames or less. Obviously, this is not accurate enough for some types of supers, but for the vast majority it is quite satisfactory.

The superimposition does not have to be done at the same time. It is wiser to take several safety takes, all with separate sync marks, and store them in clearly marked cans. In fact, the second pass does not even have to be done in the same camera if another is already set up on a suitable rig for shooting captions. Alternatively, a rostrum camera or an optical printer can be used for the second pass. Additional refinements can then be added to the caption, such as a fade in, fade out, focus pull movement, animation, and so on, and the finished result is still a first-generation negative.

Placing the Super

A white super will burn in most efficiently over those areas of the background image where the tonal values in black-and-white terms are mid-grey to black. Lighter backgrounds do not provide enough contrast for the white super. These considerations should be borne in mind when composing the background shot. An aid to accurately positioning the super is to trace imaginary lines between certain points in the frame. These can be drawn on a piece of paper indicating the area where the white super is to be placed.

In the case of a static setup, the background take should be allowed to run a few feet longer than required, so that a few frames cut off the end can be used for dip-testing. Color films can be processed in a small tank (as used for still photography) with the same developer as black-and-white films. An image produced this way may not be of high quality but it is good enough to achieve a more precise positioning of the super relative to the background. This clip is placed in the camera gate and projected (see "Rotoscoping" in Chapter 9).

However, some 35mm cameras have a provision for registering a frame of film (a clip) over the ground glass in the viewfinder. This frame can be projected by shining a light through the camera viewfinder so that the caption can be lined up correctly; alternatively, the lining up can be done visually with the negative clip in position.

In those cases where the precise position of a caption relative to the frame area is established beforehand (such as for a main title), the caption should be photographed in this position, ideally on black-and-white stock, and processed

Figure 5.6   Superimposed caption. (A) Background scene exposed on the first run through the camera. (B) White caption on black background exposed on the second run through the camera. (C) Composite negative with caption "burnt in." (D) Positive print.

by hand as before. A frame of this negative has a black caption on an otherwise clear frame so that when it is placed in the viewfinder, the background scene can be easily composed around it. Because large areas of frame are clear, the clip can be left in the viewfinder during the take to ensure a perfect match. This approach is very helpful when photographing the background to a title, even when the super is not to be done by an in-camera approach.

Colored Superimpositions

A color caption cannot be "burnt in" in the same way as a white one. An over-exposed color caption results in a dense black on the negative in the area of the title, which in turn reproduces as white when printed. On the other hand, a normally exposed color caption does not obscure those areas of the background where similar or lighter colors are to be found, resulting in "ghosting." At the points where the color superimposition overlaps other colors, a combination color is created in much the same way as when two different color paints are mixed. (See additive and subtractive color filtration [Harrison & Harrison] in the "Lighting" section of Chapter 3.)

The density of a color is greatly affected by the exposure. An increase in the density of the negative (overexposure) results in a paler, pastel hue of a specific color, while a reduction in the density of the negative (underexposure) produces a stronger hue of that same color. Consequently, a colored caption can only be reproduced successfully when it is exposed on raw stock without overlapping with other colors (see Chapter 2, "Mattes and Methods of Generating Them"). Only in those cases where there is a large, dark (preferably black) area in the background can a colored caption be successfully superimposed in the camera without additional masking.

OVERLAYS

When the picture is composed so that it includes an area of black where the negative will not be exposed, it is then possible to overlay another (complementary) image in that area on a second run through the camera. In both cases the scenes

Figure 5.7 Overlays. A and B are two different scenes exposed on the same negative in two successive passes to produce the composite C. Both scenes have large areas of black.

are exposed normally, because each image is photographed on an unexposed section of the film. Obviously, great care must be taken in the composition and the lighting of such an overlay to avoid overlaps. The choice of the subject is all important, as some are more suitable for this type of effect than others.

Double Exposures

When two scenes are photographed on the same negative in such a way that they deliberately overlap each other, the result is a double exposure. Photographing two scenes of roughly the same average density over the whole frame area, at normal exposure for each scene, would result in an overexposed negative. If each scene is exposed at normal exposure (i.e., 1/50 sec), then the negative will be overexposed by 1 f-stop (1/50 sec + 1/50 = 1/25 sec), or twice the normal exposure. Therefore, each scene must be photographed at less than its normal exposure (see Figure 7.8). The exact ratio will depend largely on the desired balance between the two scenes: if a 50:50 balance is required, then the exposure of each scene is cut down by 50% (i.e., 1 f-stop). This can be accomplished by changing the iris setting of the lens, halving the shutter opening, or placing a 0.3 ND (neutral density) filter in front of the lens.

Very often one scene is required to stand out more than the other, in which case the ratio between the two exposures would be altered as required (e.g., 40:60, 75:25, etc.), depending on the desired effect.

Excessively light or dark areas within a frame can be a problem in double exposure because of the danger of certain areas burning through while others

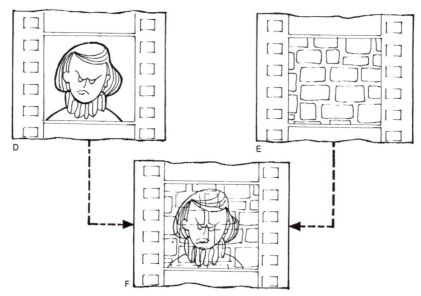

Figure 5.8 Superimpositions: Two scenes of average density (D and E) are exposed in succession on the same piece of negative but at 50% of normal exposure to produce the composite F.

remain underexposed. Scenes with a reasonably uniform distribution of middle tones are most suitable. Too much detail in both scenes can also be very confusing. Camera movement in one of the scenes can help to produce a separation between the two elements. When there is camera movement in both scenes, great care must be taken to ensure that these movements are complementary to each other.

Sectional Masking

As we have seen earlier for overlays, it is necessary that a section of the frame remains unexposed so that the overlay can be accommodated, without overlap. Very often, a relatively dark area may have some detail in it that is likely to register on the negative in the area where the overlay is intended to go. It is best to mask off that particular area to ensure that that portion of the film remains unexposed. This can be done by placing a mask either in front of the camera lens or in the camera gate itself. In either case the mask should be cut to correspond roughly to the natural outlines of the black-out area.

Mask in the Gate

Many cameras have a slot in the gate that can be used for inserting gelatin filters or masks cut out of thin black paper. Masks with various degrees of cut off, made out of thin metal plate, are often supplied with the camera, and they are easier to use in this way than masks cut out of paper. The closeness of the mask to the focal plane means that the edges appear sharp (hard edge), particularly when the lens is stopped down.

Mask in Front of the Lens

A rigid matte box is often sufficient to support a mask in front of the camera lens. The edge of such a mask is out of focus because of its nearness to the lens. This "softness" of the edge changes considerably at different iris settings, and it is advisable to check the mask lineup at the f-stop to be used for the actual take. The out-of-focus type of masking is usually required for masking off corner sections of the frame, but sometimes a central area of frame may need similar treatment. The mask is then stuck to a piece of clear glass of good optical quality and inserted in the matte box slot. In special cases, the mask can be stuck to a free-standing sheet of glass placed some distance in front of the camera (see the section on "Glass Shots" at the end of this chapter). A mask mounted on a matte box has the added advantage that it stays in a fixed position relative to the frame during a camera move.

Split Screen

In the earlier examples of overlays, no masking was required to ensure that a particular area of the frame remained unexposed. The overlay scene that was photographed on a separate run through the camera was assumed to be on a black background so that the image could be photographed in the appropriate section of the frame while the rest of the frame remained unaffected. In practice, this second run might also need some form of masking. In both these cases, the masks were really only auxiliary devices, because the two scenes already complemented each other.

However, correctly matched masks and countermasks have to be used when the frame area is split up into various sections that are then each exposed on a different run through the camera. This is, in effect, a split-screen composite.

If the mask and its countermask are cut out of the same paper, it is relatively easy to match them up when one replaces the other. Consequently, the split line can be made to match the specific outline of a shape within the frame. If the

Figure 5.9 (1) An effects disc built into the camera with a selection of masks. (2) The split-screen composite C is produced by shooting scenes A and B through their respective masks.

masking is done in the gate, however, the choice is limited to geometric cutoffs of specific proportions of the frame, such as half-frame (vertical, horizontal, diagonal), one-third, and others.

It should be remembered that if the edges of the masks overlap each other a black line is produced between the two images, its thickness corresponding to the amount of overlap. When the masks are mismatched the other way, a white line is the likely result because of the overexposure of the area in between. Of the two, the black margin is more acceptable and is often used deliberately.

Some cameras have built-in adjustable masking blades that can be positioned to mask out sections of the frame. They consist of pairs of horizontal and vertical blades. Often an adjustable iris is included that can produce circular masks of varying sizes and that can be moved to any position within the frame.

EFFECTS FILTERS AND LENS ATTACHMENTS

Since in-camera effects overlap the area of regular principal photography, there are a number of tools that are common to both, such as the effects filters and various lens attachments and specialized imaging devices.

Graduated Density Filters

The most common types of graduated density filters are of neutral color and graduated from clear to a specific density. The transition area between the two sections of the filter can be fairly narrow, dividing the filter into two parts, or it can be progressive across a much wider area. When a very bright sky needs to be darkened to create a more dramatic effect, the dividing line of the filter is lined up with the horizon. Custom filters can be made to any density ratio and gradation. Adding a small amount of a specific color to a neutral density filter can accentuate that particular color proportionally to the density of the filter. Alternatively, graduated density color filters can be prepared of any color or a combination of colors (see "Lighting" in Chapter 3). These filters are used to put life into an otherwise bleak sky or to enhance a sunset.

Fog Filters
Fog filters are made up of a multitude of finely etched spots in a glass surface that is then protected by another clear glass. The light rays striking these spots are refracted in various directions and so produce a fogging effect over the entire picture area and a desaturation of color. These filters are available in varying strengths.

Diffusion Filters
Diffusion filters are made up of tiny particles sandwiched between two pieces of optical glass. They are very useful when a deliberate softening of the overall image is required. They are also available in varying strengths.

Low-Contrast Filters
Low-contrast filters are intended to reduce the overall contrast of a scene by the introduction of a small amount of fogging and diffusion.

Star Filters
A point of light seen through a star filter has the appearance of a star with several rays projecting from it. The precise number of these rays and their geometric shape depends on the number of finely etched lines on the star filter.

Gauzes (Nets)
Silk scarves provide the best material from which gauze filters can be made. The effect is determined by the weave of the cloth and the number of layers used. Although black materials are most commonly used, it is possible to use white gauzes (with an added fogging effect) or even colored, where this is appropriate. The general effect of gauze filters is like that of combining a star and a diffusion filter.

Polarizing Filters

As a light ray travels along a straight line away from the source it also vibrates in all directions around its axis of travel. Polarizing materials selectively absorb these vibrations allowing only those in one specific plane to pass through (linear polarizers). A linear polarizing filter placed in front of a light source will "polarize" the light passing through it, and only the light rays vibrating in the polarization plane will be transmitted. When another linear polarizing filter is placed in the path of this "polarized" light, with its polarization axis matching that of the first polarizer, the light passes through virtually unobstructed. But when this second polarizer is rotated 90 degrees so that its polarizing axis is in the crossed orientation relative to the axis of the first polarizer, then no light will be able to pass through. However, before this "extinction point" is reached, the transmitted light is reduced proportionally to the angle of rotation between the two polarizing axis. This is very useful for selecting just the right amount of polarization effect required for a scene. It is also a very good way of dealing with unwanted reflections, dust particles, and other problems. It is particularly effective when a subject is photographed against a black background that needs to be a perfect, even black.

Light can also be polarized by reflection. These reflections can be eliminated with the use of a polarizing filter on the camera lens that is rotated to the point of maximum extinction (where its axis of polarization is at 90 degrees to the polarization axis of the reflected light). Sun glare on the surface of water can be eliminated so that the objects in the water can be seen clearly. Unwanted reflections in glass windows can also be lost in this way. A polarizing filter is also effective in increasing the contrast and reducing the brightness of a dull sky.

Placing two polarizing filters in line with each other in the path of a light beam produces the effect of a "light valve": one of the filters is rotated through 90 degrees and can be used to turn the light on and off with subtle gradual

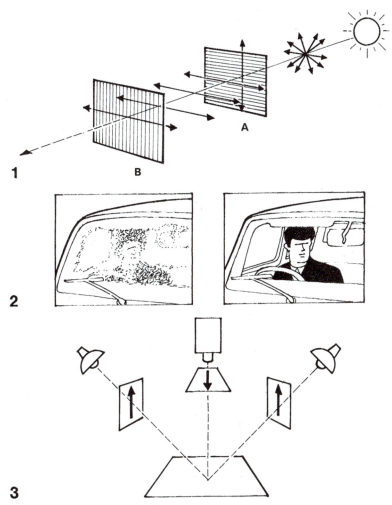

Figure 5.10 (1) Polarizing filter A allows light vibrating in only one plane to pass through. Polarizing filter B prevents light going through when its axis is set at 90 degrees to that of filter A. (2) Shot taken from the front of a car without using a polarizing screen; shows reflections of the surrounding area. The same shot taken using a polarizing screen shows interior details of the car. (3) With suitable crossed polarizers on lights and lens, it is possible to shoot shiny artwork with no reflections.

change instead of the usual "chopping" effect produced with a flag. A sheet of polarizing material placed in the scene in front of a projected image can effectively make that image visible or invisible by rotating the polarizing filter on the lens. A similar application is to deliberately reveal a reflection in the glass of a picture or painting during a shot.

Polarizing filters for use in front of the lens are made from thin polarizing materials sandwiched between two sheets of optical glass. Those used in front of the lights are mounted on a plastic base. They are available in varying strengths

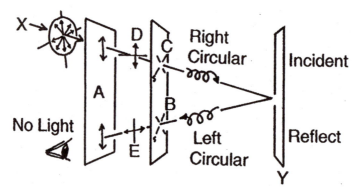

Figure 5.11   Circular polarizer consists of two elements: a linear polarizer (A) and a 1/4 wave retarder (B) whose slow and fast axis (C) are at 45 degrees to the axis of the linear polarizer (D). An unpolarized light ray (X) passing through the linear polarizer (A) becomes polarized in the vertical plane; after passing through 1/4 plate retarder (B), the light ray follows a helical (right circular) pattern of vibration. On reflection from surface (Y), the pattern of vibration is reversed and the light ray follows a left circular helical pattern; the linear polarization plane (E) is now at 90 degrees to its original polarization plane (D) and is absorbed by the linear polarization component (A) of the circular polarizer.

of polarization. However, the most efficient ones also produce color distortion and should be used only in those cases where color is not important or can be corrected sufficiently; type HN 32, 38, and 38S are normally recommended for photographic use.

Circular Polarizers

Circular polarizers have the property of adding a spin to the light vibrations passing through them so that the light rays continue to spin around their axis of travel in a clockwise or counterclockwise direction. A light ray spinning in a clockwise direction will continue to spin in the same direction after it is reflected from a surface and then bounce back towards the circular polarizer. However, the "spin" is now in an opposite direction relative to that of the polarizer, and the light ray will be blocked. A perfect example of this effect is found on the windows of limousines, which appear completely opaque from the outside but are perfectly easy to see through from the inside.

Other Filter Effects

Optical Flats

Optical flats are pieces of high-quality glass, free of any distortions or imperfections. They are used to support masks, bits of colored gelatin, and other elements. Vaseline smeared selectively on an optical flat produces a diffused vignette effect in those areas seen through the smear while the rest of the image remains unaffected.

Ripple Glass

Pieces of imperfect glass with accidental or deliberate distortions can be very effective, particularly when rotated or moved around in front of the lens during the shot. Commercially available patterned window glass can be used for this purpose. The distortions produced in this way are often very great, such that the original scene is hardly recognizable. Where possible, it is wiser to shoot the scene normally and then introduce the distortion afterwards. If the action allows it, the end of the normal part of the take can be overlapped with the beginning of the distorted part by a dissolve in the laboratory (see "A and B Roll Printing" in Chapter 6). A change of focus is also required because the ripple glass is acting as a multiple diopter lens, albeit a very imperfect one.

Clear Plastic

Shooting through a large sheet of clear plastic while it is twisted and bent can produce very interesting distortions.

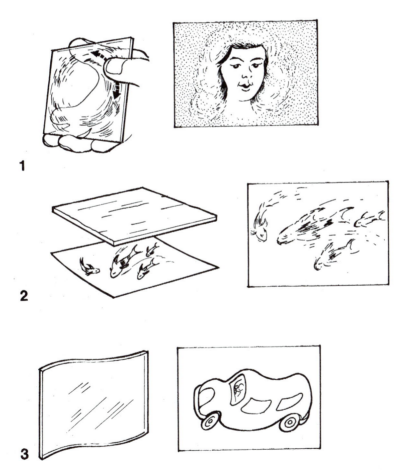

Figure 5.12 (1) Vaseline smear on a clear optical flat produces a selective diffusion effect. (2) Ripple glass produces an effective distortion or break-up of the image. (3) Twisted clear plastic is an alternative method of producing image distortions.

Prismatic Lens Attachments

Prismatic lens attachments are used to create a multi-image effect. The number of images created will depend on the number of facets in the attachment. When the attachment is rotated, the peripheral images rotate around the central one. Kaleidoscopic effects can also be created by shooting through a tube containing three front-silvered mirrors; when the tube is rotated the central image remains static. Another prismatic attachment makes it possible to rotate the full image through 360 degrees around the lens axis; the same effect can also be produced by a special arrangement of front-silvered mirrors. Other prismatic devices enable the image to be "flopped" or reversed laterally.

Split Diopter Lens

The split diopter lens is similar to the supplementary lenses used for extreme close-up photography; it is, in fact, a cut-off segment of a standard supplementary lens. It is used to bring into focus extreme close-ups in one part of the scene without affecting the rest. For best results, the optical center of a split diopter lens should be aligned with that of the camera lens, even when it is only a fraction of the circle. It is then rotated to the appropriate position where the edge is least noticeable. Moving the split diopter lens off axis affects the performance of the lens and causes color aberrations.

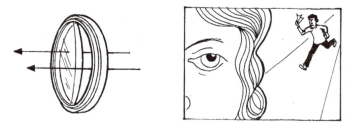

Figure 5.13 Split diopter lens in use (positive).

Positive split-diopter lenses are more commonly used. However, negative split-diopter lenses used in conjunction with prime lenses with macro-focusing capability have certain advantages over the positive types; the glass is thinner at the center of the lens than at the edges, making the join line less noticeable.

The negative split diopter lens is used in an opposite way to the positive ones. The primary lens is focused so that the nearest point is in focus; then, a negative split diopter of the appropriate power and cut-off configuration is placed in front of the primary lens to extend the focus back towards infinity in the chosen area of the frame.

Supplementary lenses with positive diopter power have the effect of shortening the focal length of the lens, and those with negative diopter power of increasing it. Therefore, a lens with a split diopter attached to it will have two effective focal lengths, each with its own depths of field. Using the standard lens formula it is possible to calculate the focal length required for the supplementary lens to produce the maximum continuous depth of field at a specific aperture. A split diopter lens can be of any focal power required.

Diopter Power

A lens that brings a bundle of parallel light rays into focus at a distance of 1M (1 meter) has the focal length of 1,000mm. This lens can be described as having the power of 1 diopter. In the following list, the A column indicates the lens power in diopters, and the B column indicates the lens focal length in millimeters.

A		B
1 diopter	=	1,000mm
2 diopters	=	500mm
3 diopters	=	250mm
4 diopters	=	125mm
5 diopters	=	62.5mm

Figure 5.14 A spherometer measures the curvature of a lens element in diopters.

Periscope Attachment

Periscope attachments are used in circumstances where it is physically impossible or dangerous to shoot with a direct view, such as close to an explosion, through narrow openings, close to a wall or some other obstruction, or at extremely low angles close to the ground. Due to the nature of their construction, periscopes are more suited for use with long focal length lenses.

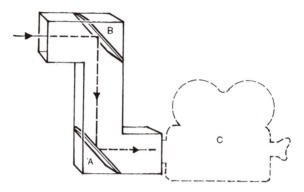

Figure 5.15   Periscope attachment. (A) and (B) Front-silvered mirrors. (C) Camera.

Snorkel Lens

There are several designs of this type of lens. The unit consists of a long tube that is attached to the lens mount of the camera. The length of the tube is determined by the design of the relay system involved. The great advantage of this system is that the prime lens is effectively moved forward away from the camera body; it can be a wide-angle lens with the correspondingly greater depth of field, or it can be a lens of a longer focal length if required.

The camera can be mounted on a transport mechanism on the gantry, which allows it to be moved in any direction. A video assist provides additional help in lining up and operating the camera by remote control. It is particularly useful for shooting miniatures; it can track along narrow streets of a model town or down the valley of a miniature landscape. A small front-silvered mirror placed at 45 degrees in front of the taking lens can be tilted up and down and rotated to produce additional moves.

The relay lens is normally positioned at the point where it will transfer the image formed by the prime lens to the film plane in a 1:1 ratio. However, it can also be positioned to produce an enlarged or reduced image at the film plane, so that cameras with different formats can be used.

Endoscopes and Modelscopes

Endoscopes and modelscopes are manufactured for medical and industrial use. They are constructed from fiber optic bundles relaying the image from a

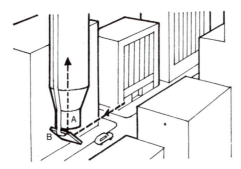

Figure 5.16a   Snorkel attachment. (A) Front lens. (B) Front-silvered mirror.

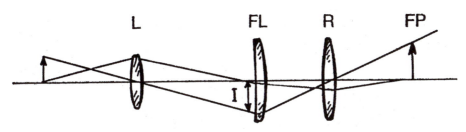

Figure 5.16b   Relay lens (R) transfers the image (I) formed by lens (L) to the film plane (FP). A field lens (FL) placed at or near the focal point.

tiny front lens along a tube to an eyepiece at the opposite end. The tube can be of rigid or flexible construction ranging in diameter from a quarter to a half inch. An adapter lens is supplied by the manufacturers for several popular makes of still cameras. This lens acts as a relay, enlarging the image to cover a full 35mm format, and can be adapted to fit one of the standard camera mounts.

There are usually no irises on an endoscope lenses, and the exposure is controlled by the level of illumination and shooting speed alone. It is advisable to test the lens and establish the effective f-stop. A useful approach is to mount the lens on a still camera with a good exposure metering system and take the appropriate reading.

There are two basic types of endoscope lenses: direct forward view (in line with the camera lens axis), and side view (at 90 degrees to the lens axis).

Because of their small diameter, the endoscope lenses can be used in situations where the larger snorkel lenses cannot. Due to the small effective aperture of the lens and the design of the system, these lenses have a very impressive depth of field. Applications are similar to those of the snorkel lens, except that they can work on a smaller scale and at a closer range: for example, tracking along a table with the lens center a half inch above the surface then moving up a glass of water and finally diving into it.

Rocking Motion Effect

An interesting use of both endoscope and snorkel type lenses is in creating the effect of a rocking motion that is particularly effective in simulating flying. The endoscope with a side view configuration or a snorkel lens with a mirror at 45 degrees to the lens axis is best suited for this. The camera tracks forward or the miniature set is moved towards the lens. The mirror is pivoted around the lens axis by a few degrees to one side and then to the other side from the forward-facing position. The extent of this displacement from the forward view will determine the degree of tilt effect produced. With a side-view endoscope this action is performed by loosening the connection from the endoscope to the adapter lens and rotating the endoscope unit.

Contact Endoscopes

These lenses are of a similar design to the regular endoscopes described above, with one major exception. They are designed to focus on the front surface of the lens so that whatever touches the lens is in fact in focus. The skin of a finger touching the lens will be in focus. This, of course, presents problems with light. The central fiber-optic bundle carrying the image from the lens is surrounded by another bundle carrying the light from an outside source to illuminate the point of contact. Contact endoscopes are available both in forward and side-view configurations.

Rotating an Anamorphic Attachment

When an anamorphic unit is mounted in such a way that it can be rotated around the optical axis of the lens, it produces an interesting distortion of the image being photographed: the image expands and contracts as the optical stretch produced by the cylindrical lens rotates. This is particularly effective when the subject is in front of a neutral background.

Mirror Effects

Ghosting

A two-way mirror placed in front of the camera lens can be used to reflect a second scene staged to one side and overlay it over the master scene photographed directly through the mirror. This is the easiest method of introducing a "ghost" into a scene, but, naturally, the area behind the actor must be blacked out. By twisting the frame holding the two-way mirror, it can be made to "shatter" (break) and so cause the "ghost" image to disappear. Shooting at high speed and/or in reverse further enhances the effect.

Two-way mirrors are available in various thicknesses and with different transmission-to-reflection ratios. For the above example, a high-transmission

WWII bi-plane flying inside a giant hanger and out through the ventilation shaft. (Still from the film *GUNBUS*. Courtesy of J&M Entertainment Limited.)

Sky Bandits/Gunbus Director and VFX Supervisor: Zoran Perisic

Format: Super 1.85

Background: Motion control VistaVision plate inside model hanger.

Foreground: Model airplane on an articulated mini pole-arm.

Compositing system: Zoptic Process.

The actor hangs on to the skids of the bi-plane as it skims the treetops. (Still from the film *GUNBUS*. Courtesy of J&M Entertainment Limited.)

Sky Bandits/Gunbus Director and VFX Supervisor: Zoran Perisic

Format: Super 1.85

Background: Aerial VistaVision plate.

Foreground: Full size bi-plane on a fixed pole-arm.

Compositing system: Zoptic Process.

Spacecraft zaps past the moon. (Courtesy Zoptic SFX.)

Space Pirates promo.

Format: Super 1.85

Background: VistaVision plate shot on an animation stand.

Foreground: Model spaceship on an articulated mini pole-arm.

Compositing: Zoptic Process. Computer controlled "motion blur."

Compositing system: Zoptic Process.

The Phoenix takes the children on a magic carpet ride.

The Phoenix and the Magic Carpet Producer-Director and VFX Supervisor: Zoran Perisic

Format: Anamorphic 2:4:1

Background: Aerial VistaVision plate.

Foreground: Carpet on an articulated pole-arm; Animatronic Phoenix.

Compositing system: Zoptic Process.

and low-reflection mirror is most suitable, because once the mirror is broken there is little change in the brightness of the scene being photographed and no compensation is necessary. In fact, an ordinary piece of good-quality glass has sufficient reflectivity to act as a two-way mirror in this case. The brightness of the reflected image can be increased by lighting the two images in the opposite ratio to the transmission reflection ratio of the mirror.

Front-Silvered Mirror

A good, flat piece of glass that has been silvered on the front reflects an image without the creation of secondary images, as is the case of conventional mirrors where the silvering is on the back surface of the glass. Breaking a full front-silvered mirror creates an interesting transition from one scene to another, particularly when it is done at high speed and at an angle so that the pieces fall towards (or away) from the camera.

Matting with a Front-Silvered Mirror

A front-silvered mirror is often used to enable a live-action section to be inserted into a miniature. This is done by placing the miniature at right angles to the lens axis so that it can be seen by the camera via a front-silvered mirror set at 45 degrees to the front of the lens. The silver is removed from the mirror in the area where the live image is to be inserted. The new image can now be seen through the clear glass and has to be lined up and lit so that it matches the miniature.

Glass Shots

A large pane of good optical-quality glass is placed some distance from the camera. Beyond it, there could be a partially completed set in the studio, while the nonexistent parts of the set (anything from a domed ceiling to foreground pillars) are painted on the glass. The camera remains in a fixed position for this type of shot. Panning and tilting moves are possible if the nodal point of the lens is positioned at the pivot point of the pan-and-tilt axis. A specially designed nodal head is required for this purpose.

When panning and tilting on a nodal head, the pivot point is coincidental with the nodal point of the lens. During a zoom shot, the nodal point of the lens travels along the lens axis and the camera has to move along the track to keep it at the pivot point of the pan-and-tilt axis.

Glass shots are used both in the studio to extend or add an element to the set, and on location where certain features in the landscape need to be eliminated or some others added. Matching color and lighting—particularly the position of shadows in the case of exteriors—means that the shooting of the composite, which may include an army of extras, has to be done during a specific time of day. In certain circumstances it is possible to use large color photographs, which are cut out and stuck on the glass. The scale and perspective have to be carefully calculated so that they match the real parts of the scene.

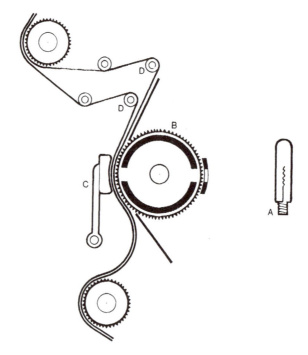

Figure 6.1a Continuous printer

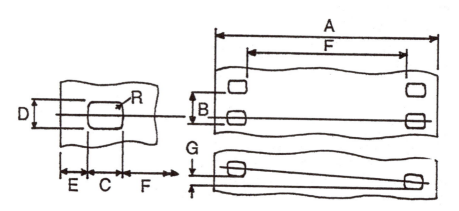

Figure 6.1b Film Perforations. Positive and negative perforations differ in "pitch" (distance from one perforation to the next) as well as in shape. However, it is possible to have positive stock with short-pitch negative perforations as used in the production of process plates. (A) Negative perforations with short pitch. (B) Positive perforations with long pitch.

The raw (unexposed) print stock is normally punched with positive perforation; because it lies over the processed negative stock on the drum, these perforations are slightly farther apart ("long pitch") than the negative stock with its "short-pitch" perforation. This is to accommodate the slight increase in diameter of the drum due to the thickness of the negative stock (see Figure 6.1).

Step Printers

Intermittent or step printers operate at much slower speeds than continuous printers do because they employ an intermittent movement. The design is very much like that of a basic camera, with a lamphouse in place of the lens and an extra magazine to carry the processed stock. The processed negative and the raw stock are held in contact by register pins during exposure to the printing light. A shutter cuts off the light during the pull-down movement in the same way as in the camera. The exposure and the color balance are controlled principally by the additive lamphouse.

Since most visual effects work involves duplicating the original negative in some way, it is essential that the quality and steadiness of the original should be preserved. Optical work is usually done with step-printed interpositives; because it is not advisable to remove the original negative from the lab due to the risk of loss or permanent damage, these interpositives are printed at the laboratory. Although all laboratories offer continuous and contact step-printer services, only a few have full optical printer facilities. Most of this type of work is to be found with specialized effects companies. (See Chapter 8, "Optical Printers and FX.")

A AND B ROLL PRINTING

A and B roll printing, or "checkerboard" printing, is a standard practice in 16mm film production due to the fact that the gap between frames is smaller that the width of a splice (a film join). Consequently, when two pieces of negative are spliced together, the join overlaps one of the frames, resulting in a disturbing flicker at every cut. This is not the case with 35mm film when using Academy (format) and 1.85:1 formats. However, in anamorphic and full aperture formats, the height of the frame is at its maximum, reducing the gap between the frames.

Figure 6.2   A and B roll printing (checkerboard)

In this case, the overlap is proportionally less than in 16mm and is somewhat helped by the projection cutoff.

A and B printing is not as popular in 35mm production, although it is equally effective and its importance is often overlooked. It is an option for creating certain visual effects of equal quality to a first generation in-camera effect because that, too, has to go through a final printing stage. Laboratory opticals can be incorporated at the printing stage, avoiding one extra generation of dupes. Very often a complex optical sequence can be simplified and even saved by eliminating one duplicating stage.

A and B Roll Opticals (Fades, Dissolves, and Double Exposures)

The negative is cut and assembled in two rolls with matching synchronization points marked on the leader of each roll. The two overlap sections that will be printed as a dissolve or a double exposure are laid parallel to each other. Black spacing is used between the scenes on each roll to make up the required length. The two rolls are printed on the same piece of raw stock in two separate runs (passes) starting from a common sync point. The start of the effect (fades, dissolves, or double exposure) is activated automatically during the printing procedure by means of a frame count in the same way as the changes in printer light.

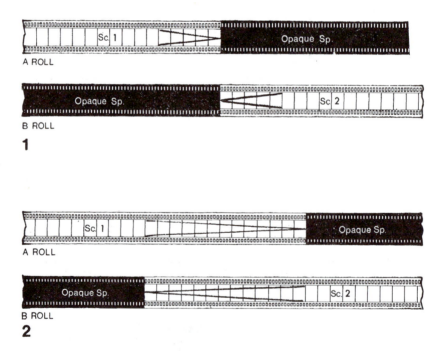

Figure 6.3   A and B roll printing. (1) Fade out on A roll followed by a fade in on B roll. (2) A dissolve (mix) from A roll to B roll.

The same A and B roll printing procedure is followed when printing the interpositive, resulting in a fully integrated master. One or more duplicate negatives derived from this interpositive master will be used for making release prints.

Naturally, if there are only one or two mixes or fades in an entire reel, this approach may not be very practical. An alternative approach adopted by some laboratories allows for creating the dissolve and double exposure opticals without A and B roll negative cutting. All the scenes are negative cut on the same roll; but at the point where the dissolve is to end, black spacing is inserted equal to the length of the optical, and the next scene is joined on at the start of the dissolve. When the dissolve-out is completed, the printer runs back to the head of the roll and the negative is pulled up (relative to the raw stock) by the length of the black spacing (optical), and the dissolve-in on the incoming scene starts at the predetermined point. After that, normal printing is resumed for the rest of the roll, or until the next optical.

Since this work is usually done on a rotary printer, steadiness between the elements can be a problem in some cases. It is wise to do a test whenever possible

FORCED DEVELOPMENT

When the light level is inadequate for a normal exposure, it is often possible to shoot with a deliberate underexposure of one or two stops. This underexposed material should be kept separate from the normally exposed material, as it requires forced development by the laboratory. It is important to state precisely the extent of the forcing required. Forced development of color negative emulsions by one stop does not create a serious color distortion, but it does affect the contrast.

PRE-FOGGING THE NEGATIVE (DESATURATING THE COLOR)

Pre-fogging the negative is an approach that is used extensively in conventional filming to desaturate colors and obtain an overall reduction in contrast. The extent of the fogging determines the extent of the color desaturation. This is done by exposing the entire roll of raw stock to a small amount of clear light before processing. It can be done either before, during, or after photography. Before or after photography, pre-fogging can be done at the lab on either a rotary or a step-printer, or by exposing the negative through the production camera under controlled conditions.

Pre-fogging in the lab after the photography has an added advantage: the extent of fogging can be finely controlled by running tests (wedges) on short sections before committing the entire roll. Pre-fogging during photography is done by means of a two-way mirror (beam-splitter) placed in front of the lens at 45 degrees to the lens axis to reflect a diffused, soft light into the camera lens (Lightflex system). This approach allows the cinematographer to see the effect of pre-fogging on a scene and make appropriate adjustments. Pre-fogging can be limited to only a section of the frame by selective masking, or varied during the take when required. Colored gels over the light can also be used to add an overall hue to a particular scene.

Pre-fogging introduces additional overall exposure to the underexposed areas of the negative and therefore affects primarily in the shadow areas of the picture, resulting in a reduction in overall contrast. There is an apparent increase in sensitivity of the film stock because details in dark areas become more noticeable. Total desaturation of color is not possible with this method; when the fogging is increased beyond a certain level, the image quality suffers.

Pre-Fogging a Duplicate Negative

Pre-fogging can also be done at the interpositive/internegative stage. For dramatic effect, the original negative can be linked by an A and B roll dissolve with a heavily fogged dupe negative of the same scene.

Pre-Fogging the Positive Print

Pre-fogging can also be done on the positive print before it is developed. The effect is the opposite of that achieved by pre-fogging the negative. This time it is the highlights in the picture that are affected. Because the brightest areas of a scene are represented as the densest areas on the negative, the least amount of light will pass through these areas to the raw stock during the printing stage to form a positive image. It is these underexposed areas of the positive image that are affected by pre-fogging the raw stock. The result is an overall reduction in contrast because the highlights are held back.

This approach is used to reduce the overall contrast ratio between the very bright and very dark areas of the scene that cannot be controlled in any other way during the original photography, as in a car shot passing through intermittent areas of strong sunlight and shadows. It is particularly useful in the production of process projection plates and/or duplicating positives (interpositives). A combination of pre-fogging the negative and the positive can produce a maximum compression in contrast by affecting both the highlights and the shadow areas.

SPECIAL DEVELOPING PROCESSES

Various laboratories offer processes specifically designed to manipulate color and contrast in the processing of color release prints and interpositive masters.

These can be used to enhance the night effect or to create a particular mood or look of a scene. They generally involve by-passing some of the regular development steps and adding additional bath.

> CCE — Color Contrast Enhancement: A bleach bi-pass that leaves more silver deposits on the film stock. The results can be a fairly drastic enhancement of blacks and a desaturation of color.

> ACE — Adjustable Color Enhancement.

> ENR — (Technicolor): This is a more subtle approach for increasing the overall contrast. After printing, the positive raw stock is put through a black-and-white bath instead of the bleach bath.

DUPLICATING FILMS

As most optical effects involve one type of duplication or another, it is well worth being familiar with the materials available. There are a number of different stocks that are specifically designed for duplicating:

> Color Intermediate films
>
> Black-and-White Panchromatic Separation films
>
> Black-and-White Fine-Grain Duplicating films
>
> Color Internegative
>
> Black-and-White High-Contrast films

Duplicating stocks are generally punched with negative perforations.

Color Intermediate (Interpositive/Internegative)

Most duplicating work is done by the interpositive/internegative method using intermediate color stock. An interpositive is first made in contact with the original negative. This positive image can then be copied again on the same intermediate stock to give a correctly balanced duplicate negative of the original scene. It is during this second duplication stage that an almost limitless number of effects can be created.

Working with a positive image is a great advantage. All other elements to be added to the original scene must also be printed on the same stock in order to maintain the color balance. Since the intermediate stock is not intended for direct photography, it is extremely slow in comparison to camera films and requires a great deal of light to produce an adequate exposure.

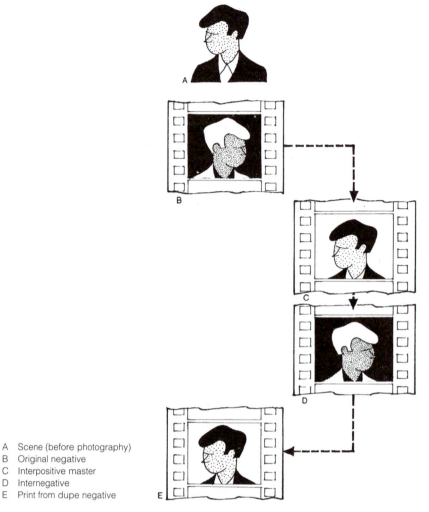

A   Scene (before photography)
B   Original negative
C   Interpositive master
D   Internegative
E   Print from dupe negative

Figure 6.4   Bulk prints for theatrical release are made from internegatives, which in turn are made from one or more master-interpositives prepared from the original cut negative.

Black-and-White Panchromatic (Color) Separation Film

Panchromatic color separation stock is used for the preparation of black-and-white separation positives from the original negative. These separations represent yellow, cyan, and magenta records of the original scene in black-and-white tonal values only. The original color negative is contact-printed three times, each time through a different color-separation filter: blue, green, and red, respectively. When this procedure is reversed, and the three black-and-white records so obtained are printed onto a color negative film through their

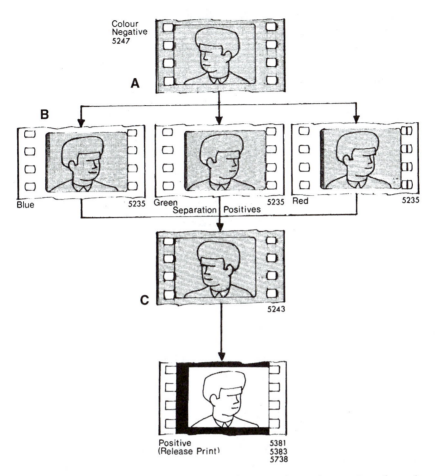

Figure 6.5 The original negative (A) is printed separately on three strips of panchromatic film (B) through color-separation filters (blue, green, and red). This produces color separation master positives representing the yellow, magenta, and cyan records of the original negative image. A duplicate color negative (C) is obtained by printing the black-and-white separation masters (B) through the same three-color separation filters (blue, green, and red) onto color negative stock.

respective color separation filters, the result is a color duplicate negative of the original.

This method of duplication offers a lot of scope for color-distortion effects. By deliberately recombining the color-separation masters through the "wrong" filter during the printing stage, a number of strange color effects can be created.

The color-separation approach is the basis of the original dye-transfer printing process, still considered by many to be the best method for producing high-quality release prints. These black-and-white color-separation masters and dye-transfer prints have a much longer shelf life than the color stocks, which are prone to fading. This process has been reintroduced by Technicolor. Color separation approach is also the basis for digital scanning and recording (see Chapter 12, "Digital Effects").

Color Reversal

This camera stock is available both in 16mm and 35mm formats. Despite some processing difficulties, color reversal stock is excellent for certain, specific requirements. It provides a less expensive way of producing process-projection plates, for example. The risk involved in using a reversal original instead of a print from a negative can be overcome in two ways:

1. by making a safety internegative of the selected take, or
2. by photographing additional backup takes (some of these can be held back and processed only in an emergency).

Color Internegative

Color internegative stock is available in both 35mm (type 5272) and 16mm (type 7272) and is used for producing negatives from color-reversal originals.

Color Reversal Intermediate (CRI)

CRI stock is no longer available. It was used for making direct duplicates from original color negatives and by-passed the interpositive stage. This meant that some opticals could be done by taking advantage of the specific characteristics of duplication by way of negative image to negative image. It required optical step printing in order to maintain the correct geometry on the duplicate negative. Contact printing CRI results in the image being flopped from left to right, because the original negative runs emulsion-to-emulsion with the raw stock. This can be very useful in certain circumstances when a reversal of geometry is required. It is hoped that this stock will be reintroduced again.

Black-and-White Duplicating Stocks

Fine-grain duplicating positive stock, type 5366 (35mm) or type 7366 (16mm), is used to produce a black-and-white positive from an original black-and-white negative. When a black-and-white positive is required from a color negative, then the panchromatic color-separation stock type 5296, should be used. A black-and-white fine-grain positive made on either of these two stocks can then be printed onto fine-grain duplicating negative type 5234 (35mm) or 7366 (16mm) to yield duplicate negatives from which prints can be made.

Black-and-White High-Contrast Stocks

These low-speed, monochromatic (blue-sensitive) black-and-white stocks register tonal values as extreme blacks and whites and are very useful in the production of optical effects. It is the sharp contrast difference between the black areas (opaque) and the light areas (clear base only) that make these stocks indispensable when it comes to titling and matting in particular (see Chapter 2, "Mattes and Methods of Generating Them," in particular the sections on travelling mattes and Chapter 8, "Optical Printer and FX").

High-Contrast Panchromatic Stock (EC5369)

This is a high-contrast stock used in the production of travelling mattes. The advantage of this stock over the regular high-contrast type is that any color can be targeted and a high-contrast matte pulled from it.

Reversal Processing

Any black and white stock can be processed as reversal, although not all laboratories are keen to offer this as a standard service.

7

Bi-Pack Camera

*The camera begat a bi-pack magazine of its
own . . . and this was even better for visual
effects.*

BASIC UNIT

The bi-pack camera is a very useful tool that offers a great deal of scope for visual
effects work of the highest quality at very modest costs. All that is required is a
standard camera with pin-registration movement, a stop-motion motor, and bi-
pack magazines. A variable shutter is a bonus. A basic bi-pack camera unit can
perform all the functions of a specially designed contact step-printer.

The Magazines

Bi-pack magazines allow for a processed piece of film to be run in contact, emulsion-to-emulsion, with the raw, unexposed negative. As the two strips of film
pass through the camera gate in a frame-by-frame operation, they are exposed to
the light source and the image on the exposed film is thus copied (printed) onto
the raw stock.

    The positive print is loaded on the outside with the emulsion side away
from the lens, and the unexposed negative is loaded on the inside with the emulsion facing the lens and in contact with the emulsion of the positive print. The
inner loop (the raw stock) is laced up one perforation shorter on both sides of the
camera gate than the outer loop (positive print).

The Light Source

A lamphouse can be used to illuminate a small area when only a step-printing
operation is required. The light reaching the camera gate is regulated by the lens

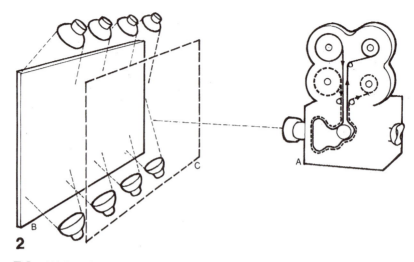

Figure 7.1   (A) Standard Mitchell camera fitted with bi-pack magazines. (B) White board illuminated by a series of lights, which serves as the light source for the step-printing operation. (C) Dotted outline of glass frame that can be used to support masks and/or artwork.

iris or at the light source. In the absence of proper optics, a diffusing material such as opal glass or ground glass can be used to create even illumination over the entire frame area. It is important that the lens is set out of focus to avoid the reproduction of the grain within the diffusing material.

A "printing light," consisting of a large, evenly illuminated white board, offers much greater possibilities for visual effects work. This is combined with a large piece of clear glass, placed in front of the backlight board, to carry masks and other artwork such as partial matte paintings, stills, or cell animation. These self-matting elements are composited on a separate pass through the camera. The glass can also be used to rotoscope outlines of objects within a scene and prepare matching cutout mattes and countermattes, which are then used to composite various elements.

An important consideration for this type of compositing operation is that any changes in focus setting, iris, and filter packs in front of the lens can affect the image size and produce a noticeable shift in the matte line.

Positive Elements

Bi-pack operation for visual effects work is usually done with color interpositives, panchromatic color separation positives, or black-and-white fine-grain positives. These elements are prepared by the laboratory so that there is no risk of loss or damage to the negative in transportation to and from the laboratory.

The Preparation

A sync mark is scratched or punched at the head of the roll, a safe distance from the section that will be printed, to allow for lacing up. This sync mark normally matches an equivalent sync mark on the work print, which also has the required visual effects marked up in wax pencil. The frame lines on the leader of the work print must be indicated clearly to enable the correct positioning of the negative in the camera gate. The sync mark on the work print is the zero point from which a precise frame count of the start and end of all effects is measured on a synchronizer.

When more than one positive element is to be printed onto the same negative, then each element has to be synced up to the zero frame. An A and B roll approach as used in negative cutting (see Chapter 6, "Laboratory Effects") is often sufficient, but on occasion each element has to be made up as a separate roll. After preparation, the material to be printed should be cleaned carefully by gently winding it through an antistatic cloth dampened with a cleaning solvent. Alternatively, and even better, the film can be treated in an ultrasonic cleaning machine, a service that most laboratories offer to customers.

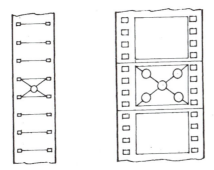

Figure 7.2   16 mm and 35 mm sync marks. Stock for bi-pack filming must be clearly marked so that all the components run through the camera exactly in sync.

BI-PACK COMPOSITING

Matte Painting and Live-Action Composites

The interpositive of a scene, which needs to have a part of the background altered or extended, is projected (rotoscoped) onto a sheet of white paper or card stuck evenly to the surface of the large piece of glass. An artist traces out the required outlines and prepares a painting in the appropriate areas of the frame, carefully matching the perspective and color to the rest of the scene. When the painting is completed, the paper is cut along predetermined lines where a join is least likely to be noticed, usually following the shape of the object in the picture. The interpositive of the scene is loaded in the camera in contact (bi-pack) with the unexposed negative. The printing light reflected from the white board can now reach the camera lens through the clear section of the glass, and the interpositive is copied onto the negative in those areas. The painted area acts as a matte so that the negative remains unexposed in that part of the frame. On the second pass, with the interpositive removed, the painting is lit from the front and photographed. Black velvet is placed behind the clear area of the glass to ensure that no stray light reflected from the white board reaches the lens. The result is a composite of the live-action element and a partial matte painting. This approach is particularly useful when actors are required to appear very small because only parts of the set in the immediate action area need to be built.

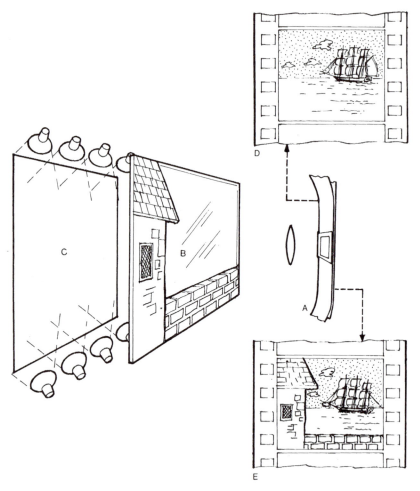

Figure 7.3 (A) Bi-pack camera. (B) Glass painting. (C) White board. (D) Interpositive scene. (E) Composite.

It is possible to use travelling mattes with this type of set-up, if the matting is to be done over the area of the matte painting. The male matte of a self-matting positive is run in bi-pack with the raw stock during the photography of the painting, then the self-matting positive is printed in bi-pack on a separate pass.

Split-Screen Composites

Some effects cameras have a variable masking device built into the camera body consisting of two pairs of blades running horizontally and vertically in relation to the camera gate. This facilitates the compositing of different elements in separate sections of the frame, in other words, split-screen.

Using the large glass placed between the camera and the printing light as described in the last section makes it possible to prepare hand-drawn matte outlines and execute very sophisticated split-screen composites. The larger the glass area, the more precise the matte outline can be drawn. Split-screen composites with sharp-edge or soft-edge mattes, overlays, animated wipes, and a variety of other effects are possible in this way. A sky shot in one location can be added to the mountain range shot in another, and a third element can represent the foreground. By masking off certain areas on the glass, a particular section of the

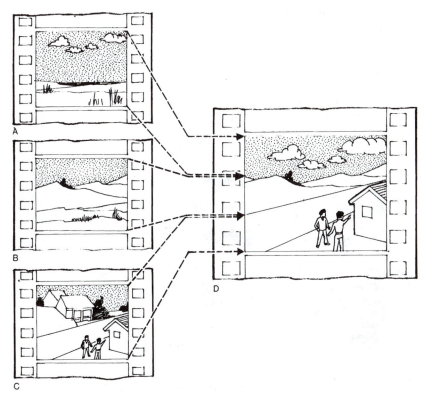

Figure 7.4 Composite D is made up from sectional printing of scenes A, B, and C.

interpositive is printed; a countermask is placed on the glass and carefully line up to the first one before it is removed, to ensure a perfect match—and then the second element can be printed, and so on.

OTHER BI-PACK EFFECTS

White Title Superimpositions

The title artwork prepared on high-contrast material such as Kodalith can be mounted on glass, backlit by the printing light (or front-lit if white lettering on black paper is used), and superimposed over a scene in separate passes. Alternatively, a high-contrast positive of the title running the full length of the superimposition is printed in bi-pack on a separate pass. This is particularly useful when there is animation in the titles. White titles are usually overexposed by up to one f-stop during the overlay pass so that they burn in on the negative.

Colored superimpositions are not possible in this way because an overexposed color title would be black on the negative (and consequently white in the final positive). The color of correctly exposed titles would mix with the colors in the background. In those cases where there are large black or grey areas in the frame, colored titles can be overlaid without a lot of difficulty. White on black (clear on black) artwork or high-contrast black-and-white positives can be used to produce a color caption with the use of an appropriate color filter.

Drop-Shadow Titles

In order to superimpose a color title over a color background without any danger of overlap, it is best to prepare a positive and negative version of the title. The

Figure 7.5   Interpositive (A) is printed on the first pass and the white high contrast title (B) is then superimposed on a second pass. The title appears white in the final print (C). When a negative (or internegative) (D) is used instead of the interpositive—the same white high contrast title (E) appears black in the final print (F).

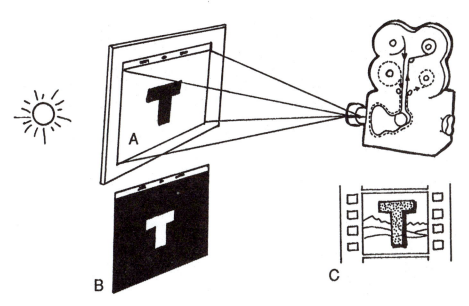

Figure 7.6   Drop-shadow titles. (A) Negative image of title (black lettering on clear background). (B) Positive image of title (clear lettering on black background). (C) Final composite: Drop-shadow title over a live-action scene.

interpositive of the background scene is copied (printed) with the negative of the title caption in position (black lettering on clear background). For the second pass the interpositive is removed and the positive version of the title caption (clear on black background) is placed on the glass (in register) and photographed through an appropriate color filter on the lens. By reducing the image of the title caption slightly and shifting it to one side, a shadow appears, making the letters stand out against the background.

FADES

If the camera is equipped with a variable shutter a fade-in or fade-out can be added to a scene during the bi-pack operation by progressively opening the shutter or closing it down.

Dissolves (Mixes)

To produce the effect of one scene dissolving into another, it is necessary to close the shutter down progressively on the outgoing scene, wind back to the sync mark (zero), load the next scene, and run the film down (with the shutter still closed) to the precise frame where the fade-out began on scene one. Printing is then resumed and the shutter is opened progressively over the same number of frames from the fully closed to the fully open position. The curve followed by the dissolve in operation has to match the curve followed by the

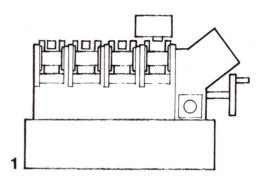

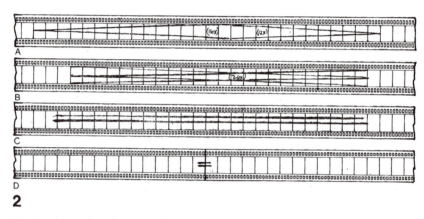

Figure 7.7   (1) Synchronizer used for checking the guide copy and the assembly of duplicating material. (2) Guide copy markings. (A) Fade-in (16 frames); fade-out (12 frames). (B) A mix or dissolve (24 frames). (C) Double exposure. (D) Cancelled cut.

dissolve out, so that there is no appreciable change in print density at the point of dissolve. Overlaying a straightforward fade-out and a fade-in does not produce a good mix (see Figure 5.5). The operation of the shutter can be manual or automatic where such a device is fitted to the camera. Automatic dissolve/fade units provide a choice of dissolve lengths of 8, 12, 16, 24, 32, 48, 64, 96, or 128 frames.

Double Exposure

The most critical factor with regard to double exposures is the density of the negative. If the optimum exposure for one scene is 100% and it is printed directly onto the negative, then the negative is fully exposed. Printing a second scene over the same piece of negative would give it twice the normal exposure (200%). Consequently, the correct way to obtain a double exposure, where the balance between the two scenes is 50:50, is to cut down the printing light by one f-stop.

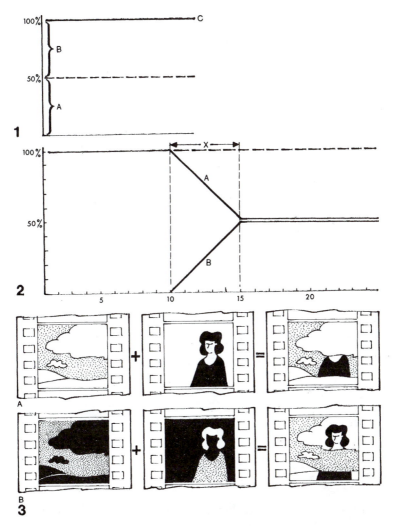

Figure 7.8 (1) The negative can be given a normal full exposure (C) by two separate exposures at 50% of the norm (A and B). (2) Graphic representation of a double exposure introduced by a mix. Exposure on scene A is altered by means of a mix from full exposure to 50% (or one f-stop less) over an exact number of frames (X). Mix out fully on normal exposure and then mix in over the same area at one f-stop less exposure. Scene B is mixed in over the same area, also from zero, at one f-stop below normal exposure. (3) Scenes (A) with large areas of white are not suitable for double exposure as positive images. On the other hand, a double exposure of the same scenes in the negative form is very successful (B).

Each scene thereby contributes 50% of the exposure to the negative with the result that the negative receives its normal full exposure (100%).

The balance between the two scenes to be double-exposed does not always have to be 50:50. However, the total amount reaching the negative must always add up to 100% to maintain normal exposure. Carefully matched scenes with large areas of black can be printed directly as overlays, as long as there is no substantial overlap of the exposed areas. In this case the two scenes could both be printed at full exposure.

Scenes representing average to dark tonal values are more suitable for double exposure than those with large bright areas. However, it is well worth remembering that in the negative form these light areas appear dark and it may be better to work with the CRIs of these scenes instead of interpositives.

When the double exposure is to be introduced some way into a continuous scene, and both scenes will have equal prominence during the double exposure, then the following procedure should be adopted. Scene A is printed normally at full exposure down to the point where scene B is to be printed over it. The introduction of scene B can be as a straightforward cut, although in most cases a mix (dissolve) works better as an introduction to the double exposure. At the start of the double exposure, dissolve-out is made on scene A over a specified number of frames.

The negative and interpositive are wound back to the start of the dissolve. Then, with the same scene (A) in the camera, but with the exposure cut down by one f-stop, the dissolve-in is executed and scene A is then printed on for as long as required. For the second pass, scene B is loaded, synchronized to the same zero frame, and wound down to the same point where the dissolve was made on roll A. With the exposure cut down by one f-stop from nominal, the dissolve-in is executed lasting the same number of frames, and the scene is printed on for the required length. The same procedure in reverse applies when one of the double-exposed scenes is to disappear, leaving the other to continue at full exposure.

SOLARIZATION EFFECT

A contact step-printed CRI (Color Reversal Internegative) print from the original negative and a contact step-printed interpositive from the same original are the two elements required to produce a solarization effect. Since CRI stock is no longer available, a color reversal stock can be used instead, to produce a negative image with the same geometry as the interpositive. (Alternatively, the internegative can be prepared at the laboratory on an optical printer.) These negative and positive records are printed in two successive passes onto the same raw negative (intermediate stock). The exposure balance between the two elements has to be determined by making a series of tests (wedges), when one element is held at a chosen exposure and the exposure on the second element is progressively altered over a selected range and on every frame. The procedure is repeated again over the next section, which has a variation in the exposure of the first element, and so on until the first element has been fully covered by the whole range of the step-wedge exposure tests. This "wedging" can also include a series of progressive color changes to produce the best results.

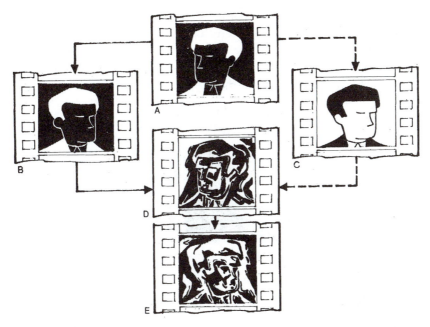

Figure 7.9 Solarization. (A) Original negative. (B) Internegative print. (C) Interpositive print. (D) Composite negative (solarized). (E) Composite positive.

Solarization of the entire shot is not as effective as when the shot starts normally and the solarization is introduced at some later point. The procedure here is much the same as in the case of the double exposure. Alternatively, the entire shot can be solarized and the new negative cut as A and B rolls with the original negative, using a dissolve to link the two scenes in the final printing stage.

Black-and-white solarization is also very effective and is produced in much the same way as color solarization, using black-and-white materials. It is also possible to use a black-and-white element in addition to the color ones, or instead of one of them.

Color Distortion (Surreal) Effect

The high-contrast stock registers tonal values in extremes of black-and-white; the result is a clear separation between dark and light areas in the scenes. This can be used effectively a produce a surreal look to the scene. A positive and a negative record of the scene is printed on high-contrast stock, and these are then composited (printed) through color separation filters onto color negative stock in two successive passes. The black and white elements of the image are each represented on the color negative by a primary color. Because of a tendency for the high-contrast stock to pull towards tonal extremes and break up any grey areas, an overlap occurs between the two records, which results in the appearance of a third color in the overlap areas as an outline — the result of the mixing of the two primary colors. When red and green are used as the primary colors, a yellow out-line emerges between the red and green shapes within the scene, giving it a very surrealistic feel.

The easiest way to obtain a pair of high-contrast positives and negatives is to contact-print one from the original negative and the other from a positive

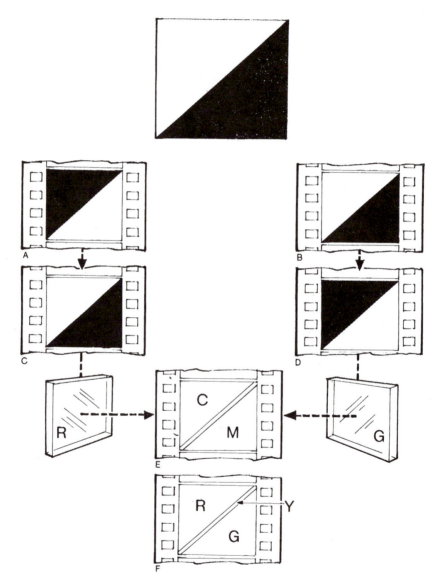

Figure 7.10 Color Tinting. (A) Original scene. A color or black-and-white negative. (B) Color or black-and-white positive. (C) High-contrast print from negative (positive image). (D) High-contrast print from positive (negative image). (R) Red filter. (G) Green filter. (E) Color intermediate stock (composite negative). (F) Composite positive. White areas in the original scene appear red, and black areas appear green. In between the overlap area is yellow.

print made from that negative. The resulting reversal of geometry can be corrected by printing the high-contrast negative cell-to-emulsion in the final marry-up, since the image is composed only of black-and-white shapes and not fine detail — which would make the loss of sharpness much more noticeable. It is also possible to have the high-contrast stock processed as reversal, in which case the geometry is not changed. Alternatively, the two high-contrast elements can be prepared on an optical printer (see Chapter 8, "Optical Printers and FX").

Tinting Distortions and Solarization Effect

The tinting procedure described above can be used to give further distortion of color following solarization. Positive and negative high-contrast records can be made from the interpositive and the CRI already prepared for solarization. Two printing generations would restore correct geometry, although this is not essential as both high-contrasts can be printed cell-to-emulsion. However, two printing generations would produce, in this case, a greater separation of tones between the black-and-white areas of the scene, enhancing the effect.

Color Separation and Distortion Effect

Black-and-white panchromatic separation positive masters are made from the original color negative by printing through color separation filters (blue, green, and red). These black-and-white records of the yellow, magenta, and cyan content of the negative are printed onto a color negative stock through the same color-separation filters (blue, green, and red) to produce a duplicate color negative (see Figure 6.5).

A visual effect element can be added at this stage. However, if the marry-up (compositing) of the black-and-white masters is done through the "wrong" filters deliberately, some very interesting color distortions can result. It is possible to obtain negative colors in a scene with a positive image.

By painting actors' faces in the negative color of the normal flesh tones (cyan) for the original photography, the color separation masters can be recombined (married-up) to produce normal flesh tones with the result that all the colors in the scene will be reversed as well. This effect can also be produced electronically.

A further development of this technique is to make high-contrast copies from the black-and-white separation positives and use them for the marry-up instead of, or in addition to, the normal procedure. The combinations in this area are limitless.

The density of a normally duplicated negative can also be increased if a regular black-and-white panchromatic positive of the scene is run as an additional pass.

From Color to Black-and-White

It is possible to wash the color from a scene so that it gradually becomes black-and-white, without any appreciable change in image quality. A color interpositive and a black-and-white panchromatic fine-grain positive are contact step-printed from the original color negative. These are then contact-printed in two successive passes onto the same intermediate color negative in a straightforward A and B roll procedure and linked by a long dissolve. In this way, a color scene will appear to change gradually to a bleak black-and-white. To accelerate this change still further, a high-contrast positive (prepared from the original negative) can be used to follow the black-and-white fine-grain positive and also be linked with it by a dissolve, so that the fine grain black-and-white version of the image is replaced by a harsh high-contrast one as the scene unfolds.

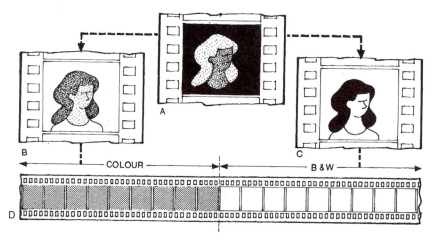

Figure 7.11 (A) Original color negative. (B) Color interpositive. (C) Black-and-white panchromatic positive. (D) Color negative stock onto which the scene is copied from the color interpositive up to a specific point; then the printing is continued from the black-and-white positive. Alternatively, a mix can soften the change from color to black-and-white.

Another approach is to leave some color in the scene, giving it the appearance of a hand-tinted black-and-white photograph. This is achieved by printing the color interpositive and black-and-white fine-grain positive as a double exposure. The exact ratio of exposure between the two elements will determine the extent to which color will be present in the final scene. Coupled with sectional masking (or wiping), it is possible to have parts of the same scene in full color gradually (or sharply) merging with the rest of the scene that is in black-and-white. For a true sepia-toned effect, the color printing has to be done with a negative image so that the black areas get the sepia tint.

8

Optical Printers and FX

*In time the printer begat a projector and
was named an optical printer . . . and this
was good news for visual effects.*

CONTACT STEP PRINTER

A printer designed specifically for contact step printing has the same basic features as a bi-pack camera and can be used in much the same way. One major difference is that in its standard configuration a lamphouse is mounted directly in front of the camera/printer. These lamphouses can be of two different types: color subtractive or color additive.

The camera mechanism is typically of the shuttle gate (Bell and Howell) type. The unit is equipped for bi-pack operation, enabling it to run a processed positive (or negative) film in contact with the raw stock. The raw stock is laced up in the normal way with the emulsion side facing the lens, and the positive stock is laced up in the opposite way so that the two pieces of film lie emulsion-to-emulsion.

The stop-motion motor normally has a selection of speeds and can run backwards as well as forwards and continuously, as well as in stop-motion, without a change in the exposure time. Variable shutter and AUTO-FADE and DISSOLVE are also part of a standard setup. All the effects described in Chapter 7, "Bi-Pack Camera," can be done on a specialized contact step printer when set up in the appropriate configuration.

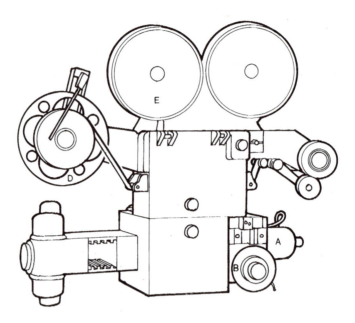

Figure 8.1 Contact step printer

The Color Subtractive Lamphouse

At its simplest, the lamphouse can be a single light source with a color temperature of 3,200 Kelvin. The optics in a simple lamphouse of this type vary, depending on the specific application. In general, they are designed to produce a flat, even illumination of the camera gate for contact printing. The condenser system normally includes a heat filter to absorb the infrared radiation. A more efficient method employs a dichroic mirror designed to transmit the visible spectrum and reflect the infrared radiation when placed in at 90 degrees to the light path. However, for best results a dichroic mirror (cold mirror), designed to reflect the light in the visible range of the spectrum and transmit the infrared, is by far the most efficient way of taking the heat out of the light beam, but it requires the light beam to be bent at 45 degrees.

Several easily accessible filter slots serve as supports for color correction and neutral density filters. The voltage supply to the lamp must be regulated because both the density and the color of the picture will be affected by voltage variations. The color correction is done by voltage control and color-correction filters placed in the path of the light beam to subtract specific colors from the light.

Additive Color Lamphouse

This is a more sophisticated lamphouse than the subtractive type. It can change the color characteristics of the light without the use of color-correction filters. There are two basic designs of color additive lamps:

1. The beam from a single light source is passed through beam-splitters to produce three separate beams of light. Each of these three beams of light is passed through a color-separation filter: blue, green, and red. These are then recombined into one beam of integrated light. By manipulating the light valves governing each separate beam, the intensity of each of the three primary colors are controlled, producing a change in the color temperature of the light reaching the film.

2. Another method employs three different light sources. The light from each lamp passes through one of the color-separation filters (or the lamps themselves are coated with the appropriate color) before it is combined into one beam of integrated light. This method offers the advantage of a greater light output and the possibility of varying the voltage supply to each light source independently.

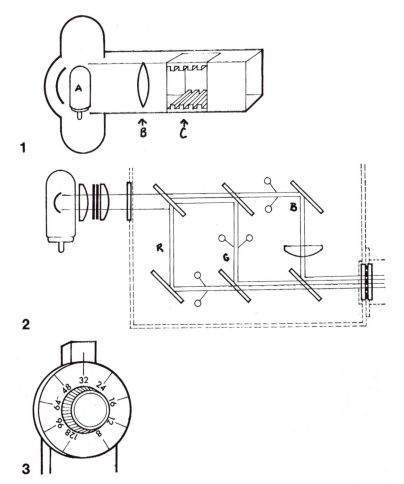

Figure 8.2 (1) Color subtractive lamphouse: (A) lamp, (B) condenser lens, and (C) filter slots. (2) Color additive lamphouse. The light from a single printing lamp is split into red, green, and blue color beams by selectively reflecting and transmitting dichroic mirrors. (3) Frame selector for choosing the length of an effect.

In both cases the appropriate color combination of blue, green, and red represented in terms of printer lights can be coded and executed automatically, producing the desired color and density changes as programmed.

CAMERA PLUS PROJECTOR HEAD

Although a great deal of visual effects work can be done with a basic contact step printer there are also a lot of limitations. With the addition of a projector head to the contact step printer (camera) the scene to be copied does not have to be in contact with the raw negative any longer. Instead, it is loaded in the projector gate where it is photographed (copied) by the camera lens and recorded on the negative. The result is an optical step printer.

The Camera

The most popular gate in optical printer cameras is a fixed-pin Bell and Howell type, or the clapper gate. The gate and the transport mechanism are usually interchangeable between 35mm and 16mm. An automatic fade/dissolve mechanism and bi-pack capability are usually standard features. In some cases, the camera can also be pivoted around its optical axis to produce image tilts of between 20 degrees and 35 degrees clockwise and counterclockwise from horizontal. The camera unit is mounted on a horizontal bench of very rigid construction and can be moved along the base independently of the lens, which is connected to it by extension bellows. Controls for the variable speed stop-motion motors, lamphouse, and other elements are built into a console at the base of the printer.

The lens is mounted on an independent carriage and connected to the camera body by means of extension bellows. The lens mount enables the lens to be moved along the vertical and horizontal axis as well as towards or away from the camera body. At zero position, the lens photographs the full image in the projector gate at a same-size ratio (1:1). To reduce the photographed image, the camera is moved away from the projector on the optical axis. To make selective enlargements of the same image, the camera is moved closer to the projector gate. The lens mount is moved independently to keep the image in focus. Some optical printer cameras are equipped with automatic focusing devices. The exposure compensation necessary at different reproduction ratios can be linked to an automatic iris controller.

The projector body is mounted on the same bench as the camera; the gate mechanism is of the same type as used in the camera and is often interchangeable. The gate can take two strips of film in contact, in the same way as the camera; two sets of take-ups are provided for this purpose. These are of the open-reel type since the film stock used in the projector is already processed.

The variable speed motor that drives the projector assembly is controlled from the console and can be run independently or in interlock with the camera

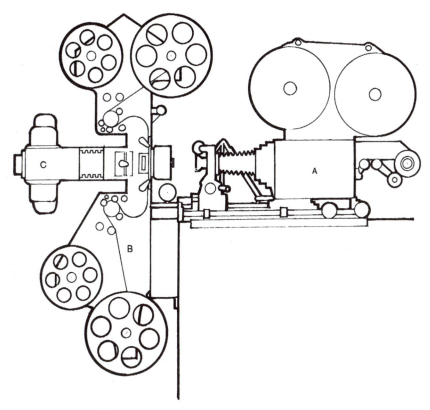

Figure 8.3 Optical printer. (A) camera head. (B) Projector head with bi-pack facility. (C) Lamphouse (standard).

motor, both in the forward or reverse mode. The lamphouse includes condenser lenses that are designed to illuminate the projector gate evenly. These can be of either "color additive" or "color subtractive" design. A filter disc with twenty-four filter slots that change automatically with each frame is a useful aid for color-correction tests.

Liquid Gate

Cell scratches on the base of a processed strip of film appear as black lines because the light rays passing through the cell are refracted differently where it is scratched. By immersing the film in a liquid whose refractive index matches that of the film base, the scratches are filled in by the liquid with the result that the light rays are refracted uniformly over the entire picture area, thereby making the scratches invisible. The liquid gate is also available on some makes of digital scanners.

The liquid gate is built around the basic shuttle gate (clapper gate) with the picture area (or aperture) enclosed by glass. Liquid is circulated through this watertight compartment in a recycling operation. Apart from eliminating the cell scratches, liquid gate printing generally produces cleaner results. Unfortunately, there is not much that can be done about serious scratches on the emulsion side.

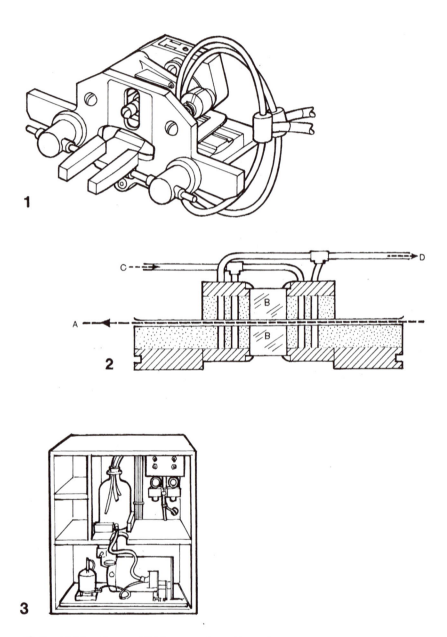

Figure 8.4   (1) Liquid gate. (2) Cross-section of liquid gate. (A) Dry film exits. (B) Glass. (C) Liquid from filter. (D) Vacuum to reservoir. (3) Liquid gate support system.

Focus Pull

Once the film being printed is removed from the camera gate and placed in the printer head instead, a lot of new possibilities open up that are not possible in contact printing. One of these is the manipulation of focus. A scene can be defocused or brought into sharp focus at a specific point during the printing operation. This can be done on all elements of a composite scene or only on selected ones. A useful effect for title superimpositions is to combine a focus pull with a fade-in or fade-out. A focus pull and a dissolve from one scene to another can also be very effective. In either case, it is important to establish the focus pull by making it last a few frames longer than the fade or dissolve.

Freeze Frame

For normal printing, the camera and projector are interlocked so that after the camera has taken one frame, the film in the projector gate is advanced to the next frame. By disconnecting the projector unit from the interlock system, the same frame of film can be held in the projector gate while the camera unit continues to copy the same frame, resulting in a freeze effect on the action. This can be done with any frame, in any sequence, and for as long as required. The action can be made to continue as normal after the freeze by interlocking the projector and camera unit again. Freezing the action suddenly may have just the right dramatic impact, but often it is too abrupt, and it is better to slow down the action gradually prior to the freeze-frame point. This is done by printing two successive frames twice, then the next two three times, the next frame four times, and so on.

Title supers are prepared on "slip-negs" (segments of a few frames in length), since only one frame is really needed. They can be repositioned, defocused, and distorted during the superimposition.

Skip Framing

Since the projector unit can run independently of the camera unit, and since both of them are operated by stop-motion motors, it is possible to "miss out" any frame in the film being duplicated. By printing only every other frame, the action will appear twice as fast. On the other hand, by printing every frame twice the action is slowed down (stretched). When a scene shot at 16 fps needs to be "stretched" for projection at 24 fps, every third frame is printed twice. Any combination of skip framing is possible at regular or random intervals.

Reverse Printing

The projector unit can run in reverse while the camera unit runs forwards. This produces a reverse action effect. This is a useful effect and can be introduced in the middle of a scene, reversing the action suddenly and then continuing in normal

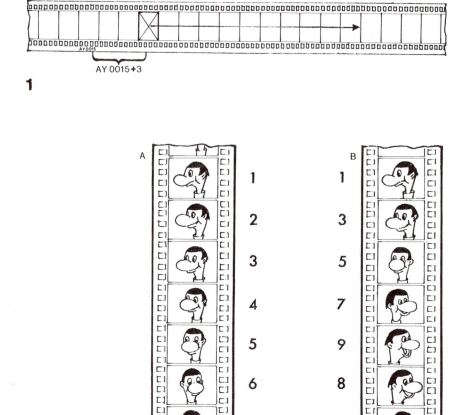

AY 0015+3

1

2

Figure 8.5 (1) Marking up freeze frames on the cutting copy guide. It is also wise to put down the exact position to be frozen in terms of edge numbers (e.g., AY 0015+3). (2) Skip framing and reverse printing. (A) Original scene in projector gate. (B) Raw stock in camera gate.

mode again. Reverse printing can be particularly effective when combined with skip and freeze framing. To extend a static scene it is best to print several frames backwards and forwards instead of freezing one frame only, as this avoids the appearance of grain.

Rippling or Strobing Effect

A subject lit by hi-contrast rim lighting against a black background is most suitable for this type of effect. The scene is printed as normal once, and on the second run it is printed again with a three-to-four-frame delay, depending on the speed of the action. Further passes through the camera, with equal delays, produce additional images of the same action, which then appear as a ripple trailing the original image.

The effect can be introduced at the start of the shot or at any point during the action. A combination of a freeze frame and ripple effect can be very effective in certain circumstances, such as when a dancer leaps across from one side of the frame to the other leaving an image trail behind. A freeze frame of the dancer at the touch down position can be held until all the delayed "ripple" images catch up and then normal action is resumed.

A   B

Figure 8.6 Subject shot against a black background and lit from the side so that only the outline of the figure is clearly visible. The effect of the progressive movement from A to B appears as a ripple movement.

Double Exposure

A conventional double exposure involving two separate runs through the camera can be varied with the introduction of additional effects on one or the other (or even both) of the scenes being duplicated. Skip frame, freeze frame, focus pull, reverse printing, and so on, can all be added to the existing facilities.

It is possible to produce the effect of a double exposure by running the two scenes in contact with one another simultaneously using the bi-pack facility of the printer head. The results of this type of double exposure are different from those made in two separate passes. Inevitably, some scenes lend themselves better to this approach than others. There is still the choice of doing the entire operation in two separate passes in order to create a different emphasis between the two scenes being double exposed, or to add a focus pull, reverse action, or freeze frame on one or both elements.

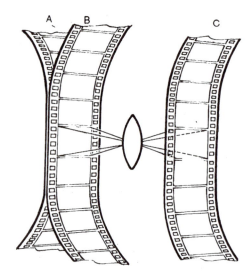

Figure 8.7   Scenes A and B are held in contact as they are copied optically to produce a double exposure C.

Geometry Reversal

It is often necessary to "flop" the image laterally, either to get around a difficult cutting problem, or simply to obtain a mirror image of a particular scene. Another reason is that the geometry of one of the elements to be used in the production of a specific visual effect may not match the others. Because the image in an optical printer is copied "optically," the film can be laced up in the projector with the emulsion either to the lens or to the light and upside down if required.

Tilting

In some cases the optical printer camera is mounted on a tilting unit that enables up to 35 degrees of clockwise and counterclockwise tilt around the lens axis. This is useful for correcting any leveling errors in the original photography and can also be used to produce a "rocking motion" effect.

Reframing

Accidental and unwanted intrusion in a frame (usually the boom mike) can be removed by selective enlargement of the picture. Reframing is also necessary when there is a change in the aspect ratio. The image can be reduced in the frame to form one element of a split-screen combination with other elements. Anamorphic material can be "unsqueezed" and printed onto Academy standards or a 1.85:1 aspect ratio with appropriate reframing, and vice versa.

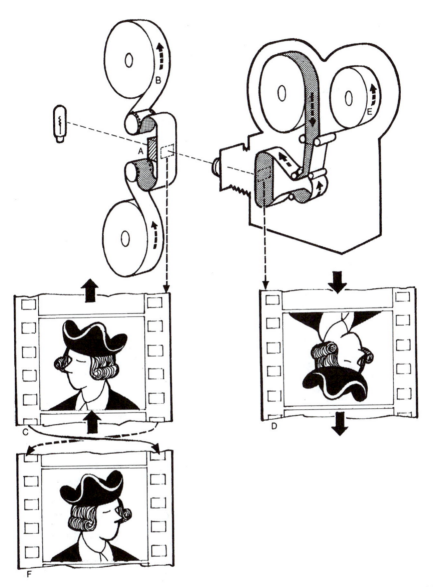

Figure 8.8 (A) Projector gate. (B) Direction of film travel (normal). (C) Image in projector gate. (D) Same image in camera gate. (E) Direction of raw stock travel through camera. (F) Reversed geometry.

Changing the Formats

As both camera and projector have interchangeable 35mm and 16mm movements, it is possible to make reductions or blowups from one format to the other. This also makes it possible to use materials on one format while shooting the composite on the other. The common example of this is to prepare the elements on a larger format and copy them onto a smaller format (i.e., VistaVision to 35mm, and 35mm to 16mm).

Split-Screening Made Easier

In the earlier example of split-screening by contact printing, each element had to have the image in the correct position, that is, corresponding to the position of that image in the composite. By using a projector head, the images of the various elements can be positioned anywhere within the frame; they can be reduced or enlarged to fit a particular shape as required. This makes it a lot easier to plan and shoot the various elements.

Moves within the Picture

A visual effect composite, consisting of several elements all shot with a static camera, can be given an extra feeling of realism by a zoom or pan within the frame area. Wherever possible, a larger format should be used for the production of the original elements, in order to avoid the problems of grain and lack of definition when enlargements exceed a ratio of 2:1 on the same format. When shooting on 16mm from a 35mm original, then enlargements up to a ratio of 4:1 produce acceptable quality.

Distortions

Because of the physical separation between the projector and the camera it is possible to insert distorting materials, image "fragmenters," and prismatic attachments that can rotate the image through 360 degrees (beyond the limitations of the camera tilt). The image can also be copied vertically with the aid of the same prism, turning the image through 90 degrees. Naturally, this means that the original has to be enlarged, with the resultant increase in graininess.

Bi-Pack Matting

When a high-contrast matte is laced up in the projector unit in contact with the positive image to be printed, it allows the areas opposite the clear sections of the matte to be photographed. As the shape of the matte changes during the printing operation, the areas of the duplicating stock that are exposed change correspondingly. On the second run through the camera a countermatte (the negative image of the first matte) is laced up in the projector unit in contact with the positive of the image to be matted in. This second positive image is now registered in those areas that were left unexposed during the first run.

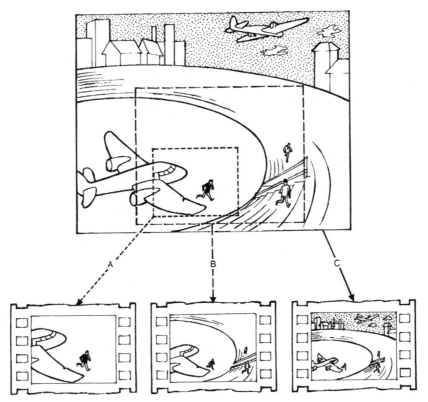

Figure 8.9   The composite picture consists of three live elements and a matte painting of the buildings in the top left of the picture. (A) Close up of the airplane's nose as it enters frame. (B) Pull out to reveal the location, as the men jump out. (C) Full view of scene as second airplane thunders overhead.

Alternatively, the image to be matted in could be self-matting (i.e., on a black background) and may not require a countermatte. It is advisable to run a clear base of high-contrast stock in bi-pack to prevent any shift in the image size. A high-contrast travelling matte of a graphic image continually changing shape can be used to produce interesting transitions between scenes. The countermatte is run on its own in the projector. The light is filtered to give the countermatte shape a color. The resultant effect is that of a colored shape appearing in the scene and progressively obscuring it altogether. This colored shape can then break up to introduce the next scene. A number of interesting wipes and other transition effects can be produced in this way.

Objects can be inlayed into a background scene with the use of a suitable matte and countermatte. The background scene is first printed in contact with a male matte of the object to be inlaid. On the second run the interpositive of the object itself is printed in contact with the female (counter) matte.

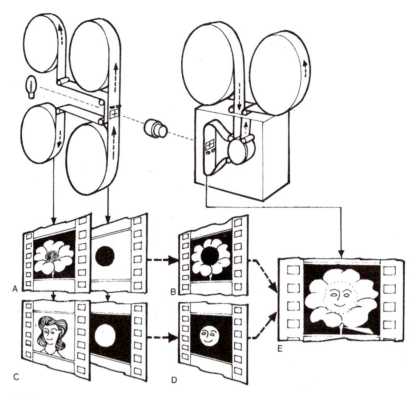

Figure 8.10   Scene A and male matte are printed in contact to produce image B. Scene C is then printed on the same negative in contact with female matte, to produce image D. E is the final composite.

Wire Removal

Often it is necessary to remove wires or other supports that could not be avoided in the original photography. This is done by the substitution method, whereby unwanted areas of the frame are replaced by the good areas from the same frame or the next one. If the wire moves across a static frame, it is first rotoscoped to produce a matte corresponding to the shape and position of the area to be replaced. The scene is copied in contact with this matte. On the second pass the same scene is copied through a countermatte, but this time the background is advanced or retarded by one or more frames while the countermatte remains in the correct relationship to the original sync mark. Since the shot is static, an area clear of the wire will now be copied in the unexposed section, held back by the matte on the first pass.

The above method can also be used in certain cases when camera moves are involved, provided there is a suitable substitution material to be pulled up from another frame. In some extreme cases it is necessary to produce a series of paintings on animation cells, which are then photographed against a black background and used on the second pass. Further color and focus adjustments can be done during the printing stage to ensure that the painted substitutes blend into the background.

Colored Inlays

Colored captions can be inlayed into a scene, without the danger of background colors mixing with the color of the inlay, by running a high-contrast print of the negative image of the lettering in contact with the background scene. The black of the lettering prevents exposure of the frame in those areas, while the rest of the scene is copied normally. On the second run through the camera the high-contrast print, with the positive image of the lettering, is laced in the projector on its own. Because of the dense black background, only the clear white letters are reproduced. By tinting the light source, these letters can be recorded on the unexposed areas of the frame in any desired color.

Drop-Shadow Titling

Neither white nor colored lettering stands out very clearly on certain types of backgrounds. In order to get over this problem a drop-shadow technique is often used. The procedure for the first run through the camera is the same as for normal color inlays; the high-contrast negative of the title is run in contact with the interpositive of the scene. On the second run the positive image of the title is reduced slightly and moved off-center. The inlayed image still falls inside the unexposed area of the frame, but as that area is slightly larger, it has the appearance of a shadow whose outline corresponds to the shape of the letters.

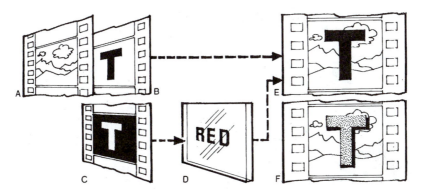

Figure 8.11 Color titling and drop shadows. Background A is printed in contact with the high-contrast negative of title (B) on the first pass. Then a high-contrast positive of same title (C) is printed through an appropriate color filter (D) to produce a composite of the color-tinted title and the background (E). Alternatively, by optically reducing the image of the title for the second pass and moving it to one side, a drop shadow effect is achieved (F).

CAMERA PLUS TWO PROJECTOR HEADS

When an optical printer is fitted with two projector heads mounted at 90 degrees to each other, more complex visual effects can be done in one pass through the camera. A matte in bi-pack with the background plate is laced up in one projector head, and the countermatte in bi-pack with the scene to be inlayed in the other. The camera can photograph the images in the gates of both projectors by means of a beam-splitter. The two images are seen as a composite, and any misalignment or mismatching of color and densities can be detected more easily than in the case of double passes.

The second projector head has its own lamphouse and a separate drive motor that can be run independently or in interlock with either the first projector, or the camera, or both.

Aerial Image Optical Printer

The second projector does not always have to be at 90 degrees to the first; it can also be in line with it, tandem fashion. The projector farthest away from the cam-

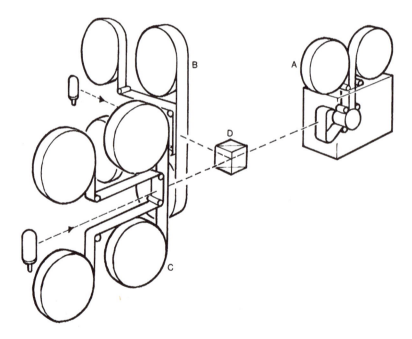

Figure 8.12 Optical printer with two projector heads set at 90 degrees to each other. (A) Camera. (B) Projector head set at 90 degrees to camera lens axis with own light source. (C) Second projector head set in-line with the camera, with own light source. (D) Beam-splitter prism.

era is the only one fitted with a lamphouse. A copying lens is set between the gates of the two projectors with the zero position equidistant from the two focal planes, so that the image from the rear projector is focused at the focal plane of the projector in front of it in a 1:1 ratio. This image is known as an aerial image, because it only exists in the air, but can be seen by the camera lens. A field lens placed close to the gate of the second projector works in conjunction with the copy lens to ensure a good reproduction of the image.

Frosted film placed in the projector gate can be used to check the line-up of the aerial image. The projectors are aligned to each other and to the camera by means of precision film clips with frame markings.

Two projector heads in tandem linked with an aerial image cannot be used in the same way as two projectors set at 90 degrees to each other. On the other hand, they offer other possibilities. A high-contrast matte can be run in the projector nearest to the camera independently of the background loaded in the other projector. Color inlays and drop shadows of static lettering can be done with only one frame in the gate of the aerial image projector. A graphic wipe can be stretched or contracted without affecting the printing of the background image; the background image itself can be freeze-framed, printed forward, or reversed with the inlay mask following an entirely different pattern. Admittedly, a second run is necessary to complete the composite. However, the freedom of movement and the facility for repositioning one image in relation to the other are useful advantages.

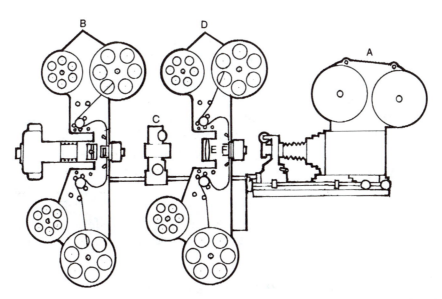

Figure 8.13 Optical printer with two "in-line" projector heads. (A) Camera. (B) Projector head with lamphouse. (C) Projector lens. (D) Second projector head. (E) Aerial image field lens. (F) Projector gate where the image from projector B is focused by lens C.

Using Multihead Optical Printers

An interesting effect that can be created with this type of equipment is to produce a gradual change in a scene from freeze-frame to normal action, so that while part of the frame is still "frozen" the rest of it is normal. Naturally, only a static shot could be used in this way until the freeze segment is concluded.

The background scene is loaded normally in the projector, and the high-contrast matte (carrying the wipe that will progressively obscure the frame) is loaded in the aerial image projector. During the printing the background remains frozen on a chosen frame as the second projector and camera run interlocked. After the picture has been entirely obscured by the high-contrast wipe, the camera is wound back to the start and the countermatte of the wipe is loaded in the aerial image projector. On the second run, both projectors are interlocked with the camera, and the scene is printed for as long as required after the end of the wipe-in. The effect can be greatly enhanced if the wipe is prepared so that it animates in an irregular line, moving slowly across the frame. The matte line should be invisible, as the print of the same scene is used for both passes. The choice of the scene and the shape and the direction of the travel of the wipe are all important.

This approach is also very useful for sectional replacement and substitution of parts of the frame, as in wire replacement, and for the elimination of other unwanted or accidental intrusions into the frame area. The best results are obtained when the matte line follows the outline of a moving shape within the action.

CAMERA PLUS THREE PROJECTOR HEADS

A projector head set at 90 degrees to the camera lens axis can be incorporated into a set-up consisting of two "in-line" projector heads. This approach incorporates some of the advantages of both "in-line" and crossed-projector configurations. The background plate and the male matte are loaded separately in the two in-line projectors. A self-matting positive on its own or the female matte in bi-pack with the inlay positive are loaded in the third projector head. The entire composite can be performed in one run through the camera. An additional advantage is that the composite scene can be viewed through the camera. However, when a countermatte has to be used, there is no flexibility for adjustment, because it has to be carried in bi-pack with the positive to which it relates.

CAMERA PLUS FOUR PROJECTOR HEADS

All the advantages of both in-line aerial image projectors and those set at 90 degrees to each other are incorporated in an optical printer with four projector

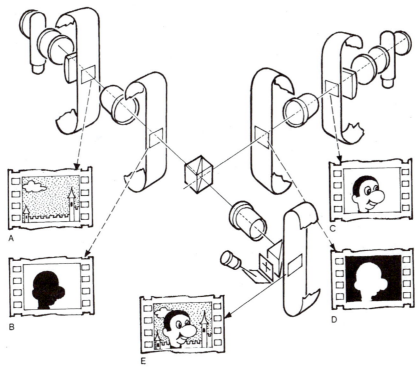

Figure 8.14 One pass marry-up with optical printer with four projector heads. (A) Background interpositive. (B) Male travelling matte (can be adjusted). (C) Foreground interpositive. (D) Female travelling matte (can be adjusted). (E) Composite.

heads. Two pairs of in-line aerial image projectors are set at 90 degrees to each other and their images are combined by means of a prismatic beam-splitter. Two lamphouses provide illumination for two basic images in the outer projectors, and the inner projectors can carry auxiliary masks or any other mattes that may need to be adjusted in some way. A color inlay of a static title could be executed in one pass with a freeze frame of the positive and negative image of the title provided as a short clip on high-contrast stock. A travelling matte composite can be married-up in one pass.

9

The Animation Rostrum
Camera and FX

*Then the camera (with its bi-pack maga-
zine) grew a support column so that it
could look down upon and have dominion
over the flat world of artwork, and it
became an animation stand.*

Although originally developed as a means of shooting flat animation artwork, the rostrum camera stand has evolved into a very useful tool for the production of visual effects.

THE STAND

Animation stands have a rigid construction, consisting of a solid metal base and one or two vertical columns (depending on the design) that serve as supports for the camera assembly to move up and down. The weight of the camera and the camera mount is counterbalanced by lead weights. In the case of the single-column stand, the counterweights are inside the column. This tracking movement is normally motorized, but it can also be operated manually. The camera can be positioned anywhere along the column so that various field sizes can be photographed, or it can be tracked continuously through the shot (zooming).

The Animation Table

In its simplest form the animation table can be an ordinary table on which the artwork is placed for photography. On sophisticated stands the animation table forms part of an elaborate compound assembly that is capable of very intricate movements with an extremely high degree of accuracy. This is very important because camera moves (panning, tilting, and rotation) are, in fact, executed by moving the artwork while the camera remains in a fixed position. The zooming action is the only camera move performed by actually moving the camera.

Registering the Artwork

The artwork is normally registered by means of pegs. Two flat pegs with a circular one between them form the basic unit. These can be either loose bars that are stuck to the animation table, or they can be made up from individual pieces that are screwed into the slots provided for them. These slots are on moving peg bars that are built into the animation table, so that their upper sides are flush with the table surface. There is a choice of two to four of these peg bars running in parallel and at predetermined distances above and below the table center. The peg bars are controlled by calibrated wheels positioned along one side of the table. The pegs are fitted as and when required, and can be placed all the way along the bar for the use of long panning cells (the celluloid sheets onto which the artwork is drawn). It is important that the cells are punched with the same standard punch that corresponds with the dimensions of the pegs.

The Cutout

The central area of the table is cut out and holds a piece of glass that lies flush with the tabletop. This is used for backlit artwork and transparencies.

The Rotation

The animation table is mounted on a rotation ring and can be rotated through 360 degrees by means of a calibrated control wheel and a gear linkage. In addition to rotation moves, it is also used for positioning the table at any angle so that the moving peg bars can be used to pan the artwork in any desired direction.

North/South Movement

The animation table and the rotation unit are in turn mounted on a set of tracks that enable the entire unit to be moved in a North/South direction. This is done by means of a control wheel that is connected to a threaded shaft.

East/West Movement

The basic compound is completed with the addition of the East/West movement. The entire assembly is placed on another set of tracks and moved by means of a control wheel and a threaded shaft.

Diagonal Panning

The artwork on the animation table can be panned in a North/South or East/West direction, relative to the camera lens, by the manipulation of either of the two basic movements of the compound. The moving peg bars makes it possible to move a section of the artwork independently of the compound move.

The diagonal pans can be done by a combination of North/South and East/West movements of the compound. On some animation stands the entire compound can be rotated on a bottom rotation (which is only used for positioning), so that either North/South or East/West movements alone can be used to

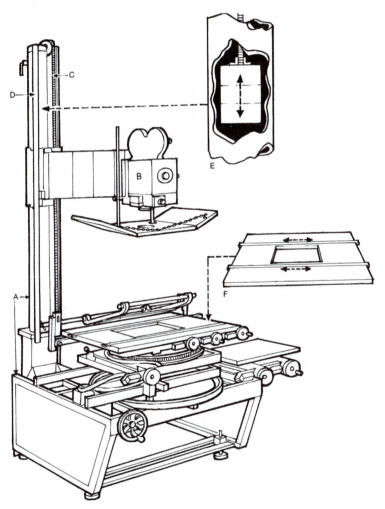

Figure 9.1 (A) Column and base. (B) Camera mount and camera. (C) Chain drive. (D) Follow-focus rack. (E) Counterweight inside column. (F) Animation table; moving peg bars are built into the animation tabletop.

perform a diagonal pan at any chosen angle. This is a great advantage in the case of manual operation: in such cases the distances from point A to point B has to be read off the counter and divided by the number of frames required for the duration of the pan, in order to obtain a constant increment by which the table must be moved for each frame. This is difficult enough for one move, but when two have to be done simultaneously, the chances of making compatible increments are very slight, without careful planning.

Added to this is the problem of "fairing." As in live-action shooting, it is very unusual to cut to a scene that pans at a constant rate from start to finish. Pans have to be "faired in" (speeded up) at the start and "faired out" (slowed down) at the end, particularly when they start or end with a static hold. All the control wheels are fitted with counters that can give readouts in actual distances; and when used in combination with the calibrations engraved on the wheels these readouts can plot distance measurements to the accuracy of one thousandth of an inch (0.001").

> *And it came to pass that the animation stand became motorized, and soon after . . . computerized . . . and this was good for visual effects.*

MOTORIZED MOVEMENTS

Although the rostrum camera is fitted with a stop-motion motor, it can shoot at continuous speeds of between 30 to 240 frames per minute (fpm). When each axis of the compound movement is motorized, the speed for each motor can be set individually and controlled by a master controller. This approach speeds up the shooting procedure enormously, but it is only suitable for stills and other straightforward work that do not require changes of cells or any very delicate maneuvers.

Computerized Movements

Computerized control of all movements takes the drudgery out of rostrum camera work. The whole operation is done by simply presetting the start and end positions of a move, and indicating the number of frames it should take and the amount of fairing required. There is also a provision for selecting the type of exponential curve required for the track. The operation can be done with the camera shooting continuously or frame-by-frame. The computer software used for driving motion control units is also used on the animation stands. In fact a motion control unit is an expanded and customized animation stand on wheels.

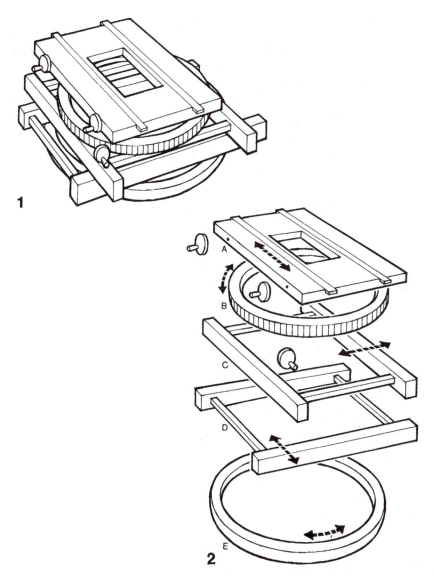

Figure 9.2 (1) Rostrum compound allows the artwork to be positioned exactly for each frame. (2) (A) Tabletop. (B) Table rotation. (C) North/South assembly. (D) East/West assembly. (E) Bottom compound rotation.

Pantograph Table

A pointer attached to the animation table moves over a small table fitted to the base of the stand; it is used to trace the movements of the animation table, enabling the execution of elaborate curves. In nonreflex cameras it is also used to indicate the relative position of the animation table relative to the lens center.

Floating Peg Bar

This peg bar lies just above the surface of the animation table and is mounted independently from the vertical column or the base with its own East/West and North/South movements. It is used to hold a piece of artwork static in relation to the background, which is attached to and moved by the animation table beneath it. It is also used to move that same artwork independently.

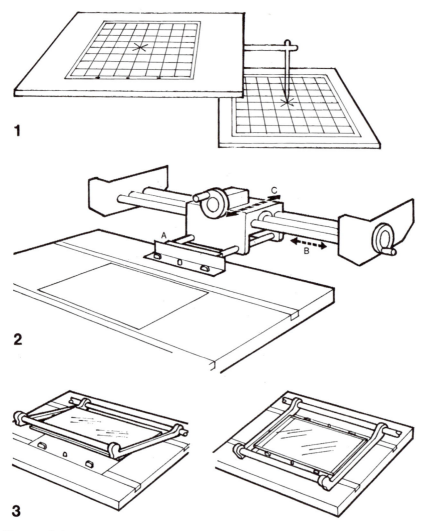

Figure 9.3 (1) Rostrum table and pantograph table with pointer. (2) Floating peg bar. (A) The peg bar. (B) East/West movement. (C) North/South movement. (3) The platen is a piece of plain glass hinged to the table. When it is down, it should hold the artwork without pressing on it too hard.

The Platen

It is necessary for the artwork to be kept flat on the animation table, particularly when several layers are being used. A piece of good quality glass (the platen) is used for this purpose. The platen has to be lifted up before any adjustment in the position of the artwork can be made. To enable speedier operation, the glass is mounted in a frame that is attached to the tabletop. It can be raised with one hand and remains in a fixed position until it is released again by the twist of a handle. The frame also ensures that the glass lies evenly across the artwork with controlled pressure.

Autofocus

The change in field size is produced by moving the camera up and down the column or by changing the lens. If the focusing had to be done manually every time a field-size change was required, it would be extremely laborious and time-consuming. A continuous tracking shot (a zoom), for example, would take a very long time. Automatic follow-focus avoids the necessity for this.

There are two basic auto-focus systems. One uses a linear cam running the full length of the camera travel, and the other uses a circular cam. In each case the cam is cut to a shape that ensures that the camera-focusing mechanism is adjusted to the correct setting for every position on the track by means of interlocking levers. The lens is mounted in a separate unit and connected to the camera body by extension bellows, enabling it to focus down to a scene-to-image ratio of 1:1. However, the best method of autofocusing is done not by moving the lens in relation to the camera body, but by moving the camera body away from the lens. This ensures that the lens moves at a constant rate throughout the zoom. (Conventional mounting results in the lens moving faster than the camera as the bellows are extended.)

The plane of primary focus can be raised from its normal position at the tabletop level so that very thick artwork, such as books, can be accommodated. This is done by altering the basic position of the follow-focus mechanism. On computer-controlled stands the camera focus becomes just one more axis that is operated by the computer.

Zoom Rates

When the camera is tracked from the largest field size to the smallest at equal increments for each frame, the resultant zoom appears to speed up progressively. This is particularly noticeable towards the smaller field sizes. This type of tracking (or zooming) is said to be "logarithmic." To make the zoom appear to be even throughout its length, the tracking has to follow an exponential curve to ensure a constant rate of increase in the image size.

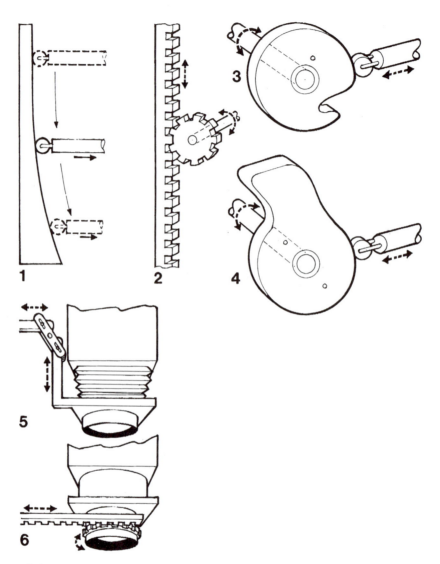

Figure 9.4   (1) Follow-focus cam running full length of the camera travel. (2) Rack and gear for rotating cam system. (3) Auto-focus cam (rotates counterclockwise when zooming in). (4) Inverted autofocus cam (rotates clockwise when zooming in). (5) Autofocus drive for normal rotary focusing. (6) Autofocus drive for lens with bellows focusing.

The calculation of this rate is made on the basis of the ratio between the largest and the smallest field size, that is, the start and end of the zoom. Naturally this results in a different increment for practically every frame. When fairing in and out are superimposed on this, it is no wonder that this type of zoom is not the most popular with camera operators. However, a computer-operated animation stand usually has this facility built in.

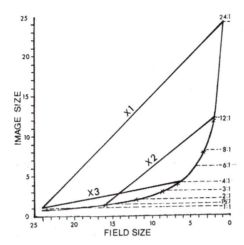

Figure 9.5 Exponential curves. As camera is zoomed in from the widest to the smallest field size in equal increments, the object photographed appears to increase in size. This increase is not equal along the track because the camera lens is responding to a logarithmic curve. When the camera track follows an exponential curve, the increase in image size is constant.

The Camera

Basically this could be virtually any camera, although the more sophisticated stands have specially designed cameras with registration-pin movements. These special cameras are similar in many ways to the cameras used on optical printers and digital scanners. Some have interchangeable movements for 35mm and 16mm. Although nonreflex cameras can be used successfully, they can present a lot of problems. Reflex viewing of some kind is essential for any sophisticated visual effects work. The most popular cameras in this field are of the rack-over reflex type.

Digital Camera

An electronic camera can be mounted on an animation stand in place of the film camera. This is particularly useful for television applications. A high-resolution digital camera of the same type used to scan in film images to digital media can be used to record the animation artwork directly, thereby bypassing one step. The electronic image can then be manipulated further in the digital form before the final output to film or tape.

Fade/Dissolve Facility

The camera shutter is normally of the variable rotary type and is used for executing fades and dissolves. This can be done manually or automatically. The length of the fade or dissolve setting varies from 8 to 128 frames.

Capping Shutter and Autocycler

In addition to the normal variable rotary shutter, some cameras have a built-in capping shutter. This consists of a metal blade that is operated by a solenoid from the control console. It is located between the lens and the normal shutter and prevents light from reaching the film gate, regardless of the position of the rotary shutter.

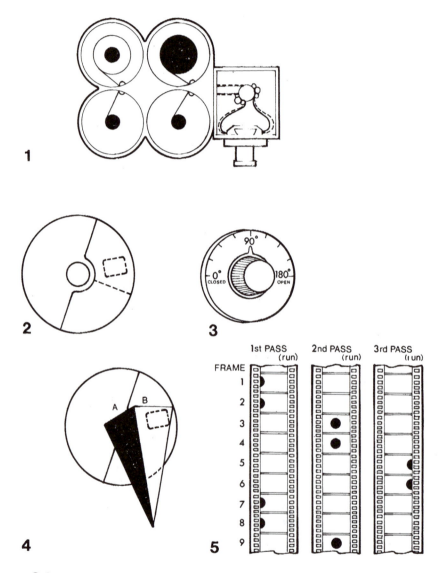

Figure 9.6 (1) Rostrum camera with bi-pack magazine. (2) Rotary shutter. The sector rotates to reveal the film aperture. (3) Manual control set at 90 degrees. (4) Capping shutter. (A) Open. (B) Closed. (5) When shooting a cycle with a capping shutter, instead of changing the artwork each frame (or two), the cycle can be shot in separate passes. The shutter is opened and closed for the appropriate passes.

During the shooting of an animation "cycle" where the same series of cells are used in a particular order, the capping shutter serves to "skip" some of the frames and allow the exposure only on the appropriate ones. On successive passes through the camera, other cells are then "slotted" into their appropriate positions within the cycle. This operation results in only a minimum change of artwork. The entire operation can be done automatically where an autocycler is fitted.

Bi-Pack Magazines

Single or bi-pack magazines are available on most rostrum cameras, both for 35mm and 16mm operation.

Camera Motor

The camera motor can be run continuously as well as for single-frame (stop-motion) shooting. The chosen exposure time remains the same in both cases. A selection of motor speeds allows for exposures of between 1 or 2 sec to 1/6 or 1/8 sec. Faster speeds, if provided, are used for rewinding or continuous operation only.

Rotoscoping

The ground glass in a rostrum camera is engraved with frame lines, a safe titling area, and frame centers. Lining up artwork is done by projecting this grid (graticule) onto the animation table by means of a lamp attached to the eyepiece. The start and end positions of the shot are noted from counters that indicate the relative positions of each of the compound movements. The shooting itself is done "blind," because most of these cameras are of the rack-over reflex type. The viewfinder, conventionally, is used only for focus checks. It also has a facility for registering a piece of film over the ground glass in the same way that it would be in the camera. For a more accurate line-up of an element that may be added later to the prefilmed scene, or simply for tracing off a particular detail, a film clip of the scene is projected onto the table.

For ultimate accuracy, rotoscoping is done through the camera gate itself. A prism is placed in the gate and, with the door open, a rotoscope lamp is directed via this prism onto the film clip threaded in the gate. A clear image is then seen projected onto the animation table. The camera motor can be made to stop with the shutter open instead of closed, and an entire scene can be projected frame-by-frame. This is invaluable where the artwork to be filmed has to match the background action and appear to be part of that background action. The artwork on the table is lined up to certain specific points in the picture and then realigned again as these points change on every successive frame. The movements to be made on the animation table are carefully noted. This is a long and tedious procedure, but very often it is the only way of obtaining a high degree of matching between the two elements. Even hand-drawn travelling mattes can be produced by rotoscoping. These are more successful, however, where regular geometric shapes are involved rather than live-action figures, except for short, quick moves.

Shadow Board

This is a board placed below the camera lens to prevent unwanted reflections reaching the lens. It is mounted on an adjustable support that in turn is fixed to

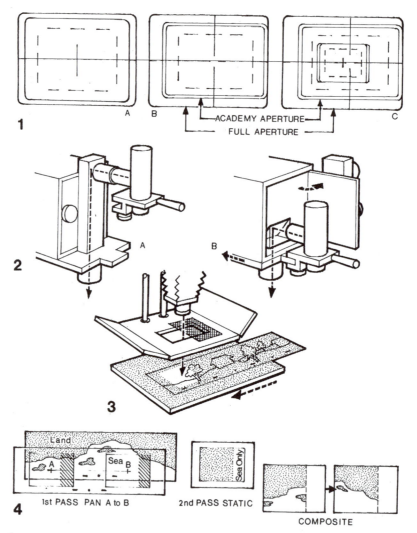

Figure 9.7 (1) (A) 16mm graticule. (B) 35mm graticule. (C) 16mm and 35mm graticule combined. (2) Rotoscope lamp. (A) Mounted for projection through the viewfinder. (B) Mounted for projection through the gate via a prism. (3) Shadow board; a simple wipe device. (4) With shadow board matte fixed, the seashore artwork is panned. Then, with the countermatte, sea only is printed in the space, so land appears to materialize from the sea as the pan continues.

the camera support so that it moves with the camera. The clear aperture cut in the board is used to carry auxiliary optical devices such as ripple glass and other elements. A clear glass placed in this aperture can be used to support fixed masks. These are used as "soft edge" mattes that stay in a fixed relationship to the frame in the camera while the artwork on the table moves independently.

A simple device consisting of a threaded shaft and a loose peg bar can be mounted on the shadow board and used to move a mask across the frame, progressively obliterating the image. A countermask (cut at the same time as the first mask and therefore an identical opposite) is used on the second pass to reveal another picture or an added element to the first picture. A soft-edged wipe is produced in this way, without interfering with the animation movements of the table or the peg bars.

Lens Attachments

All lens attachments discussed earlier in this book can be used on a rostrum camera to produce fragmentation of images, flopping, and distortion. (See Chapter 5, "In-Camera FX.")

The Halo Effect

This effect is due to the barrel distortion produced by a fisheye lens placed very close to backlit artwork such as a caption, giving lettering the appearance of being on the outside of a sphere. The letters in the center of the frame appear larger, while those at the edges appear to recede round the illusory sphere. By panning the artwork, the illusion is created of the lettering revolving around this sphere. Backlit captions can be superimposed this way over a normal photographed scene for added effects.

Figure 9.8 (A) The "halo" effect is only symmetrical when the artwork runs along the center of the fisheye lens. It can be moved up in frame either by repositioning on an optical printer, or by placing the negative one perforation out of rack in relation to the background. (B) Normal shape produced by the fisheye lens when the lettering is above or below the lens center.

DIRECT EFFECTS

Apart from shooting stills, transparencies, and animation artwork directly, a number of very sophisticated backgrounds can be produced entirely on the rostrum camera, particularly in the area of fantasy and science fiction. There is virtually no limit to the number of different passes of a shot that can be made through the camera, and the facilities for precision control are so great that the only limitation is the imagination of the operator. It is not generally known that the opening title shot of *2001: A Space Odyssey* was filmed entirely on a rostrum camera with flat artwork.

Titles

White titles can be superimposed directly onto a prefilmed scene on a separate pass. This can also be a live-action scene, shot on another camera. Alternatively, the white titles can be shot on high-contrast stock and used for color inlaying or drop-shadow treatment by the optical methods already described. The artwork can be either top-lit or backlit. Backlit material has to be prepared photographically on sheet film, such as Kodalith, with clear lettering on an opaque black background. Top-lit material is best prepared on shiny black paper or card. Normal pola-filters set up on the lights and lens ensure that the black background does not reproduce, allowing the lettering to be well exposed without danger of fogging from background reflections. In special circumstances very strong pola-filters (such as HN 22) can be used. However, this material is unsuitable for normal photography because of its adverse effect on color reproduction.

This black background is all-important because it allows numerous passes through the camera to be made without any special masking. From the simplest frame-by-frame build-up of a title to a complex break-up of letters, which eventually reassemble into a full title, the only artwork required is a straightforward white caption. Combined with distortions, fades and mixes, focus pulls, and additional masking at the shadow board level as well as on the animation table, the number of intricate effects that can be produced with the simplest artwork is unlimited.

Matting

Soft-edged mattes can be produced by masking at the shadow board, the softness of the edge being governed by the distance of the shadow board from the lens and the f-stop used. Masking with glossy black paper at the animation table level produces sharp-edged mattes. Split-screening, wipes (normal and push-off type), as well as image break-ups can all be done with the aid of this type of masking. A fluid matte effect is produced by photographing cells of specially prepared animation artwork that changes shape progressively.

Figure 9.9 (1) Each letter can be shot in a separate pass, giving it complete freedom of maneuver, until it joins up with others to form a word. (2) Split-screen. A section of the screen can be masked off with shiny black paper so that on the second run another scene can be photographed in that area, with opposite masking. (3) Flop-box. This is useful for "flopping" the image, adding to the three-dimensional effect.

Bi-Pack Matting

A graphic mask can be prefilmed on high-contrast stock and carried in bi-pack as a travelling matte. A simple shape cut out of black paper can be made to spin and move around the table, introducing a variety of shapes that can then be used as travelling mattes. Running across and zooming into sections of a high-contrast graphic representation of a face, or a similar shape, is also an effective way of producing travelling mattes. These mattes can then be used in bi-pack for direct photography of other artwork on the animation table. Alternatively, a counter-matte can be made from the original, and two or more different types of artwork can then be composited.

Bi-Pack Printing

The rostrum camera has all the basic features of a contact step printer, when adequate backlight is provided. (See Chapter 7, "Bi-Pack Camera.") It can duplicate a master positive in a straightforward bi-pack printing operation, with the additional facility that titling can be superimposed over the duplicated live scene by direct photography. Parts of the frame can be masked off to produce static mattes. These masks can also be substituted frame-by-frame and/or moved on the animation table to change the shape of the matte or even to wipe off the image completely. Identical moves can be repeated on a second pass through the camera to duplicate another scene in the unexposed areas. Apart from any additional color filtration that may be needed, it is always advisable to use a UV filter (2E) in any color-duplicating work.

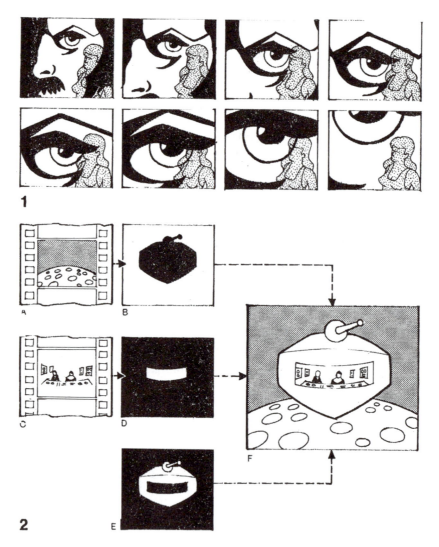

Figure 9.10   (1) Travelling matte used in bi-pack for direct photography of other artwork on the animation table. (2) Bi-pack printing. (A) Interpositive background action. (B) Cutout of spacecraft lit from behind (windows masked off). (C) Interpositive of live action to be inserted into cockpit. (D) Windows of the cutout left clear; surrounding area masked off. (E) Cutout of spacecraft, top-lit (windows masked off). (F) Composite picture.

Projected Image

Transparencies available for rostrum work are often too small to enable effects involving movements to be made within the picture area. Instead of making normal enlargements, the transparency can be projected by slide projector onto a translucent screen and the enlarged image can then be photographed. In practice, this requires that the projector be mounted in a light-tight housing incorporating a front-silvered mirror at a 45-degree angle to the projector axis, and that the back-projected material be held above the mirror by supports inside the housing. Translucent material such as Kodatrace, laid flat on a piece of clear glass, can be used instead of a conventional back-projection screen. The projection box is placed on the animation table so that all panning and rotation moves can be done as with a directly photographed transparency. When the focus plane is raised to its new level, the autofocus on the camera allows the zoom to be used as well.

Specially adapted 16mm projectors can also be used in this way to give the effect of filmed action in various areas of the frame. This can also be combined with a mask so that the moving picture appears to be part of a moving object within the frame.

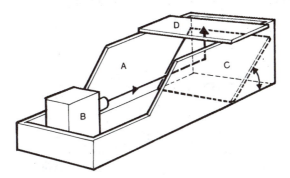

Figure 9.11 Tabletop projection unit. (A) Black wooden box. (B). Projector. (C) Front-silvered mirror. (D) Back-projection screen.

LIGHTING

Standard lighting on an animation stand consists of two lamps set at equal distances from the center of the animation table set at zero position, so that the table center lines up with the lens center. The two lamps are set at the same angle and positioned along an imaginary line, passing through the center of the table in an East/West direction. The angle of incidence is determined by the area to be illuminated evenly. Too narrow an angle produces shadows from upper layers of artwork onto the lower ones; too wide an angle is also a problem because then the camera (or specifically the shadow board) can throw shadows on the artwork. In either case, there can be an unevenness of illumination produced by each lamp, but when the two are aligned accurately this problem is eliminated. An angle of between 30 degrees and 35 degrees to the horizontal is usually the best compromise.

Filtration

Special filter holders mounted in front of the lights facilitate quick filter changes, but because the gelatins are held so close to the lights, their life expectancy is greatly reduced. Pairs of neutral-density filters and various colored filters, as well as diffusers, are stored in a large filter box when not in use. Polarizing filters, however, have to be looked after particularly well because they tend to get discolored when overheated; and if too much dust accumulates on them, they tend to absorb even more light than usual. They are practically indispensable for top-lit work. Polarizing axes have to be marked carefully so that the filters can always be inserted in the filter holder in the same position. The corresponding polarizing filter for the lens should be of the same type and set with its axis at 90 degrees to both pola-filters on the lights. Type HN 38 is the filter most commonly used for this type of work. The exposure is cut down by approximately 3 stops with the use of these pola-filters (1.5 stops for the filters over the lights and a further 1.5 stop for the filter over the lens).

Backlight

The rectangular cutout in the animation table is used to enable the light to reach transparent artwork, whether it is stills or specially prepared artwork from pieces of colored gelatin. The backlighting has to be evenly diffused over the entire area. Placing a ground glass in the cutout area is not a good solution because the grain pattern will be in focus and clearly discernible in the photographed image, particularly in the clearer areas of the frame. If ground glass is to be used to help diffuse the backlight, then it must be placed at some distance below the tabletop so that it is no longer in focus. Opal glass is another useful diffuser, but it tends to absorb too much light, and some types can alter the color temperature of the light.

Light reflected from a white card or a laminated white board can produce large areas of even illumination, provided that the lamps are lined up correctly. Where very high levels of illumination are required, such as in the case of interpositive printing, then a two-kilowatt lamp placed under the table and pointing towards the lens can be used. The fresnel lens on the lamp should be turned around, and an additional diffuser, such as ground glass, is needed. A strong fan to circulate the air over the diffuser and below the artwork is a must!

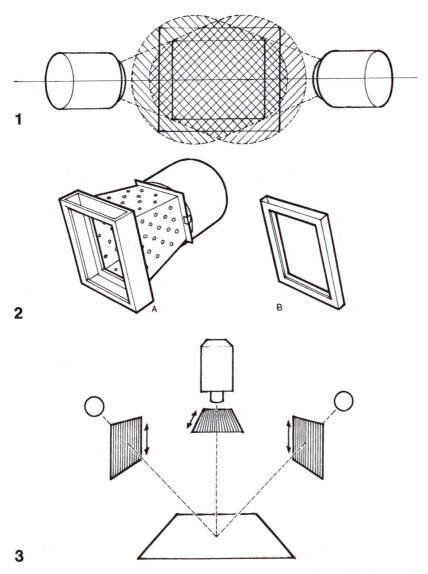

Figure 9.12 (1) When measured separately at the table center (X), each light gives the same foot-candle reading. (2) Lighting hoods. (A) Light fitted with filter hood. (B) Filter mount. (3) Polarizing filters in front of the lights, positioned so that their polarization axes are parallel. The lens polarizer is positioned so that its polarization axis is 90 degrees to the axes of the other two filters.

Black velvet (or similar material) should be used to cover the animation compound and prevent the backlight from scattering. At the same time, however, the movements of the compound must not be restricted in any way. Apart

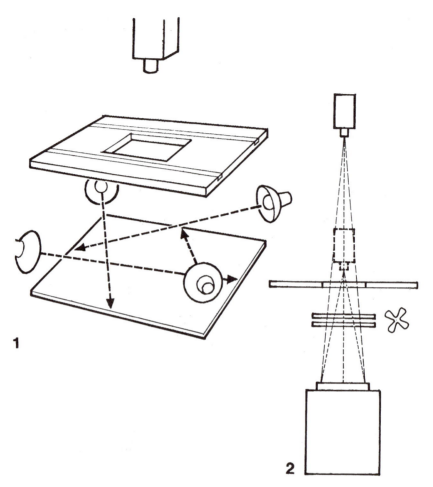

1

2

Figure 9.13   (1) Simple backlighting setup. Four quartz-iodine lamps bounced off a board with white Formica top. The lights are lined up to give even illumination over the whole area. (2) Using a 2-Kw lamp for printing. To obtain perfectly even lighting over the whole frame, the position is determined by the angle of acceptance of the lens when the size of the light source is limited. A larger working area is obtained on the tabletop with a narrow-angle lens.

from the dangers of reflection, spilled light can reach the top part of the artwork and produce a patchy desaturation effect by fogging.

When the rostrum camera is to be used for straightforward printing as a contact step printer, then a lamphouse can be fitted directly to the camera in place of the lens. In ideal circumstances the backlight should be made to match the top-light, so that an average top-lit scene and an average backlit scene have the same basic exposure. Normally, four times less light is required (in terms of foot candles) for the backlight to match the top-light because of the differences in exposure readings: the top-light is measured by incident and backlight by direct reading.

Dichroic Filters

All lamps produce heat proportionally to their brightness. The heat is in the form of infrared radiation and can be isolated with the use of dichroic filters. These are available in two basic types. One type reflects the visible spectrum and transmits the infrared, and the other reflects the infrared and transmits the visible light.

THE SLIT-SCAN

Ideally, slit-scanning should be done on specially designed equipment, but the rostrum camera lends itself extremely well to the production of this effect with very little modification. The principle of the system is to expose one frame of the picture while the camera is tracking. The technique requires that the camera motor stops with the camera shutter in the open position. An auxiliary shutter placed in front of the camera lens is opened at a precise point at the start of the track and closed at the end of it; the camera moves on to the next frame, and the operation is repeated in reverse. (A capping shutter can be used for this purpose where fitted.) This shutter is best operated by a simple solenoid motor and a microswitch that is activated by two tripping devices set at the extremes of the track.

During exposure the artwork is scanned through a slit. The shape of the slit and the ratio between the two extreme field sizes determine the final shape traced out on the film emulsion. Ideally, both the slit and the artwork behind it should be moving during exposure, but especially the artwork, since the Zoom will have the effect of changing the relative position of the slit. This can be accomplished on the rostrum camera by suspending a large and fairly thick pane of glass just above the animation table that carries the artwork. The glass is masked off with black paper except for a slit. One of the table movements is then interlocked with the tracking mechanism either by mechanical or electronic means so that both animation table and camera maintain fixed relative positions. The animation within the slit-scan effect is produced by attaching the artwork to the travelling peg bar and moving it at specific increments for each successive frame. The artwork is backlit. The effect produced by slit-scanning can be worked out by careful consideration of the following points.

During the slit-scanning a point of light becomes a line whose length is determined by the amount of tracking during the total exposure time. In theory, a "slit" is made up from an infinite number of these points of light, all following slightly different paths, and all of which can be traced accurately. However, the movement of the artwork during the scanning effectively changes the characteristics of each spot, so that colored shapes appear to flow along the myriad number of wavy streaks. Thus, a dot can become a line; a line can assume a shape; and a shape can appear to be three-dimensional.

A back-projected, prefilmed, live-action scene can be used in place of artwork, and the slit can then be mounted directly onto the tabletop and moved in a predetermined manner and in sync with the track. The entire operation can be made to run automatically.

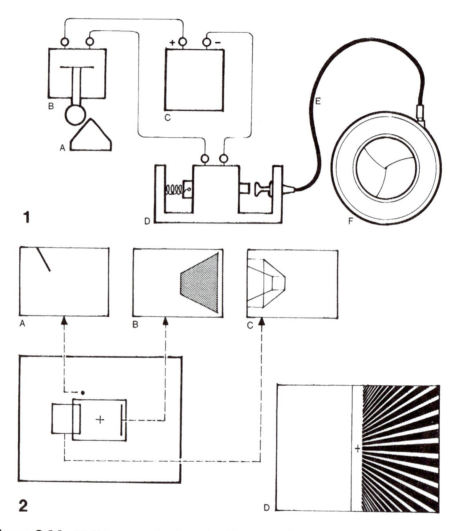

Figure 9.14 (1) Slit-scan mechanism. For this system the shutter must be held open for a measured length of time. If there is no capping shutter, a separate shutter can be fitted in front of the lens. Set at B (time exposure), this shutter can be operated by a simple solenoid system. (A) Trigger. (B) Microswitch. (C) Battery. (D) Solenoid (spring-loaded). (E) Cable release. (F) Shutter mechanism. (2) Slit-scan effects. By zooming from one field to another, different results can be achieved. (A) Dot becomes a line. (B) Line becomes a shape. (C) A shape appears to gain a third dimension. (D) An example of a simple slit-scan.

Meanwhile the optical printer became fruitful and multiplied . . . and this was good for visual effects. Then it came to pass that one of the offspring became attached to the animation stand and this blessed union begat an aerial image projector.

AERIAL IMAGE PROJECTOR

The aerial image projector has all the basic features of an optical printer projector head and is specially designed for use with rostrum cameras. A lamphouse and condenser system illuminates the film plane in the projection gate. There is also a means of inserting color correction filters and neutral-density filters in the light beam. Intermittent movements are the same as in the majority of optical printer projectors using fixed-register pins and include interchangeability between 35mm and 16mm formats (although some are available for 16mm only). The projector body is mounted on a solid bed and can be tracked along it. It is normally positioned on one side of the animation stand.

Figure 9.15   By rotoscoping each frame of a live-action sequence and tracing out key positions, it is possible to add an animated character dancing with a live-action one.

The Projection Lens

The lens is supported by its own mount independently of the projector body and can be tracked forwards or backwards along the same base. The lens also has the facility for fine movements in the vertical and horizontal plane perpendicular to the lens axis.

The Condensers

The projection beam is reflected upwards by the front-silvered mirror set centrally below the animation table. The image is focused at the tabletop just above the top surface of the two large condenser lenses fitted into the central cutout of the animation table. The maximum working area is about eleven inches. The aerial image can be viewed by placing a sheet of greaseproof paper or similar translucent material over the condensers; otherwise it is only visible through the

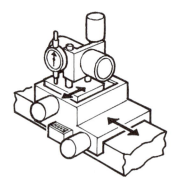

Figure 9.16   Projector lens. This may be mounted in its own compound to give precise adjustment to the selection of the frame area of the projected image.

camera lens. The camera lens has to be at a precise distance from and correctly aligned with the condensers. This means that the camera cannot track and the table cannot be panned. Built-in peg bars or the floating peg bar can make the only movements at tabletop level.

Aerial Image Zoom

By enlarging or reducing the projected image a zooming effect may be achieved while the camera remains in its fixed relationship to the condensers and the animation table. This is accomplished with the use of a copying lens in the projection lens mount while the standard projection lens is placed in another fixed mount in front of it. A field lens is used between these two lenses and it, too, is in a fixed position. A system of servomotors moves the copying lens and the projector body towards and away from each other, producing enlargements or reductions of the projected images onto the aerial image condensers. An automatic follow-focus system and an automatically operated iris are also interlocked with these movements by means of servomotors.

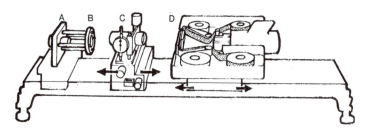

Figure 9.17   Aerial image projector with a zooming facility. (A) Standard lens (B) Field lens. (C) Copying lens. (D) Projector body.

Aerial Image and Top-lights

The great advantage of the aerial image is that it can be used for simultaneous photography of back projected images and top-lit artwork. It is possible to have an animated character inside a live-action scene without the need for travelling mattes. The animation cells are prepared so that they are opaque in the area of the artwork. They act, therefore, as their own mattes by obscuring the projected image while the rest of the scene can be seen clearly through the clear areas of the cell. Polarizing filters on the lights are essential for this operation.

Because the aerial image can be seen only through the camera, top-lights can be used at the same time without washing out the image, as would be the ease with normal back projection. This also makes it possible to check the balance between the projected scene and the top-lit artwork, both in terms of density and color correction.

Bi-Pack Operation

As both the camera and projector have bi-pack facilities, the aerial image rostrum can be used in much the same way as an optical printer, allowing skip framing, forward and reverse printing, freeze framing, etc. The added advantage is that the projected scenes can be married up with directly photographed artwork in one pass.

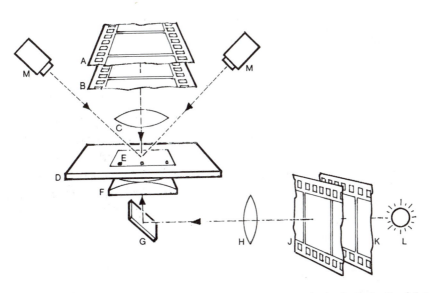

Figure 9.18 Two separate travelling mattes, cell artwork, and a back projection plate can all be used at one time. (A) Raw stock. (B) Travelling matte in contact (bi-pack) with raw stock. (C) Camera lens. (D) Table. (E) Cell artwork. (F) Condensers. (G) Front-silvered mirror. (H) Projector lens. (J) Back projection plate. (K) Travelling matte in contact with back-projection plate. (L) Projector lamp. (M) Top-lights.

The projector bi-pack facility can be used to carry traveling mattes in the same way as in the camera. Alternatively, two scenes can be run in bi-pack, producing a double exposure, which is different from printing each scene onto the same negative in succession. This is particularly useful where scenes with large clear areas of cell are involved.

10

Motion-Control Camera and FX

Then a miracle happened: the animation stand grew extra arms, raised itself on wheels, and developed a synthetic brain to control its many movements . . . and it was called motion control . . . which was good for visual effects.

A motion-control camera system consists of three main components:

1. the mechanical rig supporting the camera,
2. the motor drive system driving the mechanical rig, and
3. the computer control system.

Each of these components represents a degree of refinement and sophistication of operation. At the top end of the scale is a high-precision motion-control unit with full computer control on all its axes. This allows for precise frame-to-frame repeatability at either stop-motion or live-action speeds. Tracking shots of an actor playing two roles in the same scene can be accomplished with ease where previously this type of shot would have been tackled as a "lock off."

At the other end of the scale a very basic motion control rig can be operated manually or by direct drive electric motors. "Off the shelf" serve systems can also be used to drive some or all of the axes by remote control. This approach is only useful for stop-motion work or the most basic model shots at continuous camera speeds when great precision or frame-accurate repeatability is not required.

Any mechanical axis driven by a motor or some other actuator (pneumatic or hydraulic) can be controlled in this way. The precision of movement is governed by the resolution of the potentiometer or encoder used, as well as the maximum range of travel. For example, a standard ten-turn potentiometer will have a lower resolution if it is geared to represent 100 turns of the drive shaft than if it represents only 10 turns. However, the distance traveled will also be proportionally greater.

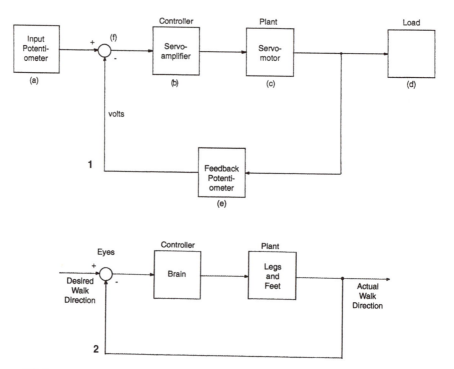

Figure 10.1 A typical "off the shelf" closed-loop servo system. (1) Input potentiometer (A), built into the control panel or attached to an input device, sends the power via a servo-amplifier (B) to the servomotor (C), driving a mechanical axis (D). Potentiometer (E) attached to the mechanical axis or the motor shaft provides the feedback information, indicating the extent of movement on the axis. (F) Error detector. (2) Human equivalent to the closed-loop servo system.

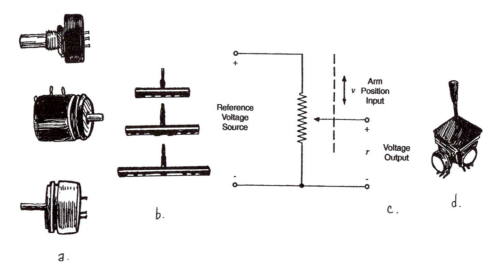

Figure 10.2 (A) Rotary potentiometers: "single turn," "multiturn," and "continuous rotation." (B) Linear potentiometers are available in various lengths. (C) Schematic diagram of a potentiometer. (D) Dual-axis joystick potentiometer.

THE MECHANICAL RIG

A typical motion-control rig can be thought of as an animation stand on wheels, designed specifically for use with three-dimensional objects instead of only flat artwork. It is a natural evolution of an animation stand with the East/West and North/South compound table removed from the support column and adapted into a "model mover."

In fact, some of the earliest versions of motion-control units were just that—animation stands placed on wheels with the camera mounted on a pan-and-tilt head. A more refined version of this added a boom arm to the support column. The camera could now move on three axes: East/West on the floor track, North/South on the boom arm, and up/down on the support column.

Other designs opted for a fixed vertical support and a crane arm with the entire compound being able to rotate around its vertical axis. All this mobility combined with frame-accurate computer control has resulted in these motion-control rigs becoming an indispensable tool for shooting models and miniatures, as well as live-action elements.

Although the majority of motion control rigs are custom built, there are a number of standard units such as Gazelle, Graphlite, and Zebra (Sorensen Design International) and Mark Robert's "Milo."

MOTION-CONTROL MOTOR-DRIVE SYSTEMS

Motion-control evolved out of technology developed for automated machine-control systems used in various manufacturing processes. These control systems employ either DC servomotors or stepper motors. Consequently, the motor drive packages used for motion-control cinematography are either DC servos or stepper motors. Some versions allow for interchangeability between DC servo drive and stepping-motor cards. Recent developments in AC servo systems have the advantage of speed and torque relative to weight.

Power Amplifier

The electric current driving a servomotor is generated by a power amplifier in response to a command signal, typically an analogue signal in the range of +/–10 volts. The current produced is directly proportional to the input voltage from the encoder. However, in the velocity mode it is the signal from a tacho-generator that provides the reference for accurate speed control.

An incremental encoder acts as a position sensor, indicating the position of the motor shaft or the drive shaft of the axis. In order to enable the controller to detect the direction of rotation, the encoder generates two sets of signals (from 100 to 500 per revolution) that are phase-shifted by a quarter of a cycle (90 degrees). A reference signal is also generated once per revolution. The resolution of the encoder is defined by the number of divisions on the disc, since they determine

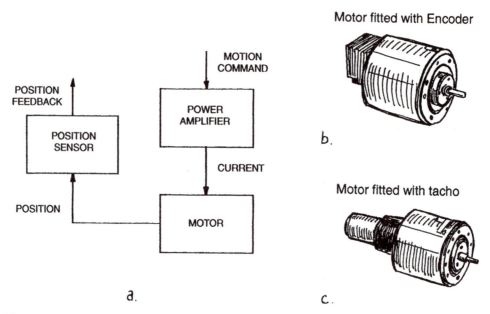

Figure 10.3   (A) Block diagram of power amplifier and motor relationship. (B) Motor fitted with an encoder. (C) Motor fitted with a tacho.

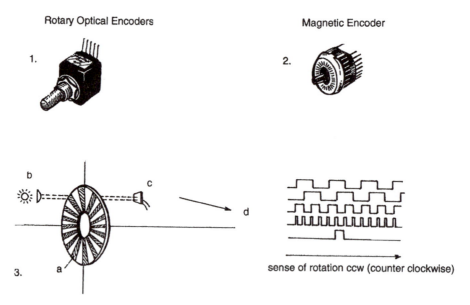

Figure 10.4   (1) Rotary optical encoder. (2) Magnetic encoder. (3) Optical encoders have a transparent disc divided into clear and opaque strips at regular intervals (A). A narrow light beam from an infrared LED (B) passes through the disc to a photo diode (C) positioned behind the disc. As the disc turns, the opaque strips block the light intermittently and the diode generates a signal to indicate movement on the axis. The final output of the encoder is in the form of a square wave (D).

the number of pulses generated per revolution. The greater the number of pulses per revolution, the greater the resolving power (accuracy) of the encoder.

Stepper-Motor Drives

The key design characteristic of stepper motors is that they move in "steps" in response to an input signal. Each electrical pulse applied to the winding produces a specific angle of rotation of the motor shaft (a "step"). The result can be a "cogging" effect at slow speeds. However, microstepping motors have extremely fine steps so that the cogging effect is eliminated for all practical purposes. These motors are extremely accurate but cannot match the speed and torque of DC servos of comparable size.

MOTION-CONTROL COMPUTER UNITS

The computer hardware required to run a motion-control unit is either a stand-alone unit or is made up of a host computer and a motion-controller. The host computer runs the main motion-control program and records/plays back the information received from the encoders on all axes of the mechanical rig. The motion-controller is a computer processor that interfaces directly with the motor drive units. It has certain specific functions programmed into the memory and performs the commands issued by the host computer.

Motion-control equipment suppliers generally provide the computer processor and motor-drive package as well as the software. A standard computer with adequate memory to run the software can be used, provided that motion-control logic boards are installed in a slot in the computer to enable it to output informa-

Elements of a Servo System

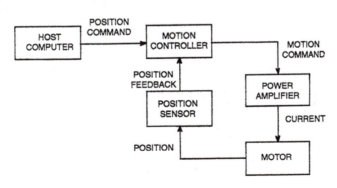

Figure 10.5 Elements of a servo system

tion regarding step and direction to the motor-drive package. A typical motion-control unit can run from 1 to 32 axes. Common configurations are 8, 16, and 32 axes.

Computer Software

It is the computer software that provides an interface between the user and the motion-control equipment. Each software package offers a number of different ways of programming a motion-control shot from real-time live action to stop-motion. Time lapse exposure, overcranking, undercranking, streak, slit-scan, and smear effects are some of the additional options available.

Programming Methods and Shooting Modes

The camera motion can be programmed by a combination of techniques, including all of the following:

1. *"Teach by example" real-time encoding.* This method is ideal for live-action programming. The camera is operated manually with the motion-control rig moved physically along the desired path of motion. The computer records the information from the encoders on all axes. The recorded information is then played back by the computer, which recreates the move. The record and playback can be done at different speeds.
2. *Joystick operation.* A joystick is used to control one or more axes when shooting "on the fly" in real time. This allows the operator to improve the smoothness on the chosen axis or to improvise a move while all other axes are controlled by the computer in playback mode. The joystick can also be used to input one or more axes at a time in order to build up a complex move.
3. *Keyframing.* This option allows the operator to select a number of "key" frames of a complex move and position the rig for each frame so that it can be recorded by the computer. During playback the computer software creates a continuous move on each axis by filling in the "in-between" frames. This option is particularly useful when a motion-control shot is to dissolve into or out of a live-action shot with a matching camera move. The line-up of "key" frames can be done using film clips in the camera viewfinder, or by freeze-framing video playback of the scene and overlaying it over the image from the video assist.
4. *Curve-fit.* The operator can fit a smooth curve to a set of points to vary the speed at different parts of the camera move without altering the overall length of the shot. These points may be defined by entering points from the keyboard, or by positioning the camera in the same manner as in "keyframing."
5. *Point-edit (graphics approach).* A graphic representation of the camera move allows the operator to analyze, modify, or create data files on a point-by-point basis.

6. *Numeric input.* Camera motion may be defined or modified using mathematical formulae.
7. *Target track.* The target track mode enables the camera to hold a specific target on a model or graphic centered in the frame during the shot. The target point may be static or in motion.
8. *Scaling a move.* In multipass operation it is sometimes necessary to scale up or scale down a move in order to maintain a match between the elements, as in a composite shot requiring a camera move on a live-action element photographed on location and a miniature set photographed in the studio. The software program will compute the relative camera positions for the model pass from the information recorded during the live-action shot or vice versa. This option also allows for the addition of a two-dimensional graphic (matte painting) to a three-dimensional shot while still maintaining the perspective.
9. *Taper-in/Taper-out.* A "taper-in" and "taper-out" of varied durations and characteristics can be added to a move to smooth out the transitions. These can be linear, sine, cosine, logarithmic, or exponential.

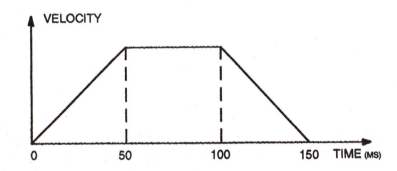

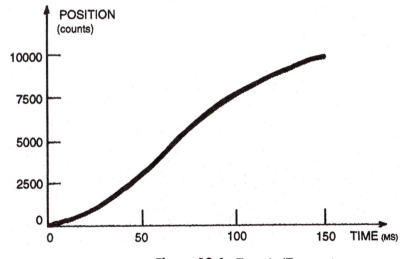

Figure 10.6 Taper-in/Taper out

10. *Nodal head compensation.* A nodal head pan-and-tilt can be simulated on a regular camera head by programming an offset of the physical position of the camera lens relative to the pivot point of the pan-and-tilt axes of the gear head.

11. *Go-motion.* Stop-frame photography produces clear, crisp images that are likely to strobe when a fast move is involved. "Go-motion" emulates the live-action "motion blur" produced by a fast move. There are two approaches: "expose-then-move," and "move-then-expose." In the "expose-then-move" approach, the motion-control rig moves on before the camera shutter is closed. The extent of the smear is controlled by the proportion of exposure time used for the "move."

12. *Streak photography.* A streak in the form of a blurred trail left behind a moving object is produced by a variation on the "go-motion" approach. The "streaking" effect on a model moving inside a miniature set is best done in two passes. The first pass photographs the composite move as a regular stop-motion shot. With the film wound back to the start position, the second pass is done with the illumination on the model only and the set blacked out. The camera is moved on during exposure starting at the matching position for each frame "streak." For very long streak trails it is necessary to move the camera back for the start of each successive frame.

    The streak effect can also be accomplished using the "travelling matte approach" to composite the two elements. It requires a separate pass on the miniature set without the model to produce one element. and another pass on the model alone to produce the other element complete with a streak. The drawback to this approach is that the color of the model is likely to mix with the color of the background in the area of the streak, making it difficult to extract a good matte.

    The stop-frame, motion-controlled, front-projection approach to the streak effect produces a composite image with a realistic, transparent, streak. It requires a background plate of the miniature set to be shot first. The model move (and the streak) is created during compositing. A capping shutter on the projector cuts off the projected background at the start point of the streak move.

13. *The strobe effect.* Unlike the streak effect, where the trail is a smeared blur, the strobe effect produces a trail of staggered images, behind the main image, that are sharp and clear. Using a multipass approach, this effect can be created by repeating the move with the miniature set blacked out and only the model illuminated, as in the earlier example. The film in the camera is advanced three or four frames ahead of the start frame for each successive pass, which is superimposed over the original take.

    For the travelling matte approach, the model is shot as a straightforward matting element and then overlaid in the compositing stage (pulled back three or four frames for each successive overlay) to create the strobe effect. The strobe image can also be fully matted in if required.

A motion-controlled front-projection approach achieves the strobe effect by compositing the model with the background plate on the first pass, and then repeating the camera move without the projected image and with the film advanced in the camera by three or four frames for the subsequent strobe passes.

14. *Slit-scan.* A slit-scan effect is achieved by exposing a frame while moving the camera towards (or away from) a backlit slit. Artwork consisting of colored patterns is moved in sync with the camera to produce a variety of patterns that are scanned onto the film frame. This technique first came into prominence in Stanley Kubrick's *2001: A Space Odyssey.* For more details see Chapter 9, "The Animation Rostrum Camera and FX."

15. *Zoom-and-track effect.* This effect can convey the feeling of an emotional disturbance when used in the appropriate context. It involves a zoom in one direction and a synchronized track in the opposite direction, that is, a zoom in and track out (or vice versa). The field of view at the point of primary focus (i.e., the actor) remains the same size while the background appears to expand or shrink. Although this effect can be done "on the fly" using manual controls, it is much easier to execute accurately with motion-control.

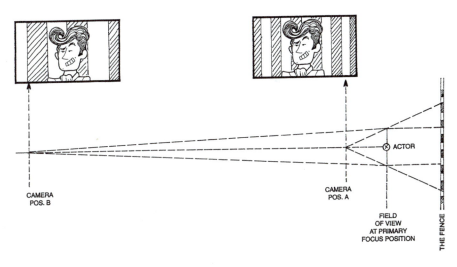

Figure 10.7 Zoom-and-track effect. (A) Image at camera position A in "zoomed-out" position (25mm). (B) Image at camera position B in "zoomed-in" position (240mm).

Motion-Control Recording Methods

The encoder information from the axis of the mechanical rig and the camera can be stored by the computer on a floppy or hard disc or by other storage options to be played back at a later date. Ideally the same motion-control rig should be used for playback, otherwise appropriate corrections need to be made to the recorded data in order to reproduce the move accurately. This is particularly important for multipass work when the subsequent passes may be done at a different time, at a different location, and even at a different scale. Allowances also have to be made for mechanical backlash.

A simpler version of a motion-control computer stores the encoder information in memory only and can be used for playback, but the information is lost once the computer is switched off. It is useful for executing a complex "single pass" move that may need to be "memorized" at a slower than real-time speed and executed at real-time speed (or vice versa).

Another method offers the option of programming certain characteristics to a drive axis and burning it into the memory. This is useful for altering the ratio between the input and output potentiometers in direct-drive controllers, acting as an "electronic gearbox."

Field Recording

A basic field-recording unit consists of a computer and a motor-drive package. It is used to record and playback the camera operation, pan, tilt (rotation), zoom, and focus. It is a useful tool for shooting background plates and other shots involving a simple motion-controlled move.

Motion Capture

In its simplest form motion capture consists of a computer and encoders only without the motor-drive package. The camera moves (pan, tilt, zoom, and focus) are recorded by the computer for later use in playback or as reference for digital animation. Visual markers placed within the photographed area are also helpful in tracking the move as well as perspective changes. (Both Panavision and Arriflex have encoded gear heads available for rent.)

For more complex applications encoders can be placed on all mechanical axes that affect the camera moves (e.g., crane arm, dolly, etc.). This way the position of the camera in three-dimensional space can be recorded and later played back on a motion-control system or used as a reference for CGI (computer-generated image) work.

Another aspect of motion capture relates to the encoding of movements made by actors and used to control a computer-generated character in real time (see Chapter 12, "Digital Effects").

Video Assist and Motion-Control

Video assist is of great importance in motion-control work because a lot of the time the camera is remotely controlled and not easily accessible for direct viewing through the viewfinder. It also allows the operator to preview the composite elements in multipass operations. With the addition of a chromakey, it is possible to preview a travelling matte shot.

The image from the video assist can be recorded by a (Perception) digital video recorder at non-real-time camera speeds and played back in real time.

Video playback is also used to generate the START CUE for synchronizing motion-control and live action in multipass work.

Model-Movers

Supplementary rigs are used to move models in synchronization with the camera moves. These model-movers are programmed and controlled by the motion-control computer as additional axes. They can be programmed separately or at the same time and in the same manner as the camera rig.

MOTION-CONTROL APPLICATIONS

1. *Animation stand.* A motion-control computer and a motor-drive package can be used to control any animation stand on all its axes.
2. *For live-action shots.* Motion-control camera equipment is used in live-action shots, to repeat identical camera moves for different elements in a multipass operation, and to encode a complex move for reference in CGI work.
3. *For model and miniature shots.* Motion-control camera equipment is used to repeat scaled, live-action moves to match the scale of the miniature, and to create and repeat complex camera moves at real and non-real time.
4. *For travelling matte elements (blue/green screen).* Motion-control camera equipment is used to match a camera move on a travelling matte element to the camera move on the plate, and to create a movement of a subject within the frame for insertion into a background plate.
5. *For process-projection compositing.* Motion-control camera equipment is used to encode a camera move on the background plate and repeat it during process compositing with the foreground subject (particularly useful with mini f.p. [front projection] units), and to create real-time motion control in front projection (see "Zoptic 'Moving Stills' Projector" in Chapter 11).
6. *For servo-driven animatronics.* Motion-control camera equipment is used to control and record servo-driven axes of an animatronic character, including jaw movements of an actor for perfect lip sync in "playback" mode.

11

Process Projection

And lo, another miracle happened: the optical printer split in half and begat process projection . . . and it was good for visual effects.

Process projection is a self-matting method for visual effects compositing of live-action or model elements and prefilmed backgrounds. There are two basic approaches to process projection: rear (or back) projection and front-projection. The two systems share certain basic characteristics: they utilize a projector and camera running in interlock.

A great advantage of process-projection is in terms of perspective line-up and lighting, because both the foreground element and the projected plate can be seen as they will appear in the final composite. It also allows for subtle manipulation of focus and the depth of field, so that the focus on the background can appear as a continuation of the natural focus fall-off towards infinity, or vice versa, as is the case in nature. Focus pulls from background to foreground object can also be done when required.

THE PROCESS PROJECTOR

Either a still or a moving picture can be used for process projection. The Mitchell rear-projector, utilizing the same type of mechanism as the Mitchell cameras, was the state-of-the-art projector in its day. When front-projection became possible due to the availability of the highly reflective directional screen, the Mitchell projector was initially adapted for this purpose, then specially designed front-projection units were produced.

Projector Mechanism

Process projector intermittent mechanisms are designed with register pins in much the same way as those of a camera. The pull-down-to-stationary relationship is generally 50/50 (i.e., equal to a 180-degree shutter).

Specially designed "fast pull-down" mechanisms allow for longer "dwell" periods and shorter pull-downs. This offers the advantage that the projected picture can be seen for a short time before and after the pull-down during photography with a camera using a reflex mirror shutter. The background image is faint, but it can be of great help in synchronizing foreground action to the action on the background plate. Another advantage is the latitude for synchronizing the camera shutter, which is normally 180 degrees.

Process Projector Motor Drives and Synchronization

The methods for interlocking the camera and the projector are the same for both techniques. The original rear projectors used a three-phase interlock system, which has now been largely superceded by the use of an electronic sync box designed to keep the camera motor running in phase with the projector. The sync box offers a selection of preset speeds as well as the standard 24 fps, but the speeds cannot be varied during the take. Most production cameras provide a sync pulse that connects to the sync box. A pulse generated by the projector is also fed into the sync box. Camera and projector motors are crystal-controlled and run up to speed independently. The sync box adjusts the phase of the camera motor so that it matches that of the projector. (The line-up is normally done at the center of the pull-down.)

The "selsyn" interlock system is perhaps the most convenient, allowing the greatest versatility. This system offers shooting speeds from 1 fps to 32 fps that can be varied during the shot, as well as a stop-frame facility and an option to interlock several projectors at the same time. The "selsyn" motors work on the principle of master-slave: the master selsyn is driven by another motor, and the slave repeats the movements of the master. A three-phase current is generated by the motors themselves to provide one-to-one interlock, although the primary voltage is standard.

When the main drive motor is used for driving the projector directly as well as the master selsyn, a mechanical or magnetic clutch is required to enable the camera and projector to be set in the correct synchronous position to each other, as well as to disengage the projector when it is required to run the camera alone. A better solution is to use a bigger master selsyn and two slave motors, one on the projector and one on the camera. This makes it possible to place the main drive motor, the master selsyn, reversing switches, and other controls in a separate control console. Stepper motors can also be used. Although somewhat less versatile than the selsyn type, the steppers are smaller and lighter.

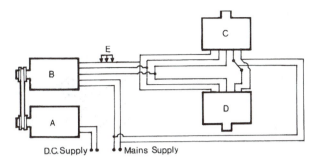

Figure 11.1 Basic selsyn interlock system. (A) Main drive motor. (B) Master selsyn motor. (C) and (D) Slave selsyn motors. (E) Three-phase interlock. All three selsyns energized by the mains supply.

Projector Shutter

Unlike cameras, the shutters on process projectors are only required occasionally and are usually disconnected during photography. Normally, a shutter is used only during the line-up to check the balance on the projected plate; however, this can result in a false impression, because the eye sees the projected image only 50% of the time, but the foreground is seen 100% of the time. A better approach is to set the sync 180 degrees out of phase and run the mirror shutter camera (empty). The flicker of the camera shutter affects the whole image seen by the eye and not only the background.

Three-Bladed Shutter

A three-bladed shutter is sometimes used as a crude means of synchronization. Although there is an increased chance that a camera and projector running wild can hit a sync point than with a 180-degree shutter, this is still very much a hit-and-miss approach that does not produce reliable, consistent results. In addition, it reduces the effective light output of the projector.

A three-bladed shutter is often used when more than one projector is required to run in sync with the camera. In those cases where the reproduction of the secondary plate is not critical, such as in shooting the reflection in the windshield of a car, the primary projector is in proper interlock with the camera and the secondary projector runs wild with a three-bladed shutter.

The Capping Shutter

This is required primarily for stop-motion operation to protect the film from excessive heat during the pause time between frames. It is in the form of a blade built into the lamphouse system. It is operated by a solenoid that is activated at the same time as the single-frame shot is taken. Alternatively, a 180-degree shutter driven by a servo motor (or selsyn) slaved to the projector motor can be used for this purpose.

PROCESS CAMERA

Any reflex camera can be interlocked with a projector with the use of an appropriate motor and an interlock system. The projected image will not be seen during the photography, when a mirror-shutter reflex camera is used with a standard projector mechanism with a 50/50 ratio between pull-down and dwell time. Rack-over reflex cameras can also be used in certain circumstances, particularly in animation and model work.

A pellicle reflex camera is ideal for process work, because it allows the projected image to be seen during the photography both in the camera viewfinder and on a video monitor. The advantage is that it makes it easier to execute complex interactions between the foreground action and prefilmed action on the plate. In addition, it provides instant preview of any changes in perspective line-up and lighting changes that need to be synchronized with the background plate. The disadvantage is a slight loss in exposure, which needs to be compensated for; this is typically 1/3 of an f-stop.

Video Assist

A small television camera attached to the reflex viewfinder can be used to display the image on several monitors, so that other members of the crew, apart from the operator, can see the composite image. The video picture can be recorded both during the rehearsal and during the actual take when a pellicle reflex camera is used, and played back to the actors to help them interact with the projected image. It is also useful for selecting takes to be printed.

PROCESS PLATES

Process plates are made on step printers in those cases where steadiness is of paramount importance and on continuous printers when this is less critical. In either case, the positive film stock used can be perforated with either negative or positive perforations, depending on the projector mechanism to be used.

The advantage of positive perforation plates is that prints can be made on continuous rotary printers. However, positive perforations are not made to the same tolerances as negative ones and are more likely to be unsteady. Rotary printing also contributes to this unsteadiness.

Ideally, front projection plates should be made on negative perforation stock (short pitch) in contact with the original negative on a step-printer.

Often additional effects such as skip- or freeze-framing can be incorporated in the printing stage. The steadiness of a process-projection plate can be checked by looking through the camera and observing certain points in the projected image against a fixed object in the foreground. A better way is to place a fixed marker, like a flag stand, in the projector beam and observe its shadow on the screen relative to the projected image. Static background shots against foreground sets show up unsteadiness much more than shots involving movement. Naturally, the camera used in the original filming must have perfect registration, but the same applies to the projector.

When shooting background plates it is essential not to lose sight of the fact that it is only one element of a final composite and not the final shot. Therefore, if the correct line-up results in odd-looking framing, leave it alone; that's how it should be. You may have to do a lot of explaining to the uninitiated, but that is preferable to the alternative — a bad composite. It is only the composite image that will be seen by the audience, not the plate. A helpful tip is to draw the outline of the foreground element on the video assist monitor (or use a paper cutout).

Ideally, the whole sequence involving process projection should be storyboarded and detailed sketches prepared for each composite shot.

Preparing Process Plates

Process plates can be made on either normal or low-contrast stock, depending on the specific requirements of the scene. In terms of density, lighter prints allow more light to reach the screen, resulting in greater exposure and, eventually, a denser negative. It is advisable to make tests in order to establish the best grading for front-projection plates.

A color chart and a grey scale should be included whenever possible on every take in the original filming of the plate. In addition, five seconds of a standard grey scale and color chart should be added at the head of each front-projection plate, preferably occupying only one side of the frame. This can then be used to match up to a grey scale and color chart in the studio. It is important that this section of the front projection plate is always printed at the same printer light. It then represents a constant against which all other variations can be checked — including laboratory processing, which is not always infallible!

Special processing and pre-fogging can also be used in controlling the quality of the process plates. A five-second line-up grid at the head or tail of the plate is used for accurately lining up camera and projector. It can also act as a focus chart for fine-focussing the plate on the screen.

Protective Coating

A coating applied on the emulsion side of the process plate provides protection from scratching and increases the number of times the plate can be run through the projector. As a consequence, only one backup plate may need to be printed instead of the customary two when no protection is used.

DAY-FOR-NIGHT PROCESS SHOTS

When a scene requires a "day-for-night" approach, it is best to shoot the background plate at normal exposure (as for day) and print the plate at normal density. The density and color balance between foreground elements and the background plate is also done as if for daylight. Additional "night effect" filtration is added to the overall scene, and the composite scene is photographed stopped down (typically 2 f-stops) to create the desired underexposure.

BACK (REAR) PROJECTION

In rear projection the actors perform in front of a translucent screen onto which the Background picture is projected from behind. Either a still or a movie projector can be used.

The back projection screen is set at right angles to the axis of the projector lens, and the camera is set in line with the projector. The line-up is not absolutely critical, although sharp deviations result in fall off and "keystoning" effects (image distortion produced when the projector is offset from the axis perpendicular to the screen; one side of the frame rectangle is larger than the other due to the fact that it is farther from the projector lens). As the projector and camera have to be considerable distances apart, back-projection setups are normally horizontal, with the screen erected vertically. Angling the screen makes it sag, with consequent loss of focus.

The key requirements for the best result with rear projection are the following:

- maximum density screens
- long focal length lenses ("long throw")
- small screen area

The Screen

The rear-projection screen is made of translucent plastic material and is available in different densities and two basic types. One is dark grey and more tolerant to ambient light, and the other type is white.

A denser screen material absorbs more light but is more diffused and, with a good optical system in the projector, produces a flat, evenly illuminated image. It is also less restrictive in terms of viewing angle. A back-projection screen made of thinner material has a high transmission ratio but is prone to light falling off at the edges.

The highest transmission is possible with a rear-projection screen made from a partially diffused, rigid plastic material engraved with fine Fresnel grooves. This type of screen acts as a lens in bending the peripheral rays towards the camera and is, consequently, very directional—with a viewing angle limited to the center line. This screen is available in relatively small sizes of up to three feet square.

In general, the more efficient the rear-projection screen is the more directional its performance. The ultimate means of capturing a rear-projected image without any loss of light or the introduction of grain is to use a large diameter positive lens. This is the basis of aerial image projection (see Chapter 9, "The Animation Rostrum Camera and FX").

The Hot Spot

The biggest problem with back projection is the "hot spot." It manifests itself in two ways: either as a bright spot at the center of the screen, where all the light appears to be emanating from, or as a vignette with fall off at the edges.

Conventional cinema projectors often have a pronounced fall off at the edges of the frame, which is not normally noticed by the viewer. However, when rephotographed, this fall off is compounded. The optics used in process projectors are required to have a high degree of uniform illumination over the entire frame area.

Many different methods have been tried over the years to eliminate the hot spot but without any real measure of success. Screens have been made so that they are more opaque in the center than at the edges. Black discs have been placed in the condenser systems or in front of the projection lens to reduce the brightness of the picture in the center. Even back-projection plates were specially prepared so that the central areas were more burnt in and, therefore, denser on projection. As a general rule, wide-angle lenses produce a greater degree of vignetting than lenses of long focal lengths, and this applies both to projector and camera lenses. This inevitably means that for best results the projector and the camera have to be some considerable distance from the back projection screen. Often this requires the use of front-silvered mirrors to bend the projected light beam where the studio space is restricted.

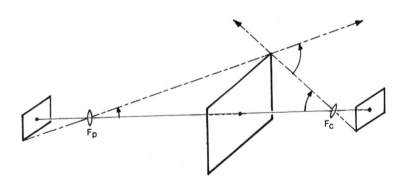

Figure 11.2 Bend angles for rear projection.

Projection Lenses

High-speed, long focal length lenses are most suitable for rear projection. In some cases it is possible to make special adapters to take regular camera lenses.

A long focal length lens ensures that the angle at which the peripheral light rays hit the screen will be closer to perpendicular than is the case with wide-angle lenses. When a long focal length lens is also used on the camera it results in a good "bend angle" at the screen plane.

Because the focus is restricted to a narrow plane at the screen, it is possible to use lenses of very high apertures and consequent shallow depth of field. It should be remembered that one f-stop gained in projection lens aperture is equal to reducing the light output by half (and therefore the heat output by the same amount). Another way to look at this is that gaining two f-stops in projection efficiency is equal to doubling the size of the projected image at the same relative exposure.

A combination of a long focal length and a low f-stop results in a fairly massive lens. An F2 lens of 300mm f. length has a front element of 150mm.

The Lamphouse

A great deal of light is needed for back projection, and therefore very powerful light sources, such as arcs, are often employed. Unfortunately, the arc lamps are not an ideal light source for photography, because the radiation in the visible spectrum does not match that of color film, even when the color temperature has been corrected with conversion filters. For best results, it is advisable to use the same type of light source for both foreground illumination and process projection.

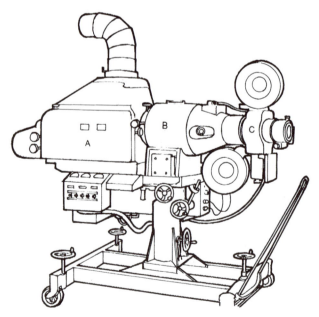

Figure 11.3 Mitchell background projector. (A) Arc lamphouse. (B) Optical condenser system. (C) Projector head.

The increase in the output of visible radiation is accompanied by a similar increase in heat radiation, which can be harmful to the film plate. Heat radiation can be eliminated to a certain degree either by the use of dichroic filters to deflect the infrared radiation, or by heat-absorbing filters or water-cooled units within the optical system, or by cooling the film in the projector gate with forced air. It is interesting to note how small a proportion of the entire machine, in the case of the Mitchell projector, is taken up by the projection head and magazines; all the rest is the lamphouse and the condenser system. This, of course, makes it rather unwieldy.

When a 4,000-watt Xenon arc lamp is fully color-corrected to 3,200 Kelvin the actual amount of useable light it produces is the same as a 2,000-watt tungsten halogen lamp without any correction. The heat output of the 2,000-watt tungsten halogen lamp is half of that produced by the 4,000-watt arc lamp.

USING BACK PROJECTION

Live Action: Car Shots

Conventional uses of back projection involve projection of backgrounds, usually filmed on location, to blend in with the foreground sets in the studio. The most common use is for car shots, particularly when these involve dangerous stunts or night scenes that would otherwise be difficult to do on location. When the lens angles and perspective of the background plates match those of the studio setup, the results can be undetectable as visual effects.

In those cases, for example, where the background action is to be seen through a window only, it is wiser to shoot slightly more than the window area on a full frame. The lens angle used for shooting the background plate relative to the lens angle used in compositing will determine whether the composite looks realistic or not. If, for example, a telephoto lens is used to photograph the area seen through a window, objects in the background will appear nearer than if a wider-angle lens is used. It is most important therefore that the specific effect required in the final composite is known and understood by everyone concerned. A longer focal length projection lens can be used to project the entire plate area in the window from position B (in Figure 11.4) seeing all four trees, but if the plate is shot with a wider-angle lens from position A, the result will be a mismatch in perspective.

Rear Projection and Models

Rear projection is widely used with miniatures to incorporate "live' images in parts of the scene, such as the windows of miniature buildings. If the miniature is made to a reasonably large scale, so that the window area is represented by a

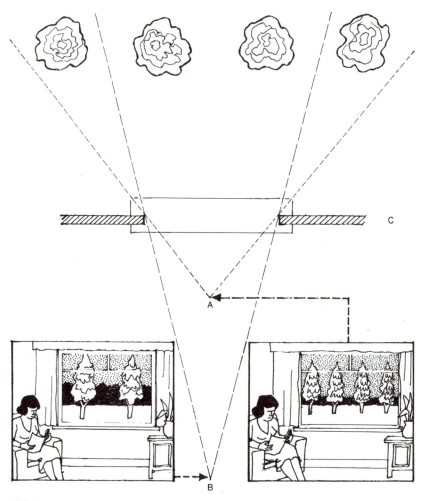

Figure 11.4   Preparing background plates. Shooting through the same "window," the background appears different when shot on wide-angle lens (A) then when it is shot on narrow-angle lens (B)

fairly large back-projection screen, it is possible to create the illusion of going through the window and following an intricate action inside the building. This is done by prefilming the action on a set, as it would appear through a window, and then tracking into the actor on the set or even following him around from room to room. This "plate" is then projected onto the back-projection screen, which coincides with the window of the miniature set representing the exterior of the house, garden, and even parts of the town, if necessary. The camera pans across the miniature, ending up with a close-up of the window area and continues to copy the back-projected picture image, which may contain a tracking shot inside the building. When the action is properly synchronized, a convincing illusion that the camera has tracked in through the window is created. Once the photographed area is clear of the window an A and B roll dissolve can be made from the composite scene to the matching point on the original negative and the scene may continue.

When setting up the shot a grid is projected and the camera is lined up with an identical grid in the gate at 1:1 reproduction point. It is also advisable to shoot this type of action in reverse, since the line-up at the transition point will be most critical. Often an action within the scene can be used to make a jump-cut from the projected (rephotographed) segment to the original (e.g., a person walks across the frame partially or fully obscuring it).

Back Projection and Matte Paintings

A matte painting can be used as efficiently as a miniature set for certain scenes. The painting is done on a large piece of glass leaving a clear area where the back-projected image is to be inserted. The back-projection screen is set at some distance behind the glass to prevent the light used to illuminate the painting from washing out the projected image. The use of polaroid filters on the lights and the lens helps to control spill light as well as to eliminate unwanted reflections.

Figure 11.5 (A) Background projector, projecting a picture onto a translucent screen (B) which is set some distance away from a large glass supporting a painting (C). The camera pans across the painting from right to left, ending on a close-up of the window area and the back-projected image. The camera can appear to go through the window, following whatever action is inside, if this action is already on the projection plate.

FRONT-AXIAL PROJECTION

Front projection compositing is a self-matting process. A subject placed in front of the front-projection screen provides its own matte because the projected light is prevented from reaching the screen by the subject. The shadow produced by the subject on the screen is in fact the male matte.

The actors perform in front of a highly reflective screen that has the special property of reflecting the light rays back towards the projector lens. The picture is projected via a two-way mirror acting as a beam-splitter and set at a 45-degree angle to the axis of the projector lens. The composite picture is photographed by the camera lens, which is positioned behind the two-way mirror in line with the reflected beam. The projector and camera lenses are effectively on the same optical axis.

The reflectivity of a front-projection screen is 500 times greater than that of a regular white surface, consequently the projector light falling on the subject is rendered invisible. Even when the subject is dressed in white clothes, it photographs as a silhouette (or a matte) against the projected image at the correct exposure. When the subject is lit appropriately to match the projected image, the composite is complete. The result is the same as with a self-matting positive, except that it is instantaneous.

This system has largely superceded back projection for most applications. Much wider screen areas can be covered with less powerful lamps and, as the camera and projector are on the same side of the screen, the studio space required is only half that needed for rear-projection. Because of the flexibility of screen construction, it is possible to set up front projection at any angle from vertical up to vertical down and all points in between.

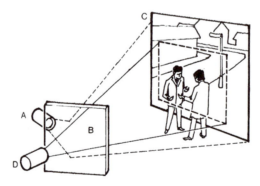

Figure 11.6   Front projection. (A) Projector. (B) Beam-splitter. (C) Front-projection screen. (D) Camera.

Front-Projection Screen

The front-projection screen is made up of a multitude of tiny glass spheres. Each sphere is aluminized on half of its outer surface and embedded in a plastic support with the clear surface facing outwards. Each of these "beads" acts as a retroreflector producing total internal reflection. A light ray entering the clear "window" area of the sphere at any angle is reflected internally by the coated back surface, reemerging through the "window" and travelling back along its own axis.

The industrial applications of this principle are less precise but still produce very directional reflections, such as in the case of car headlights on road signs, reflective safety strips for clothing, and "Cat's eyes" lane dividers on roads.

The front-projection matting system depends very largely on a basic principle of optics: that light rays can coexist in the same plane while travelling in opposite directions. Light rays from the projector lens occupy the same plane on reflection from the screen as they do going towards the screen, because each light ray is redirected back along its axis by its own "bead" (sphere).

Although the front-projection screen has a grey appearance in ambient light, it photographs black because of its reflective properties. It is more tolerant to ambient light the farther the light source is from the camera/projector lens axis.

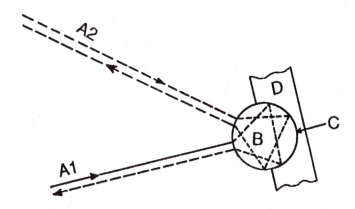

Figure 11.7 Light rays (A1 and A2) go through total internal reflection by glass bead (B) and emerge at the same point where they entered the bead, to continue in the opposite direction of travel. (C) Reflective coating. (D) Plastic backing.

Beam-Splitter (Two-Way Mirror)

A beam-splitter is a piece of optical quality, distortion-free glass, partially coated (half-silvered) so that a proportion of light is reflected while the rest is transmitted. The ideal ratio between transmission and reflection is 50:50. However, in practice, it is nearer to 40:60. This is not critical, because the advantage gained by using a more reflective beam-splitter is lost by the corresponding reduction in transmission. In certain circumstances it is advantageous to use a low-reflectivity/high-transmission ratio (e.g., when panning off the mirror).

Two-way mirrors can be made in thicknesses of between 1mm and 4mm. Thicker mirrors are prone to ghosting produced by secondary reflections. On the other hand, extremely thin mirrors cannot be handled safely in large dimensions and can be distorted easily by uneven pressure from the support frame. Because regular glass has a green bias, the water-white type glass is more suitable for this purpose.

The beam-splitter mirror is always used with the coated (partially silvered) side towards the projection lens. Ideally, the uncoated side should be treated with an antireflection coating.

Fringing

The exit pupil of the projection lens is that point in the lens from which the light beam appears to emanate. On reflection from the front-projection screen the projection beam converges again towards a spot beyond the beam-splitter mirror. With the camera removed, this spot can actually be seen and examined by introducing smoke in the path of the projection beam. The entrance pupil of the camera lens should be coincidental with this point where the reflected light beams converge.

When the camera and projector lenses are not lined up correctly, the camera lens will not see the subject from exactly the same point as the projector lens and will therefore see the subject's shadow in the form of a black fringe. To correct for a black fringe on the left side of the subject, the camera needs to be moved slightly to the right, and vice versa. A fringe around the upper part of the subject is corrected by lowering the camera.

The misalignment is not restricted to the vertical and the horizontal planes only; it can also be lateral (along the lens axis), giving the appearance of the matte (shadow) being too big or too small for the subject. When the matte (shadow) is too big, a black fringe is visible all around the subject, and when it is too small the fringe appears as white ghosting. This is corrected by sliding the camera towards or away from the beam-splitter mirror until the fringe disappears completely.

Fringing and Focus

Focus is an important element affecting fringing. The projection lens has the same optical properties as the camera lens and is subject to the same laws. Because conventional projection lenses usually have no iris, the concept of depth of field is often overlooked as focus is intended to be in one plane only. However, it is the depth of field of the projection lens that determines the sharpness of the shadow produced by the subject.

The depth-of-field rules apply to the projection lens in the same way as to the camera lens. The factors determining depth of field are the same as with any lens: focal length of the lens, object-to-lens distance, and the aperture used.

When the subject is further away from the screen and nearer to the projector/camera assembly, the edge of the shadow appears soft and fuzzy; when the subject is moved nearer to the screen, the edges of its shadow become sharp and clear. The best results in front projection can, therefore, be achieved by the following:

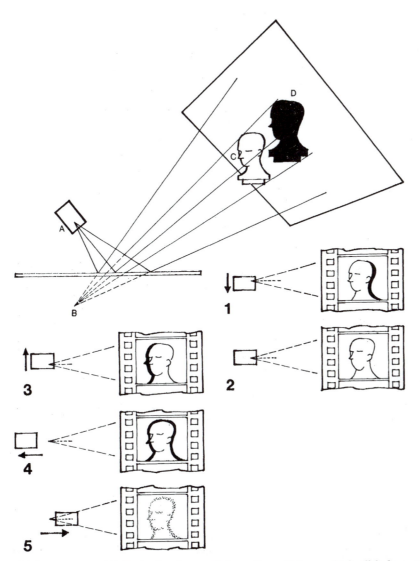

Figure 11.8 Fringing. (A) Projection lens and the exit pupil from which all light appears to emanate. (B) Light beams converge at this point on their return from the screen. Entrance pupil of the camera lens should be coincidental with this point. (1) Lens too far to the right. (2) Lens in correct position (no fringe). (3) Lens too far to the left. (4) Lens too far back. (5) Lens too far forward.

1. The subject should be placed as close to the screen as possible, allowing sufficient room for lighting.
2. The lens aperture of the projection lens should be stopped down as much as possible to achieve the maximum depth of field.
3. Projector focus should be set at the hyper-focal distance for the chosen f-stop instead of at the screen distance.
4. Focal lengths should be as short as possible, consistent with even illumination.

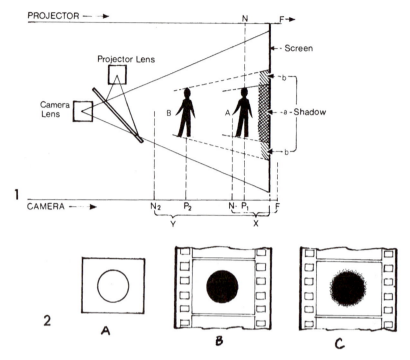

Figure 11.9 (1) Depth of field and fringing. Primary focus of the projection lens is set at the screen (P). Depth of field at a given f-stop will have a near focus point (N) and a far focus point (F) (beyond the screen). Subject A is within the near focus point of the projection lens, therefore its shadow will appear sharp. However, the shadow of subject B will have soft edges because the subject is farther from the screen and outside the "depth of field" range of the projection lens. (2) (A) Subject in sharp focus; (B) sharp-edge shadow; (C) soft-edge shadow.

Fringing and the Zoom Lens

When identical lenses are used on the projector and the camera, it is easier to line up the exit and entrance pupils; their positions are practically equidistant from the beam-splitter. However, when lenses of different types and focal lengths are used, the angles of view and entrance pupils have to be matched.

In the case of a zoom lens another problem arises. The entrance pupil of a zoom lens moves along the lens axis during the zooming action; this can be a considerable distance, depending on lens design and zoom ratio. In order for the entrance pupil of the zoom lens on the camera to remain in the correct relationship with the exit pupil of the projector lens, the panning and tilting action during the zoom requires the front nodal point of the lens to coincide with the pivot point of the nodal head. Since the nodal point also moves along the lens axis during the zooming action, this requires the camera to be mounted on a nodal head. The nodal point of a zoom lens is not necessarily at the same physical point as the entrance pupil. In practice, this means that it is necessary to adjust the position of the nodal head relative to the beam-splitter mirror, or the position of the projector relative to the beam-splitter.

Fringing and the Anamorphic Lens

The original anamorphic lenses consisted of an attachment that was placed in front of the prime lens. The modern anamorphic lenses have the cylindrical lens elements built in, forming an integral unit with the prime lens. There are two basic designs, depending on the position of the anamorphic unit relative to the prime lens unit:

Front anamorphs have cylindrical elements at the front of the prime lens.

Rear anamorphs have the cylindrical elements at the rear of the prime lens.

Either type of anamorphic design is suitable for front projection when the lenses are matched using the same format. However, when an anamorphic lens is used on the camera and a spherical lens on the projector (VistaVision to 35mm) it becomes more difficult. This is due to the fact that anamorphic lenses have two effective focal lengths—one for the horizontal, and the other for the vertical plane—and, consequently, two entrance pupils. The spherical lens has only one entrance pupil. Rear anamorphic design is more suitable in this situation, because the physical distance between the points is not as great as with the front anamorphic ones. For general work it is best to line up the spherical pupil between the two anamorphic pupil points. For extreme close-ups it is often necessary to match to the vertical or the horizontal depending on the subject being photographed.

Pincushion and Barrel Distortions

Different lens designs produce different "flatness of image" characteristics. The image produced by a simple spherical lens is not flat but spherical. Since the film plane is flat, it is necessary to include field flatteners in the design of complex lenses to make the image plane flat also. This is hardly ever an entirely successful endeavor, resulting in some spherical distortion of either a "barrel" or "pincushion" type. This can produce disturbing fringing results in front projection when the two lenses have opposing characteristics. The result is that when there is a perfect match in the center of frame, a fringe appears when the subject moves to the side of the frame.

Camera Mount

The camera is mounted on a support plate that allows it to slide forwards and backwards in a straight line along the lens axis. A second sliding support plate mounted transversely over the first one allows the camera to be moved sideways on an axis set at 90 degrees to the lens axis. In addition, the camera can be raised or lowered in the vertical plane either by adjusting the height of the camera support plate or by moving the projector towards or away from the camera in the horizontal plane, parallel to the lens axis. This way the projection beam is raised or lowered as the intercept point changes.

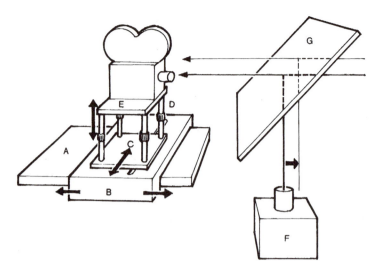

Figure 11.10   Camera support. (A) Base plate. (B) Support plate for sliding movement to and from the beam-splitter (with guides). (C) Support plate for traverse movement, held in position by a keyway. (D) Left- and right-hand studs for raising and lowering the camera plate. (E) Top-plate supporting the camera. (F) The projector: sliding the projector towards and away from the camera mount has the same effect as raising and lowering the camera. (G) Two-way mirror (beam-splitter).

The most flexible solution, however, is to mount the beam-splitter mirror on a sliding support that enables it to move along the camera lens axis. Additional adjustment is provided by pivoting the mirror; ideally the pivot point should be set at the intersection of the projector and camera axis.

The Nodal Head

On a conventional camera head the camera body is usually mounted centrally in order to achieve the best balance; as a result, the camera lens traces an arc as it moves during the pan-and-tilt operation. The exact dimensions of this arc depend on the distance from the nodal point of the lens to the pivot point of the camera head. In front projection, a conventional pan-and-tilt camera head cannot be used because it would move the camera lens off axis.

However, when the camera is mounted with the nodal point of the lens coincidental with the pivot point of the camera head for both pan and tilt, the lens always stays on-axis. A nodal head is designed specifically for this purpose. Checking the correct line-up of the lens on the nodal head is best done by placing two targets, one behind the other, at some distance from the camera and from each other. When the nodal point of the lens is correctly lined up with the pivot point of the nodal head, the targets will not move in relation to each other during the pan-and-tilt operation.

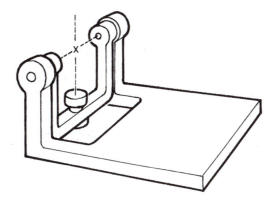

Figure 11.11 Basic nodal head. (X) Pan-and-tilt center. Nodal point of the camera lens should be coincidental with this point.

Line-Up Procedure

Fringing checks should be done at the correct focus and f-stop setting for both the projector and the camera lenses. This is because the effective focal length of the lens is altered progressively as it is focused closer from infinity.

Another method is to cover the "fringe disc" with front projection material, then, by using the white light only from the projector, the line-up can be checked. The fringe disc is also used to check the farthest points back and forward of the primary focus when the scene is lit with the background plate running in the projector.

Setting Up a Front Projection Shot

It is important to know the lens used in the original shooting of a background plate as well as the height, inclination, and lighting conditions, so that the correct perspective match can be achieved in the studio. It is also advisable to have a stand-in in the position of the actor for a few feet at the start of the background plate shot, to ensure a perfect match in the studio later, both for lighting and perspective line-up. "Markers" can also be placed in the frame, particularly in the areas that will be masked off by foreground set pieces.

Panning Off the Beam-Splitter

It is possible to make camera moves within the front-projected picture, if the camera is mounted so that the nodal point of its lens coincides with the pivot point of the pan-and-tilt head. The action can therefore be followed, as in conventional shooting. This inevitably means that the projected picture is enlarged, unless of course a larger format is used for the background plate. On occasion it

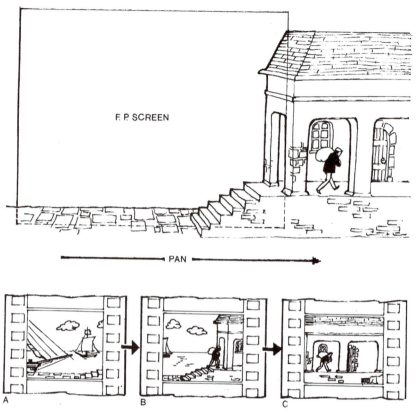

Figure 11.12   Panning off the mirror. (A) Front-projected picture with a little foreground. (B) Halfway through the pass, the edge of the mirror is lined up with the edge of the house. (C) Studio set; camera has panned off the front-projection picture completely.

is possible to pan from the front-projection picture to a continuation of the set by panning off the beam-splitter mirror.

The edge of the beam-splitter mirror is cut at an angle to produce a straight line, which can then be lined up with a suitable point in the background. The edge is not invisible because it is out of focus. However, the beam-splitter absorbs light and therefore a mirror with a high transmission-to-reflection ratio is more suitable for this purpose. The lighting on the set is modified, so that no change in the exposure is discernible during the pan.

Going "Behind" Foreground Objects

When a secondary front projection screen is placed in front of the primary screen, part of the projected background will be reflected from it instead of the main screen. This approach enables the actors to go behind objects within the projected scene. For example, a foreground wall can be reflected off a small screen placed in front of the main screen, so that the actor can go behind it. Apart from adding realism to a scene, this approach can also be used to create additional visual effects. For example, graffiti can appear to animate on the wall as the actor goes behind it (animated lettering painted directly on the wall and photographed stop-motion would, of course, be done in the original shooting of the plate). A nodal pan across the picture following the actor makes the scene even more convincing. A variation on this is to apply the front-projection material to a section of the set; this offers great possibilities for really zany composites. The main consideration with this approach is focus sharpness of the foreground image. This sharpness is determined by several factors:

1. The depth of field of the projection lens
2. The choice of projector lens
3. The projector lens f-stop
4. The distance of the foreground screen from the main screen

The secondary screen (or part of the set with front-projection material) used to reflect the foreground image, will appear brighter than the main screen because it is nearer to the camera/projector assembly. Neutral-density filters, carefully cut to match the shape of the foreground screen, can be used in front of the projector lens. Cutting down the reflectivity of the front projection material itself by spraying antireflection coating onto the foreground screen, or using a batch of screen material of lower reflectivity value, can help to balance the two parts of the image. Alternatively, the original exposure of the background plate can be held back on the foreground part of the scene to compensate the subsequent increase in brightness in this area during front-projection compositing.

Figure 11.13 Foreground wall is reflected off a small screen placed in front of the main screen so that the actor can go behind it. This method can be used to create certain "impossible" effects. Graffiti can appear to animate on the wall as the actor goes behind it.

Masking Off

Front-projection material is sometimes used to mask foreground objects, such as a crane arm holding up a car. All the problems mentioned above apply to this technique also. With certain backgrounds this type of masking can be successful, but it is far from being foolproof.

For vertical or near vertical downshots, front-projection material can be applied to an overhang platform to support an actor above the main front-projection screen laid out on the stage floor. Front-projection material can also be used on the floor in certain circumstance for actors to walk on, although, this can present a considerable lighting challenge. Generally, however, it is better to build real floors for actors to walk on and use the overlapping slats for the corner joins.

Front Projection and Matte Paintings

Matte paintings on glass can be used in conjunction with front projection in much the same way as with back projection. The glass has to be angled a little to avoid

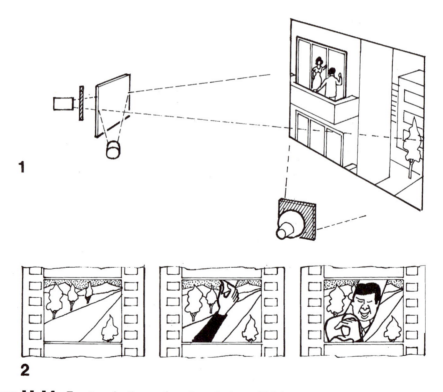

Figure 11.14   Front projection and matte paintings. (1) Matte paintings on glass can be used in conjunction with front-projection. The glass has to be angled a little to avoid reflections. If a polarizing filter is used in front of the camera lens and polarized lighting used for the illumination of the matte painting, then the front-projection material can be at the same level as the painting. (2) A hand can peel off the front projection material to reveal another scene.

flare from the projection beam. The front projection material can be at the same physical plane as the painting, when polarized lighting is used for the illumination of the matte painting. A polarizing filter is placed in front of the camera lens.

The front projection material can be applied over a painted area and then cut out and peeled off as desired. This approach makes it possible to achieve some interesting transitions. For example, a hand is seen to peel off a section of front projection material and the "live" scene can be replaced by the painting in that area. It can also be used in conjunction with a rear-projection screen placed behind the glass. The scene to be revealed could also be part painting and part "live."

Ghosting

When the camera and the projector lie in the horizontal plane at 90 degrees to each other, it is possible to photograph another image set directly in line with the projector axis and reflected into the lens via the beam-splitter mirror. Because there is no matting involved, the image appears transparent. A "ghost" can be made to move in and around a front-projected scene, which may include other actors in front of the front-projection screen. The ghost image has a reversed geometry because it is seen via the mirror.

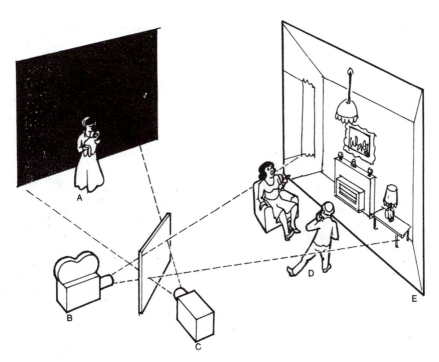

Figure 11.15   Ghosting. (A) Image set at 90 degrees to lens axis. (B and C) Camera and projector in the horizontal plane at 90 degrees to each other. (D) Live actors. (E) Front-projection screen.

The most common configuration in front projection is for the projector and camera to be mounted at 90 degrees to each other in the vertical plane with the projector pointing upwards. The projector beam is redirected by the beam-splitter mirror towards the front-projection screen, and the "wasted" portion passes through the beam-splitter onto a light trap above (usually black velvet). A full mirror (front-silvered) placed above the beam-splitter can be used to pick up the ghost image.

Flame Overlays

The same setup as above can be used for simulating flames to create the effect of a building on fire. The outlines of the building are traced onto a large sheet of glass placed in front of a black background at right angles to the front-projection screen. A black paper mask is placed over these outlines with cutout sections to correspond to the areas of the building that are on fire. Gas burners are placed at strategic points and the flames adjusted as required. A nodal-head pan across the composite adds an extra dimension to the effect.

Front Projection and Miniatures

Using the same setup as above, miniatures can be incorporated into a front-pro-jected shot that also involves actors. The miniature is placed in front of a black backdrop and is effectively "self-matting," and a male matte corresponding to its

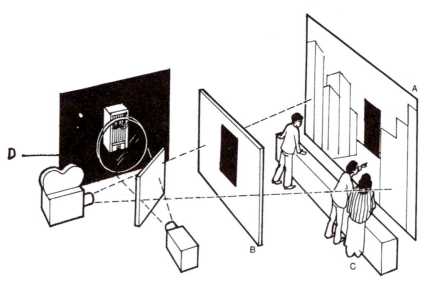

Figure 11.16   Front projection and miniatures. Miniatures can be incorporated into a front-projected screen using the same setup as above, but the miniature is masked off to prevent ghosting. (A) Front-projection screen. (B) Male matte painted on glass. (C) Live actors. (D) Supplementary lens.

outlines is placed between the projector and the screen, so that it does not appear as a "ghost." This is particularly useful when the building represented by the miniature is to be destroyed by an explosion or fire. To make the miniature appear sufficiently large in the frame and still keep it in focus, it is often necessary to use a supplementary lens. This large positive lens is placed as close to the camera lens as possible, beyond the two-way mirror, so that only the focus of the secondary image (the miniature) is affected.

Foreground action has to be staged outside the matted area, otherwise the actors will disappear behind the miniature. A photograph or a painting can also be used in this way in place of the miniature.

Dual-Screen System

In a standard setup roughly half the amount of light from the projector is reflected by the beam-splitter towards the front-projection screen and the other half is transmitted. This wasted portion of the projection beam is usually absorbed by a black velvet light trap. However, by placing a secondary front projection screen in the path of this transmitted beam, the projected image can be captured and redirected back towards the beam-splitter and the camera lens.

If this secondary front-projection screen is placed closer to the beam-splitter than the main screen, the projected image will be out of focus. A large diameter supplementary lens placed above the beam-splitter is used to bring the secondary image into focus at a relatively short distance from the beam-splitter, thus requiring a much smaller secondary screen, which can then be attached to the projector/camera assembly. By masking the images reflected from the two screens with complementary male and female mattes, the camera sees a composite image.

As the secondary screen is very much nearer to the projector than the primary screen, the image reflected from it is much brighter. Neutral density filters are used to achieve the correct balance.

The advantage of this setup is that scenes that would normally require very large front-projection screens can be filmed using smaller screens, provided the action is restricted to the area of the primary screen. It also makes lighting easier, because the spill light has to be kept off a smaller area and the lights can be brought in nearer to the subject. Consequently, front lighting is possible to a greater degree than if only one large screen were to be used.

The drawback to the dual-screen system has to do with the quality of the image from the secondary screen. Because the secondary beam has to pass through the clear glass of the beam-splitter before being reflected into the camera lens by the coated side, a small amount of light is reflected by the uncoated glass surface of the beam-splitter, producing a faint double image ("ghosting"). This results in a deterioration of image resolution in that part of the frame. This effect can be minimized to a certain extent with antireflection coating on the non-reflecting side of the beam-splitter, or by the use of extremely thin beam-splitters.

Another drawback with dual-screen front-projection is the difficulty of matching the masking used to matte out the unwanted areas on the two screens. Masks placed at equal distances, on either side of the beam-splitter, normally have equally soft edges. However, when the mask for the secondary screen image is placed between the supplementary lens and the secondary screen, it will appear sharper and will not match the soft edge of the complementary mask (countermask) placed at the same distance from the beam-splitter in front of the main screen. This mask has to be moved away from the camera lens until the softness of its edge matches that of the second mask. Once this is achieved the two images can be blended together relatively easily.

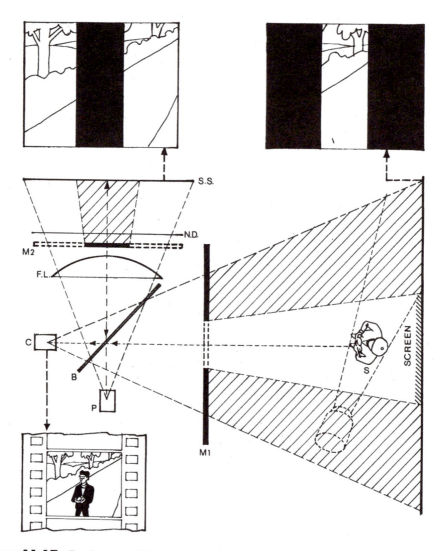

Figure 11.17   Dual screen. (P) Projector lens. (C) Camera lens. (B) Beam-splitter. (M1) Mask (male). (M2) Countermask (female). (F.L.) Field lens. (S.S.) Small screen. (N.D.) Graduated neutral-density filters. (S) Subject.

Zoptic Dual-Screen System

This system uses an alternative approach to masking between the two screens, employing a front-silvered mirror with sections of silvering removed in specific areas. The beam-splitter mirror is turned around so that the reflecting surface is facing upwards, and the light trap is placed in front instead of above it. A front-silvered mirror placed above the beam-splitter redirects the projected image to the primary screen. By removing the silvering from the mirror surface in chosen areas, the projected image is able to pass through the clear glass to the secondary

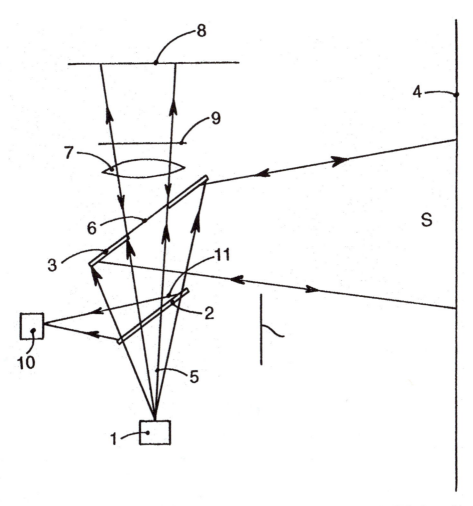

Figure 11.18 Zoptic Dual Screen System (U.S. Patent No. 4,609,253). The light beam from projector lens (1) passes through the beam-splitter (2) and is reflected by the front-silvered mirror (3) towards the screen (4). Part of the light beam (5) passes through the clear area (6) and is brought into focus by the lens (7) on the secondary screen (8). Neutral density filters (9) are used to match the brightness of the secondary screen to the primary one. The light beam reflected from both screens is redirected towards the camera (10) by the reflecting surface of the beam-splitter (11). (S) Subject to be composited with the projected background.

screen and is focussed by a supplementary lens. This self-matting method offers certain unique advantages. The images from both screens are reflected from the same side of the beam-splitter, avoiding the problems of double reflections. The same matte line serves as a matte and countermatte, thus eliminating the problems of a mismatch.

Lightweight Projectors

The earliest front-projection units were looked upon as replacements for back projection with the added advantage of larger screen sizes and smaller operating space requirements. The same cumbersome back-projection equipment with its massive arc-lamp was modified for front-projection. Consequently, all the restrictions commonly associated with back-projection were simply transferred to front projection, such as static, horizontal setups with the projector fixed in a rigid position, and limited panning or tilting on a nodal head. By replacing the arc lamp with a tungsten halogen lamp, it became possible to produce purpose-built front-projection units that are small, compact, and easily maneuverable.

The benefit of switching over from an arc light source to tungsten halogen is not only in size but also in the quality of color reproduction of the background plate. The best results in matching color reproduction of the foreground objects to the color of the projected image are obtained when the color temperature of the projection light matches that of the studio lights.

With these compact lightweight projectors, it is not only possible to shoot at any angle, but also to move the camera/projector assembly during the shot. This type of compact unit can be mounted on a conventional dolly and used for combining conventional filming with front projection. For example, a scene can be shot of an actor, with a front-projection screen behind him, apparently talking to another actor (or even himself) who has been prefilmed on the front projection screen. From this composite, the actor walks away from the projected area and into the set with the camera following him, as it pans off the two-way mirror. Once the camera is off the mirror, the camera dolly can be moved anywhere within the set, continuing to follow the actor as in conventional shooting.

Moving the Front-Projection Assembly

If the front projection assembly is mounted on a dolly, which is set on tracks parallel to the screen, then the entire assembly can be crabbed during the shot. Seen through the camera, this crabbing movement is not noticeable on the background plate; however, the foreground set appears to glide across the frame, although it is, in fact, standing still. In this way a boat can appear to sail across the frame in the foreground, while an appropriate seascape plate is projected in the background. If the projector/camera assembly is mounted on a rotation ring, then the sailing-boat effect can be produced by simply panning the entire assembly from side to side. (Tilting the projector/camera assembly makes the boat appear to bob up and down on the waves.)

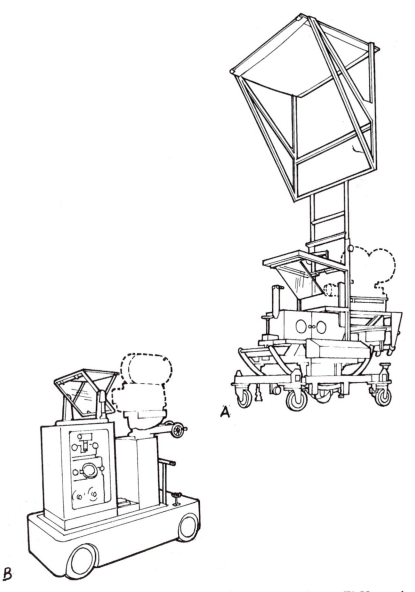

Figure 11.19 (A) Neilson-Hordell dual-screen front-matte projector. (B) Hansard mobile front projection unit.

The "keystoning" effect of the projected picture is automatically compensated for by the camera lens, so that the photographed image looks the same as when the projector is at right angles to the screen. The inherent depth of field of the projection lens ensures that the side of the picture affected most by keystoning remains in focus. In addition, the properties of the front-projection screen material are such that the reflectivity remains the same within a considerable range of viewing angles. In practice, both crabbing and panning would be used in the above shot, because crabbing produces a change in perspective. In addition,

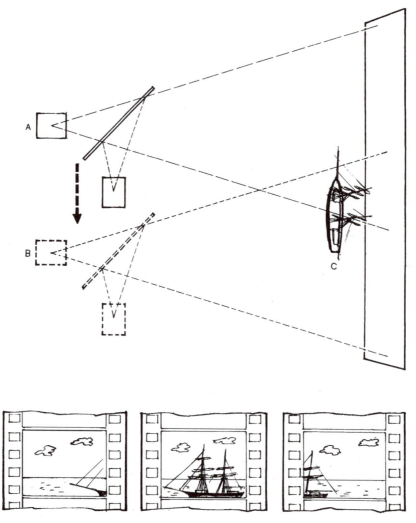

Figure 11.20 Tracking the front projection unit from position A to position B creates the effect of the boat (C) sailing across the frame. Alternatively, the front-projection unit can be panned left to right to produce the same effect but without the change of perspective.

a prefilmed movement on the background plate enhances the effect further. As the boat is really in a stationary position, it is possible to introduce additional rocking and pitching movements to add to the effect of a violent storm created in the safety of a studio environment.

Rotation Effect

A front-silvered mirror is placed at 45 degrees above the front-projection unit and supported independently from it. The front-projection unit is mounted on a rotating platform, with the center of rotation coincident with the axis of the projection lens. The beam-splitter mirror is flopped with the reflective side facing up. At zero position this setup acts as a large periscope; but when the front-projection unit is rotated, the image on the front-projection screen rotates in a clockwise or counterclockwise direction, because the front-silvered mirror remains static. Seen through the camera lens (which is locked on the projected background at all times), it is the foreground subject that rotates while the background remains unaltered.

A 180-degree rotation results in the subject appearing to be upside-down in relation to the background. (This is a useful setup for producing the effect of actors walking on ceilings.) A full 360-degree rotation creates the effect of the subject spinning within the frame. Additional pan-and-tilt movements can be created by suspending the front-silvered mirror on a movable gimbal. With the use of an appropriate support system an effect of free-fall or floating can be created.

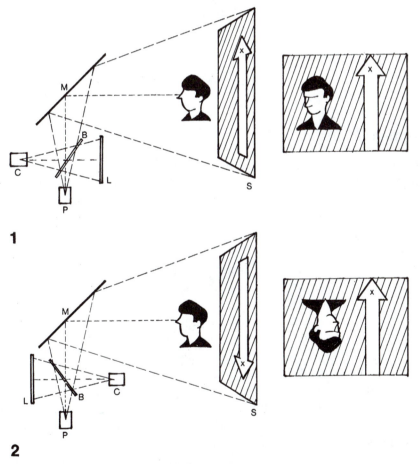

Figure 11.21   (1) Subject and background normal way up. (2) Subject appears to be upside down. (C) Camera lens. (P) Projector lens. (B) Beam-splitter. (L) Light trap. (M) Front-silvered mirror. (X) Projected image.

Double Pan-and-Tilt Heads

A compact front-projection unit can be mounted on a conventional pan-and-tilt head and operated with the same degree of freedom as a conventional camera. Two pan-and-tilt heads placed on top of each other allow for a rocking movement to be added to the pan and tilt.

Figure 11.22   Miniature front-projection units can be mounted on two geared heads for greater flexibility.

Movement in Depth

For the subject to appear to move inside the picture in one plane—up, down, sideways, or even to rotate—the front-projection unit simply has to be moved in the opposite direction. However, when it comes to movement in depth, such as when the subject is meant to move towards or away from the camera as well, then the problem becomes altogether more difficult.

In conventional front-projection, if a subject is to appear to fly "in depth," the subject has to be moved physically towards the camera. This can be done on wires that are later removed optically or digitally. Apart from the difficulties with stability and control, this approach involving physical movement creates another more fundamental problem: fringing. In order to achieve an effective movement in depth, the subject has to travel a considerable distance away from the front-projection screen and closer to the camera (or vice versa), making it very difficult to eliminate the fringe.

The restrictions created by a combination of fringing problems and wires make it impractical to attempt this type of effect in conventional front projection, particularly for live-action work where the subject has to move at considerable speed. It is necessary to resort to the travelling matte approach. However, the Zoptic Front Projection System overcomes all these restrictions, enabling the subject to appear to move in depth with ease while actually remaining in the same place.

ZOPTIC FRONT PROJECTION

The Zoptic front-projection system creates the effect of movement in depth without the need for the subject to move relative to the screen and the front-projection unit. This is achieved by means of two identical zoom lenses, one on the projector and the other on the camera. The two lenses are set so that the camera lens is copying the full frame projected by the other lens. The zoom drives of the two lenses are interlocked, and the zooming operation is synchronized throughout the range of the zoom (10:1). Consequently, when the widest picture is projected on the screen, the camera lens is photographing the same size image.

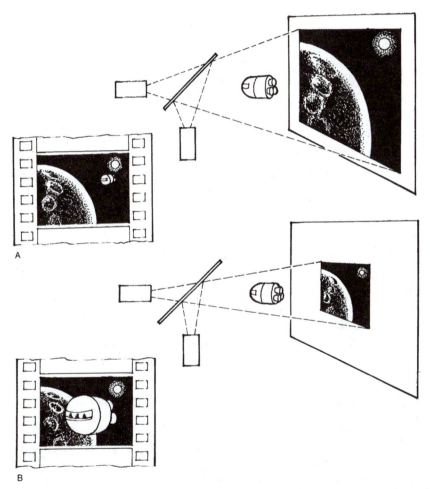

Figure 11.23 Zoptic effect. (A) Projector lens projecting a large picture on the front-projection screen (wide-angle) and camera lens set on wide angle. The subject appears small against the background. (B) Projector lens zoomed in, projecting a small picture on the front projection screen and camera lens zoomed in correspondingly. The subject appears much bigger than in A, although the backgrounds appear the same.

When the projector lens is zoomed in, the camera lens is also zoomed in and copying this same image, which is now projected on a smaller area of the front-projection screen. In the camera viewfinder the projected scene looks unchanged throughout the zoom range, while a subject placed in front of the front-projection screen appears small against the projected background at the wide end of the zoom and much bigger at the opposite end of the zoom. Because of this apparent increase in size, the subject appears to move closer to the camera.

During the Zoptic zoom it is, in fact, the background that moves by changing size while the subject remains static, creating the illusion that the subject is moving and the background remains unchanged. When pan, tilt, and rotation are added to the movement in depth, a totally fluid flying effect is achieved.

The Flying Rig

A lightweight front-projection unit equipped with the Zoptic system and mounted on a flying rig with pan/tilt and rotation capability is the ultimate method for producing flying effects. The flying rig can be tracked and moved up and down on a crane in addition to the pan/tilt and rotation movements to produce totally fluid flying effects. With the subject suspended at the end of a pole pushed through the screen, additional pitch, yaw, and rotation movements are added.

The flying rig pan/tilt and rotation axis can be operated manually or remotely from a servo console, or by a combination of the two. In addition, a motion-control computer unit, slaved to the projector frame-count, makes it possible to program moves for each axis individually, or to record them all from manual input and replay in real time or in any other camera speed from 1 fps to 32 fps and higher. Computer operation makes it possible to rehearse a shot and make subtle changes to each axis (including the pole-arm controls) and then shoot a composite with very intricate moves in one "take."

Computerized Zoptic operation also allows for repeat moves to be made with absolute accuracy, combining the advantages of motion control with that of front-projection.

Zoptic without Zooms

The Zoptic effect can also be achieved by using fixed focal length lenses instead of zooms. This requires the front projection unit to be tracked towards the screen. A servomotor system controls the autofocus of both lenses, as well as controlling a progressive reduction in light output. This system is much less flexible than using zooms and more suitable for model work than live action. The apparent speed of the movement in depth for live-action shots is limited by the physical speed of the projector unit on the tracks. However, it has one major advantage: the zooming range is limited only by the size of the stage.

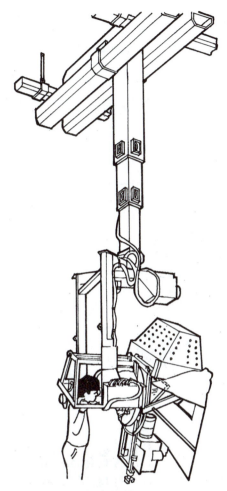

Figure 11.24 The flying rig. Lightweight front-projection unit equipped with the Zoptic system, for producing flying effects.

Shot Planning

The Zoptic effect can be worked out in detail on paper because it follows strict geometric rules. The path along which the subject appears to move in depth through the picture is the extension of a line drawn from the center of the frame (optical axis) through the center of the subject. Two more lines drawn from the frame center to the extreme points of the subject and extended to the edge of the frame give the wedge-shaped path along which the subject appears to travel.

This is particularly useful when people or objects are required to shrink or grow while standing in a specific spot. If the actor is fully in frame at the start of the shot with his feet on the bottom frame line, and is required to "shrink" to a

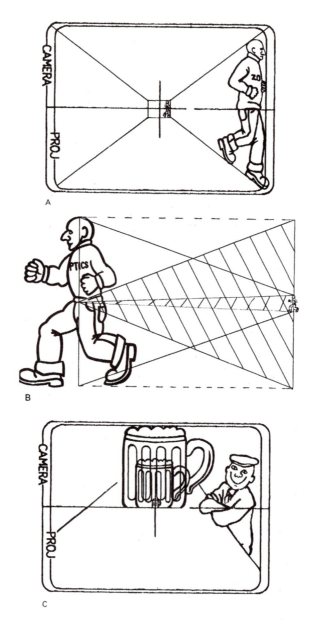

Figure 11.25   (A and B) Two ways of calculating and representing a 10-to-1 zoom on a man running. (C) No compensation is needed for a glass to grow when positioned with its base on the horizontal center line with the vertical line cutting down the center of the glass.

very small size on the same spot, then the camera/projector compound has to be tilted upwards during the zoom out in order to keep his feet in the same position within the frame.

The position of the object relative to the vertical centerline is also of equal importance. A girl (as in *Alice in Wonderland*) standing on the vertical centerline with her feet on the horizontal centerline will grow or shrink on the spot during a zoom, without the need for any compensation. However, if she is standing to the right of the vertical centerline with her feet still on the horizontal centerline, she will drift towards the right edge of the frame as she grows, and her feet will appear to slide along the horizontal centerline. In this case, a left-to-right pan of the camera/projector compound is required.

This type of compensation is not difficult to achieve since the actual effect can be seen as it is being created. Nevertheless, it is best to use motion control on the pan-and-tilt axis linked to the zoom drive.

Using the Zoptic system camera is changing constantly, as would be the case in real life. Because the Zoptic effect can be seen as it happens and is infinitely variable, it enables the creation of very realistic effects as well as those of total fantasy.

MIXING FORMATS

Using larger formats, both in the original shooting and in the preparation of the plates, is one way of increasing the definition of the projected image. Projecting a VistaVision format (8-perforation pull-down) or 65mm format and shooting on 35mm (or projecting 35mm film and shooting on 16mm) makes it easier to produce a well-balanced image, as opposed to projecting and filming on the same format. Even when the original photography of the background plates is done on 35mm, the composite image will benefit if the plates are blown up in the printing stage to VistaVision format.

Stills Projectors

A typical stills projector designed for front projection utilizes 5″ × 4″ or 10″ × 8″ transparencies. It incorporates a lightweight Nodal Head for panning and tilting inside the composite image (foreground set and projected still). A zoom lens can be used on the camera, when the zoom control is linked electronically to a facility for moving the camera along the lens axis, in order to maintain the nodal point of the lens at the pivot point of the Nodal Head.

On some projectors the transparency can be rotated 360 degrees to create a tilt on the background or a rocking motion during the shot. For best results, the transparencies are sandwiched between two sheets of heat-resistant high-quality glass. A dichroic filter in the lamphouse system ensures that as much of the heat-producing infrared radiation as possible is taken out of the light beam before it reaches the transparency.

A 5″ × 4″ unit is of compact design and can be mounted on a heavy-duty geared head, which in turn can go on a dolly, a crane, or a high hat, as required for ease of positioning. Extreme up and down angles are accomplished with the use of a wedge on the gear head or by means of a front-silvered mirror.

Zoptic "Moving Stills" Projector

The Zoptic "Moving Still" projector is an extremely compact unit mounted on a heavy-duty geared head. It can accommodate transparencies of various sizes up to 10" × 8".

A motion-control computer moves the large-format transparency in East/West and North/South directions in precise, real time, and synchronized with the panning and tilting movements of the geared head, while only a part of the transparency (equal to a VistaVision or 2.25-inch format) is projected at any one time.

The best way to visualize this is to imagine that the entire 10" × 8" transparency is being projected on the front-projection screen, but we are looking at only one section. As we pan and tilt inside the composite image, the transparency is moved by the motion-control computer in real time, so that the projection lens is always projecting the appropriate section of the transparency.

The great advantage of this system is the ability to pan over an extremely wide range of horizontal angles—up to 360 degrees, well beyond the confines of conventional front-projection. Transparencies shot with wide-angle lenses and/or with panoramic cameras are ideal for this approach. The projector and camera lenses are matched up to copy the correct horizontal angle represented by the segment of transparency being projected. Thus, if the ten-inch transparency was shot with a 60-degree horizontal angle and the camera/projector is set to copy two inches horizontally, then the lens with a horizontal angle of 1/5 of the original will match correctly (i.e., 12 degrees). On the other hand, a five-inch transparency shot with the same horizontal angle of 60 degrees will be matched by lenses with horizontal angles of 24 degrees.

The projected still (transparency) can also be moved during the shot independently of the movements of the gear head if required. It can also be rotated through 360 degrees. A 3:1 zoom lens can be used on the camera. An automatic compensating track maintains the relationship of the entrance pupil of the camera lens to the exit pupil of the projection lens.

Zoptic Blue/Green Screen Projector

This projector is designed to project an extremely narrow band of light in either the BLUE or GREEN area of the spectrum suitable for the production of color-difference mattes.

It utilizes a light source that is biased to the blue or green part of the spectrum (as required). Additional cutoff filters are placed in the light path to isolate a specific bandwidth, producing maximum exposure over a narrow spectral range.

Reversed Projection Method

The projector and camera are positioned at 45 degrees to each other with the beam-splitter placed between the subject and the front-projection screen.

Figure 11.26 Reverse Projection method: (P) Projector; (C) Camera; (B) Beam-splitter; (S) Screen; (X) Composite Image.

Because the subject is in front of the beam-splitter and is no longer throwing a shadow on the screen, the fringing line-up is eliminated, but the subject is still self matting. Panning and tilting is possible with the nodal head.

The disadvantage of this approach is that it is harder to achieve a precise line-up of the camera and projector lenses. It also requires a static setup.

Regular glass beam-splitters are limited in size, and these can be used only for relatively small objects and close-ups. Live action requires very large beam-splitters that are difficult to manufacture. A plain sheet of glass can be used in certain circumstances. This approach is well suited to the front-projected blue or green process for deriving color-difference mattes.

Concave Mirror

A concave mirror can be used in place of a front-projection screen. When lined up correctly the mirror acts as the most efficient retroreflector. The focal length of the mirror determines the position where the exit pupil of the projector should be placed, in order for the return beam to coincide with the same point. Different focal length mirrors are required for different setups.

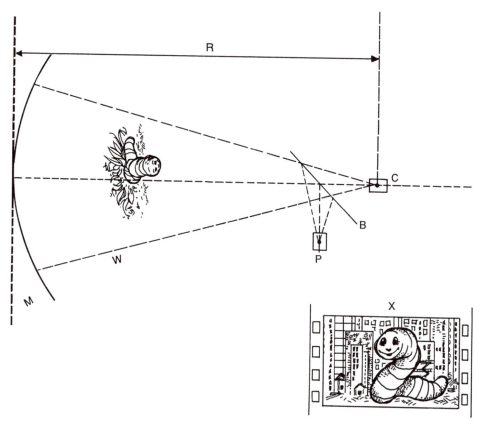

Figure 11.27 Concave mirror as retroreflector. (C) Camera. (B) Beam-splitter. (P) Projector. (M) Concave Mirror. (R) Radius of curvature. (W) Worm. (X) Composite image (cityscape with giant worm in foreground).

The great advantage of this approach is that a very small amount of light is required because of the retroreflecting efficiency of the mirror. It is ideal for extreme close-ups or very small setups involving insects or similar live creatures.

Front-Silvered Mirrors

Extreme vertical angles, as well as some of the more difficult setups, are achieved more easily with the use of a large front-silvered mirror (four by five feet).

In this case, the beam-splitter mirror in the front-projection unit is flopped so that the reflecting side is facing up. The blackout is moved from its normal position above the mirror and in line with the projector to the front of the mirror and in line with the camera. With the front-projection unit tilted forward at 45 degrees and the front-silvered mirror also at 45 degrees in front and above, it is possible to get a direct vertical P.O.V. (point of view).

SUSPENSION METHODS

The Pole

The best way to suspend a subject for front projection is by means of a pole pushed through the screen. The camera/projector assembly is set up in line with the pole so that it is automatically masked off by the subject it supports. A screen of rigid construction is preferable because it is easier to cut holes in it for the pole arm. The pole is attached to a freestanding support tower at the back of the screen. When heavy weights are involved, such as a full-size aircraft, the pole support base should be extended under the screen for counterbalance. The sub-

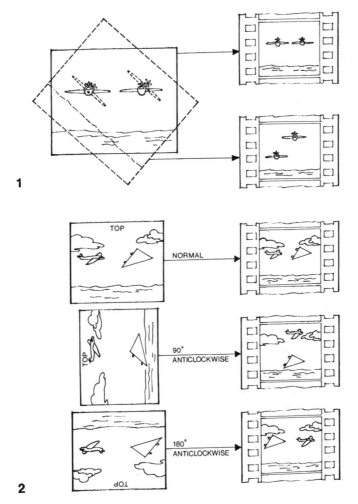

Figure 11.28 (1) By rotating the model aircraft in unison with the camera/projector unit, the aircraft appear to float relative to each other, as though they were not supported on rigid poles. (2) A full 180-degree counterclockwise rotation creates the illusion that one aircraft has overtaken the other.

ject can be attached either directly to the end of the pole or via a set of mechanical joints that enable the subject to be manipulated up and down as well as sideways. The pole can also be constructed so that it rotates, thus giving yet another
movement to the subject.

Multiple Pole Arms.

More than one pole support can be used at the same time, provided that they all
point towards the camera lens.

Wires

The subject can also be suspended in front of the front-projection screen on wires.
This method works fine with light objects, because very thin wires can be used.
Thicker wires, such as those used for supporting the weight of a person, cannot
be used successfully in front projection without resorting to wire removal.

Vibrating wires can be made to look less obtrusive, but their performance is
inconsistent when they are used to manipulate the subject, instead of merely
keeping it suspended in one place.

Painting Out Wires (Wire Removal)

In those circumstances where wires have to be used in a front-projection shot,
they can be eliminated using optical or digital wire removal. Inevitably, this
means a duplicating stage where the bad sections of the frame (those with wires)
are replaced with the good sections from a clean duplicate print. It is best to
shoot a "cover" take on the background plate alone, at the same time as the wire
composite is made. This avoids possible differences in framing and color balance, which can complicate matters further.

LIGHTING FOR FRONT PROJECTION

The front-projection screen can tolerate a considerable amount of ambient light
but not too much spill light. Front projection is more suited to side and back
lighting than flat, frontal lighting, which makes it difficult to keep the spill light
off the screen. In certain circumstances where the subject is close to the screen,
the spill light falling on the screen can be neutralized with the use of polarizing
filters on the lights.

Skylight

This is a very useful aid in lighting for front projection because it raises the general level of illumination and can be kept away from the screen. It is made up of
rows of photoflood lamps wired up in several combinations, so that the light out-

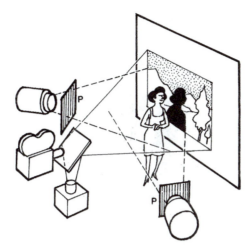

Figure 11.29 Polarized lighting. It is possible to light the subject more directly from the front when polarizing filters are used (P) over the lights.

put can be varied. A layer of greaseproof paper below the lamps acts as a diffuser, and the whole assembly is mounted in a frame. Black drapes around the sides of the frame and a slight inclination away from the screen can help to contain the light in the required area.

Exposure Balance

Establishing the correct exposure can be a problem in front projection, as the projected image cannot be measured in the normal way. The best approach is to establish a basic match between a grey scale on stage and a standard projected grey scale at the head of the plate. Based on this test, the foreground set is lit to a chosen f-stop and the background is fine-tuned to match the foreground. A grey scale placed in the key light can be used to check the balance of the various segments of the projected picture. When basing the shooting f-stop on the incident reading at the set, an allowance should be made for the absorption factor of the beam-splitter.

With the camera removed, a spot meter can be placed at the point of convergence of light rays and used to take a reflected reading of specific points within the picture. Alternatively, a mirror placed between the camera lens and the beam-splitter can be used to redirect the light beam to the side, where it can be read easily. Yet another approach is to take the reading in the camera gate itself, with the help of a fiber-optic probe and a clip of frosted film.

A useful rule of thumb for calculating the exposure and changes in the size of projected image is, when the size of the image is doubled, the light output drops by two f-stops, and when it is reduced by 50%, the light output increases by two f-stops.

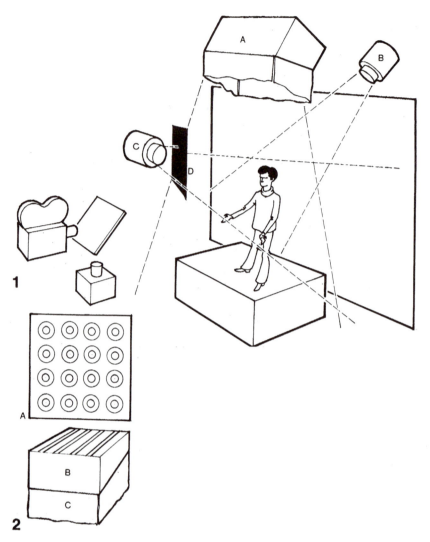

Figure 11.30 (1) (A) Skylight is positioned so that no spill light reaches the screen. (B) Back light. (C) Sidelights should be positioned so that the shadow produced by them falls just outside the field of view. (D) Gobo. (2) Skylight. (A) Bulb arrangement. (B) Diffusing material. (C) Black skirting.

Color Balance

The color temperature of the projector light source is extremely important for achieving a good color balance between the foreground set and the projected plate. A tungsten lamp with a color temperature of 3,200 Kelvin, matching the lighting used for the illumination of the foreground set, requires less color correction than, for example, an arc lamp. However, even with the most suitable light source, a certain amount of color correction is required. This is because the front-projection screen material itself has a slight green bias and requires magenta correction. A certain amount of color correction can also be built into the plate at the printing stage.

Blending In the Foreground

A large format is preferred for the background plates (VistaVision or 65mm). The resultant increase in the resolution of the projected image makes it compatible with the first-generation quality of the foreground elements.

A successful blending of foreground elements and the background image is achieved with the use of low-contrast filters, fogs, or gauzes. Ideally the filters should affect the foreground image only, particularly in blending the density of the shadow areas.

Producing controlled, even fogging over the entire frame area is another way in which this blending of foreground and background can be achieved. The extent of the fogging can vary for different types of scene and should be determined experimentally. This approach reduces contrast, but it also desaturates the color and is equivalent to pre-fogging the negative. The ideal use of this method is to fog selected areas only.

FRONT-PROJECTION SCREEN CONSTRUCTION

Photographic-quality, front-projection material is manufactured by 3M, with adhesive backing, and is available in rolls 50 yards long (two feet or four feet wide). There are two basic types: No. 7610 and No. 7611. The latter has a somewhat thicker base.

The rolls should also be tested for any possible variation in quality between the start and the end of the roll and between one side and the other. The material used for front projection must be of the highest quality and with a minimum variation in reflectivity between rolls in a particular batch. The material is overlapped when applied. It is advisable to follow the advice of the manufacturer as to the best methods of application.

The ideal screen would have no joins in it at all. This, however, is restricted by the maximum width of the rolls.

Horizontal Application

A layout of the screen is prepared, taking great care to match the rolls as well as possible by their reflectivity readings. It is advisable to apply every other strip running in the opposite direction so that the same sides of the roll are always adjoining each other. This ensures that the effect of any fall off in reflectivity between one side of the roll and the other is minimized.

The strips are overlapped at the joins, and provided that there is no drastic difference in reflectivity between the strips, these joins are normally invisible.

After some time, however, dirt tends to collect at these points, and they can start to show up as black lines in the photographed picture. The screen can be washed with detergent and clear water to remove the dust and grime accumulated from the atmosphere.

It is best to cut the rolls into the required lengths and to allow them to adjust to the ambient temperature before application. This reduces the risk of buckling and the appearance of air bubbles. Incidentally, these air bubbles cannot be seen during projection. However, after a certain amount of time, the dust accumulated on the screen will be distributed unevenly over the bubbly areas, creating patches of unequal reflectivity.

Patchwork Application

Horizontal joins are preferable to verticals ones, but diagonal ones are least likely to be noticeable. However, any uninterrupted straight line across the screen is likely to show up under certain conditions, particularly with light areas. The patchwork approach provides for both ease of application and an elimination of continuous straight lines.

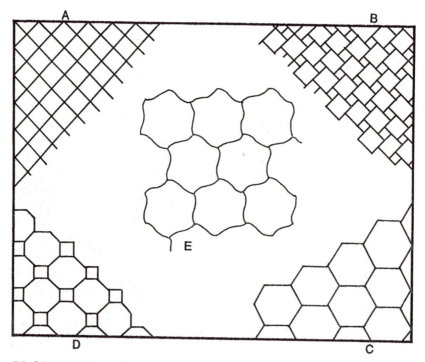

Figure 11.31   Typical patchwork applications of front-projection material. Ideally, the overlaps should be radiating outwards from the center of the screen, consequently, the application should start at the corners. (A) Diamond pattern, (B) a combination pattern of large and small diamond shapes, (C) hexagonal pattern, (D) a combination pattern of large octagonals and small squares, and (E) hexagonal curved line pattern.

Soft Backing

Under normal circumstances an old back projection screen can be used as the backing for front projection material. Such screens are very useful because they already have rigid frameworks onto which the screen is stretched. The application procedure is also relatively simple.

The screen material used for making theatrical projection screens is also a good backing for the application of front projection material. The tiny holes in the screen material help to avoid air being trapped during application.

Hard Backing

A solid, flat surface is an ideal backing for a front-projection screen and patch-work application is most suited for this purpose. A front-projection screen on a hard backing is particularly useful when pole arms are used for supporting the subject. A hole can be cut anywhere in the screen and later plugged in again and recovered with front-projection material.

Patching Up

It is most important to save a certain amount of spare material from each roll so that a damaged area of the screen can be patched up. A layout of the screen prepared during application is used for reference to ensure that the replacement piece of front-projection material comes from the same roll as the original.

Curved Screens

Panning and tilting the front-projection unit is possible because the reflectivity of the screen remains constant over a wide range of angles. A curved screen reduces both keystoning and projection focus fall-off.

Keystoning itself is not noticeable in the projected background because the distortion is cancelled out by the camera lens, which is subject to the same keystoning effect. It is only a problem insofar as a larger screen has to be used to ensure that the part of the picture farthest from the unit does not disappear off screen. Focus fall-off on the side of the frame farthest from the front projection unit can be a more serious problem, when the depth of field of either or both lenses is very shallow.

The Shaking Screen

Work with miniatures requires the use of a relatively small screen area, and therefore the overlap joins can be more noticeable, particularly with light backgrounds (i.e., clear sky). Wherever possible it is best to use a screen made up of a single piece without joins. In those cases where both small and large areas of the screen are to be used (as in the Zoptic zoom process) a shaking screen approach is the best solution.

The screen is prepared as a patchwork on a solid surface resting on springs or air cushions. It can move freely in two axes only: up/down and side-to-side. An eccentric weight attached to the shaft of an electric motor, mounted centrally at the back of the screen, provides the shaking movement. The speed of the motor determines the speed of the shake and the displacement of the eccentric weight determines the extent of the shaking movement. It is best to shoot a test with a suitable subject matter, such as a page of newsprint attached to the screen surface. This test can be done without the use of front-projection equipment.

Patchwork application of the front-projection material involving diagonal joins only is best for this approach. Screens of thirty feet wide and twenty feet high can be shaken quite successfully. Because the amount of actual physical movement is very small, the shaking screen approach makes it possible to use pole arms pushed through the screen to support models and miniatures.

Spinning Screen

A front-projection screen constructed in the shape of a circle can be rotated with less effort than a shaking screen. A patchwork approach with join lines radiating from the center is a good way of applying the front-projection material. This is a much quieter operation than the shaking screen. The drawback is that only one centrally mounted pole arm can be used, provided the screen is mounted on a bearing with a large inner diameter.

12

Digital Effects

> *And lo, another miracle happened: the optical printer became attached to the digital camera and begat a digital scanner . . . and this too was good for visual effects.*

Virtually all complex visual effects require some film duplication at some stage, which is done either by "photographic" or electronic (digital) means.

The current cost ratio between the two approaches is 16:1; that is, the cost of duplicating one 35mm frame digitally is equal to duplicating one foot of 35mm film optically (16 frames per foot).

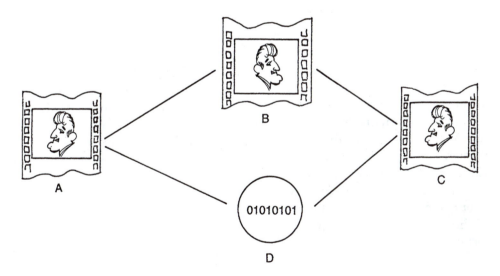

Figure 12.1 Film duplication methods: (A) original negative; (B) duplicating positive (interpositive); (C) duplicate negative; (D) digital media.

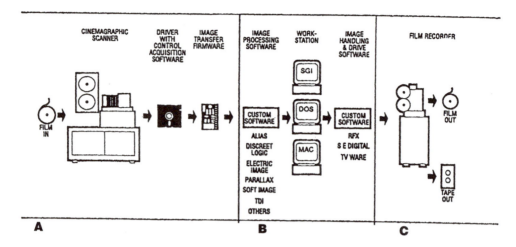

Figure 12.2   (A) Film Input Stage. (B) Digital Processing Stage. (C) Film Output Stage.

Digital FX work for film is divided into three stages:

1. Film-to-digital transfer
2. Image manipulation in digital form
3. Digital-to-film transfer

FILM-TO-DIGITAL TRANSFER

This first stage of the digital process is done either from a negative or an inter-positive. Although there is little risk of damage to the negative in the actual transfer process, there is always some risk of loss or damage involved when the negative is removed from the laboratory. It is advisable to make a safety inter-positive as insurance and hold it at the laboratory when the original negative is taken out. Alternatively, the interpositive can be used for transfer to digital instead. For best results, the interpositive is printed on an optical or contact step-printer, although in certain circumstances a rotary printer may be used. (See Chapter 6, "Laboratory Effects.")

The transfer to digital media is done on a digital scanner. A commonly adopted procedure is to do the "scanning" (film-to-digital transfer) at an outside facility that acts as a "digital laboratory." These facilities often use proprietary technology.

Digital Scanner

In principal, a digital scanner is an optical printer with the film camera module removed and replaced with an electronic camera. In fact, the earliest versions of the digital scanner were just that—modified optical printers. The majority of digital scanners use the same film gate as the optical printers, the ever-popular "shuttle gate" with static-pin registration, manufactured by Oxberry (yes, folks, the same guys that brought you the optical printer and the animation camera).

The design of all digital scanners follows the basic layout of an optical printer: a lamphouse and condenser system illuminate the film frame registered in the gate; and a lens transfers this image optically to the image plane where it is picked up by an array of electronic sensors—the "chip" of the CCD camera. The CCD chip (Charge-Coupled-Device) is made up of thousands of tiny electronic sensors that convert natural light into electrical current, which is then turned into digital information. The tonal and color values of the film image are converted into a series of binary digits, or bits, and represented as a series of "0" and "1." This digital information is stored in a variety of file formats and used for image manipulation on a computer workstation. Finally, the digitally processed image is converted back to a film image via a digital recorder.

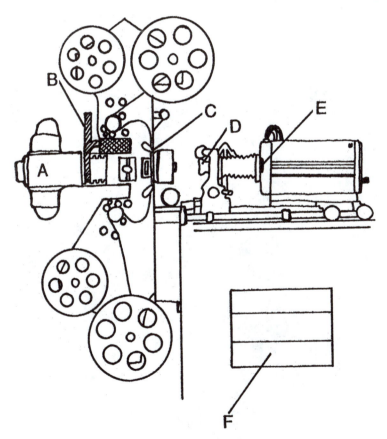

Figure 12.3 Optical printer-based Digital Scanner with a CCD camera: (A) lamphouse and condenser system; (B) R-B-G color wheel; (C) film gate; (D) lens; (E) CCD chip (at image plane); (F) electronic storage.

CCD Chip Camera Approach

Many digital scanners use a high-resolution black-and-white CCD chip camera and the "color separation" approach to digitize a film image. A film frame is scanned once through each of the three color-separation filters (red, green, blue) to produce three separate panchromatic records of the picture (i.e., three "color separation masters" in digital form). This is an electronic version of the "color separation" approach used in film-to-film duplication (see Figure 6.5). The three black-and-white panchromatic records of the image in digital form are recombined electronically by the scanner into a full-color image before being stored on

Figure 12.4   The Oxberry Cinescan range offers a choice of fixed array CCD camera with resolutions of 1.5K × 1K; 2K × 2K; 3K × 2K; and even 4K × 3K (1K = 1,000 pixels).

a chosen storage format for use on a computer workstation in digital image manipulation. Alternatively, they can be stored as separate layers and combined at a later stage.

The resolution is determined by the choice of the camera, that is, the number of elements (samples) on the CCD chip and consequently the number of pixels (individual dots of light in an image) that can be digitized. It is commonly accepted that the theoretical minimum number needed to resolve 35mm negative film stock is between 3,000 and 4,000 samples per line. This in turn determines the scanning speed per frame: the higher the resolution, the longer the scan time.

A major advantage of an optical-printer-based digital scanner like the Oxberry Cinescan 6400 is that it can perform a lot of the functions of an optical printer during the scanning stage without sacrificing digital resolution of the scanned image. In addition to the X-Y-Z movements (sideways, up-down, in-out) of the camera and lens mounts, the camera can also be rotated up to 100 degrees, making it possible to do zooms and panning moves within the frame, sectional enlargements as well as reframing to accommodate changes in aspect ratio or to eliminate an unwanted area of the frame. Changing formats is done in the same way as on the optical printer, by changing the film gate (from 16mm to 70mm). A difference in film pitch and perforation type can also be accommodated with the appropriate gate. "Wet gate" can also be used in the same way as on an optical printer. (See Chapter 8, "Optical Printers and FX" and Figure 8.4.)

The Single-Line CCD Array Approach

The "line scanning" approach utilizes a single-line CCD array consisting of 4,096 elements per line in the case of Kodak's "Lightning" and 6,000 (5,760) elements per line in the case of Quantel's "Domino."

Domino Scanner

The "optical printer" part of Quantel's Domino scanner comprises a lamp-house and condensing system, the Oxberry pin-registered "shuttle" gate, and a copy lens. The color wheel with red-green-blue (R-G-B) color-separation filters is built into the light path. A 6,000 (5,760) element CCD single-line array is used to scan the image. The CCD array is physically moved across the image plane three times per frame, each time with a different color-separation filter (red, green, or blue) in the light path, producing three black-and-white panchromatic records of the image. This digital information is then recombined into a full-color image and outputted to a storage device. Using pixel interpolation (average values of two adjoining pixels) the digital information is reduced from 6K (5,760) per line to 3K (2,880) per line. The result is an overall resolution of 3K × 2K.

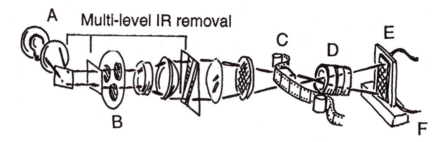

Figure 12.5 The Domino Scanner. (A) Lamphouse, (B) R-G-B color wheel, (C) Film gate, (D) Lens, (E) CCD array, (F) Linear motion table.

Tri-Linear Array

The color separation on Kodak's "Lightning" and Imagica's "IMAGER 300V" scanners is accomplished with the use of a "tri-linear" CCD array with an R-G-B color separation filter in front of each of the three lines. This way all three black-and-white panchromatic records of the image are scanned in one single operation. Each line of the tri-linear array is made up of 4,096 elements.

With Kodak's "Lightning" the tri-linear CCD array remains stationary during the "scanning" process. A custom designed film gate is moved physi-

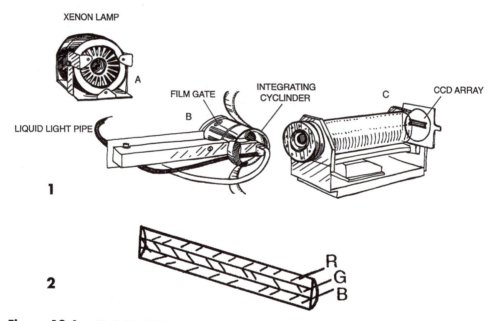

Figure 12.6a Kodak's "Lightening" Scanner. (1) (A) Xenon Lamp, (B) Rotating film gate, (C) Tri-linear CCD array. (2) Detail of the tri-linear CCD array with color-separation filters.

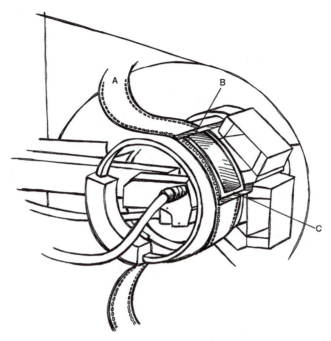

Figure 12.6b   Detail of the rotating film gate. The film (A) is held in position around the drum by register pin (B) as the gate rotates clockwise in order that the full height of the frame can be scanned by the lens. At the end of the scan the holding pin (C) engages the film as the register pin (B) retracts and the gate-drum rotates back to the start position so that the next frame can be engaged.

cally across the image plane, holding the film frame in register. Each line of the tri-linear array produces a panchromatic color-separation record of the image; these are recombined electronically into a full-color image file and outputted to storage.

Resolution

Resolving power is said to be a combination of the ratio between shadow and highlight detail (dynamic range) and the effective image sharpness ("grain" structure).

Dynamic Range
There is no digital film scanner at present that can extract the full range of latitude of a camera film negative, which can be up to 11 f-stops! The usable dynamic range of digital scanners is around 6 f-stops and is more in line with the dynamic range of the film print stock. This is adequate for the majority of film

work, but it does mean that a certain amount of "timing" has to be done at the scanning stage to ensure that the correct tonal range is covered, allowing for any over- or underexposure in the original photography.

Film "Grain" Structure

The sharpness of a photographic image is affected by the grain structure of the film emulsion. The finer the grain — the more grains per frame, resulting in more detail being recorded and consequently a better image sharpness — the higher resolution. Since the resolving power of the imaging lens is greater than the resolving power of the film emulsion, an image occupying a larger area on the negative will result in higher image sharpness because it is made up of a greater number of grains than a smaller one (e.g., a VistaVision frame has double the area of a standard 35mm frame). The digital parallel to the film "grain" is the "pixel" (the smallest element making up a digital image).

Film Formats and Digital Resolution

Digital resolution refers to the total number of pixels in an image. The resolution of a digital scanner is determined by the total number of elements (pixels) at the "receptor" side of the scanner. Scanners utilizing the full image approach are limited by the total number of elements on the CCD chip of the digital camera, and those (scanners) using the "line scanning" approach are limited by the number of elements per line in the CCD array and the range of the scan. The 35mm film formats differ not only in the aspect ratio of width to height of the frame but also in the amount of physical space the image occupies on the film. A digital scanner set up to cover the full aperture format will produce maximum resolution at that format but will utilize fewer elements (pixels) when scanning the Academy format. Some "line" scanners have a provision for adjusting the size of the image optically so that it matches the length of the line array for all standard formats. This ensures that all formats are scanned at the maximum resolution.

Film Format	Aspect Ratio	Image Size in mm	Total Number of Pixels @ 4K Res	Total Number of Pixels @ 2K Res.
Full Aperture	1.32:1	18.672 x 4.576	4,096 x 3,112	2,048 x 1,556
Academy	1.37:1	15.984 x 21.936	3,656 x 2,664	1,828 x 1,332
Cinemascope	1.17:1	18.674 x 21.936	3,656 x 3,112	1,828 x 1,556
Wide screen	1.85:1	11.858 x 21.935	3,656 x 1,976	1,828 x 988
Super 1.85	1.85:1	13.653 x 24.576	4,096 x 2,214	2,048 x 1,107
VistaVision	1.50:1	24.576 x 36.864	4,096 x 6,144	2,048 x 3,072

Figure 12.7   Digital resolution chart of 35mm film scanned at "Full Aperture" setting for all aspect ratios. (Kodak's "Lightning" tri-linear scanner.)

Relationship between 35mm formats and total number of pixels scanned with a 4,096-element CCD tri-linear array at full resolution (4K) and at half-resolution (2K).

Full Resolution versus Half Resolution

The advantage of working in half resolution is obvious in terms of storage and memory requirements, both at the scanning stage and, more importantly, at the digital image manipulation stage of the process. The effective difference between 4K and 2K resolution is in the ratio of 4:1. The half resolution scanning at 2K is often done with the same scanner as the 4K resolution utilizing pixel interpolation. The record of two adjoining pixels is averaged and combined into one before it is outputted to storage.

In practice, the full 4K resolution is used only when fine detail is involved such as hair. The vast majority of digital scanning is done at 2K resolution.

The Domino system scans the image with a 5,760-element CCD array (6K), which is then interpolated to produce a digital record with 2,880 pixels per line of the image (3K). The "copy ratio" between the image on the film in the gate and the aerial image at the image plane of the CCD array is adjusted for each format so that the width of the frame is always sampled by the full array of sensors — 2,880 pixels per line.

Film Format	Aspect Ratio	Image Size in mm	Total No. of Pixels @ 3K
Full Aperture	1.32:1	24.576 x 18.672	2,880 x 2,181
Academy	1.37:1	21.936 x 15.984	2,880 x 2,102
Cinemascope	1.17:1	21.936 x 18.674	2,880 x 2,461
Wide screen	1.85:1	21.935 x 11.858	2,880 x 1,556
Super 1.85	1.85:1	24.576 x 13.653	2,880 x 1,556

Figure 12.8 Digital resolution (pixels per frame) for standard 35mm formats scanned by "Domino" line scanner at full (3K) resolution.

Film Format	Aspect Ratio	Image Size in mm	Total No. of Pixels 4K x 3K	Total No. of Pixels 3K x 2K
Full Aperture	1.32:1	24.576 x 18.672	4,055 x 3,072	2,703 x 2,048
Academy	1.37:1	21.936 x 15.984	4,095 x 2,989	2,805 x 2,048
Cinemascope	1.17:1	21.936 x 18.674	3,594 x 3,072	3,072 x 2,625
Wide screen	1.85:1	21.935 x 11.858	4,095 x 2,213	3,072 x 1,660
Super 1.85	1.85:1	24.576 x 13.653	4,095 x 2,213	3,072 x 16,60
VistaVision	1.50:1	36.867 x 24.576	4,095 x 2,730	3,072 x 2,048

Figure 12.9 Pixel resolution with a fixed area-array CCD: 4,096 × 3,072 (4K × 3K) and 3,072 × 2,048 (3K × 2K).

Telecine Transfers

Telecine machines can transfer film to digital format in real time, which is only a dream with digital scanners. Unfortunately, with a typical resolution of around 720 pixels per line, the telecine transfer is far short of the 2,000, 3,000, and 4,000 pixels-per-line produced by digital scanners. A resolution on 720 pixels per line is inadequate for film work when a transfer from digital to film is required, but it is perfectly satisfactory for film transfers where the final output is to a video standard.

The difference between video and film requirements is best illustrated by direct comparison: a video picture on the NTSC Television standard, digitally captured in R-G-B at a pixel matrix of 640×480 equals 307,200 sampling points. At 2K resolution, a 35mm full aperture format digitally captured at a pixels matrix of $2,048 \times 1,556$ equals 3,186,688 pixels, which is 10 times larger — and at 4K resolution (12,746,752) it is more than 40 times as large!

However, the latest developments in telecine transfer technology indicate the potential for real-time film-to-data transfer at 2K resolution in the near future. Several models already have 2K resolution capability but are still short of real-time transfer speed. Spirit DataCine High Resolution film scanner from Phillips has a $2K \times 2K$ film-to-data transfer capability. Cintel's C-Reality offers 2K scanning at $2,048 \times 1,536$ pixels in each of three R-G-B channels. And Sony's multiresolution Telecine FVS-1000 uses a Hi-Def camera with $1,920 \times 1,080$ pixel chips.

Quality Control

Digital scanners are equipped with electronic calibrations that are used to maintain quality control in the same manner as the laboratories use sensitometric film strips. A "clear white light" test is particularly useful for detecting any irregularities in the CCD or the light path. A standard color and density filmstrip scanned at the head of each scene provides a base reference.

Monitoring

As each frame is scanned it is displayed in real time on a high-resolution, color-balanced monitor. The timing controls of the scanner can be used at this stage for color correction, to eliminate color bias, or to compensate for variations in the exposure of the original negative. The scanned images can also be played back directly from the disc storage and viewed on the high-resolution monitor, before they are copied to tape for transfer to the workstation.

Image File Formats

The file format is determined by the hardware and software of the computer platform to be used for the manipulation of the files. A number of different file formats are supported by various scanners as standard: Cineon, SGI, TIFF, and more. Other image file formats can usually be converted when required.

Tape Formats for File Transfer

A variety of storage formats are supported by the different scanners. Domino uses either D16 format or high-speed direct computer interface (DCI) which enables direct image transfer to SGI equipment. Lightning supports Exabyte, Ampex DST, Metrum, DTF, and DLT.

Color Depth

The color depth of a picture refers to the maximum number of colors that an image can contain. This is dictated by the resolution of the image and usually described in terms of bits: either 8, 16 , 24, or 32 bits. An 8-bit image can have a combination of 256 different colors; a 16-bit image can display up to 65,536 colors; and a 24-bit image has 16 million different colors. Color depth is sometimes referred to as "bit depth" or "pixel depth," because it is directly related to the number of bits that each pixel can represent.

DIGITAL IMAGE MANIPULATION

In principal, the scanning (film-to-digital) and recording (digital-to-film) has evolved into a digital laboratory process and is handled as a separate operation even by the effects facility companies that have the full range of equipment. Standardized file and storage methods are used to move data from the film scanner to the workstation and from the workstation to the film recorder.

The image-manipulation phase is where the digital effects are actually created. Virtually all visual effects that can be created using film-to-film technology can also be accomplished digitally. In addition, certain visual effects elements can be originated in digital form and composited with other elements originated on film.

A workstation for digital image manipulation consists of three basic elements:

1. A computer platform, comprised of:
   — an electronic imaging mainframe,
   — pen-and-tablet workstation with keyboard, and
   — color-balanced high-resolution monitor.
2. Film-resolution digital storage units.
3. Graphics software programs.

Computer Platforms

The computer is a vital piece of hardware required for digital image manipulation. It can range in power and speed from a modest PC or Mac to the supercomputers like the Crey series. The choice of computer hardware determines the resolution level and often the type of software that can be used, and therefore the type of effects that can be tackled.

High-end computer platforms with graphics capability suitable for image-manipulation work at film resolution are manufactured by Silicon Graphics, IBM, and Macintosh. Several other computer companies supply platforms employing standard processors and operating systems that offer impressive performance at competitive prices. Computer platforms with sophisticated graphics capability are also available for hire.

The main considerations in choosing a suitable computer platform are:

speed of operation (determined by the processor and the operating system), and

memory capacity (affecting the relationship of the resolution level, the complexity of the effect, and the length of the shot).

High-Resolution Monitors

A major advantage of digital video manipulation is that the result can be viewed as it happens. For realistic comparisons, the image displayed on the video monitor screen should have the same qualities (the "look") as the projected film print. The color temperatures of the monitors should be matched to the color temperature of the film projector (usually 5,400 Kelvin). In addition, all monitors within the system should also be matched to each other.

There are several ways of achieving and maintaining consistent color between the image displayed on the video monitors and the final image recorded on film, utilizing software and hardware specifically designed to measure luminance, density range, and Correlated Color Temperature (CCT) in Kelvin degrees. The resolution of video monitors is also an important factor in maintaining quality control.

Anamorphic Squeeze

An anamorphic image has a 2:1 optical squeeze along the horizontal axis that is unsqueezed in projection. However, it is scanned as a regular spherical image by the digital scanner and appears as a distorted, "squeezed" image on the video monitor. In order to see a normal, unsqueezed, image it is necessary to miss-out every other horizontal line displayed on the monitor screen. When the work is completed, the image is reconstructed again and outputted to film as an anamorphic, squeezed, image.

Some of the work like compositing and wire removal can be done with the squeezed image. A more serious problem arises when compositing anamorphic and computer-generated images. It is also difficult to use motion-control data accurately for tracking camera moves because the computer can handle only one nodal point, whereas the anamorphic lens has two nodal points.

Storage Systems

With a requirement of close to one gigabyte per second of 35mm film (24 frames), storage of digital data plays a very important part in image manipulation. Storage requirements are governed by the length of the shot, the number of frames to be processed, the level of image resolution, and the speed of access. A number of storage systems are available as stand-alone units that can be interfaced with various computer platforms.

Key characteristics of a digital storage system are:

Capacity—measured in kilobytes (KB), megabytes (MB), gigabytes (GB), and terabytes (TB)

Data Transfer Rate—measured as KB/sec, MB/sec

Access Time—measured in milliseconds (1/1000 of a second)

Transfer speeds of some of the available storage system are from 40 to 100 times faster than that of the CD-ROM drive.

Archiving
Often digital information is stored out of the system on tape or disc so that it can be recalled at a later date and the work continued without tying up the system in the meantime.

Software

Graphics software is the key to digital image manipulation, and many versions and packages are available for all the main computer operating systems. Because of the specific processing requirements, many of the companies supplying graphics software offer a complete hardware package as well, which includes the computer platforms, digital storage systems, and, in some cases, digital scanners and recorders. These may not all be of their own manufacture, but they have been selected to form an integrated package.

Apart from the basic graphic programs a variety of specialized software programs are available for all the different functions, from basic image editing to compositing and 3-D digital animation. There are dozens of 2-D effects and paint software programs and even more 3-D modeling and animation programs available on the market, with still more in development. Incidentally, the widespread reference to 3-D in computer graphics has nothing to do with stereoscopic vision. It is a method of defining and shading a computer-generated character to give it a feel of "roundness," of a real three-dimensional object as opposed to a flat, two-dimensional drawing.

Method of Operation

The digital information produced by the film-scanning process is transferred to digital storage where it can be accessed by the computer. An appropriate graphics program is used to manipulate the digitized image as required. In practice, several software programs are used either simultaneously or sequentially to achieve the desired effect.

The digitized image is manipulated at pixel level to achieve extremely subtle changes to the image as well as the more obvious ones. A variety of visual effects can be accomplished, ranging in complexity from simple optical wipes to compositing of computer-generated images and live-action scenes.

Options for Digital Image Manipulation

1. Image enhancement:
    a. color and contrast correction/distortion
    b. restoration of faded images
2. Image alteration
    a. pull, squeeze, stretch, scrunch, and other image distortions
    b. wire and other artifact removal
3. Electronic matte painting texture mapping
4. Computer Generated Images (CGI)
    a. 3-D animated characters and photorealistic creatures and objects
5. Compositing
    a. of color-difference (blue/green screen) elements
    b. with elements originated on film or in digital form
6. Digital tracking
    a. of images (shapes) in the scene to generate mattes and camera information
    b. from motion-control encoded information of camera moves
    c. of motion control-camera moves from encoded information
7. Digital rotoscoping
    a. integrating software, soft edge, and so on
8. Motion capture
    a. of live-action to control movement of computer-generated characters

Digital Sources

There are three sources of digital data that can be used for image manipulation:

1. Film Images (photographed on film transferred to digital data)
   digital film scanner
   telecine scanner
2. CGI (Computer Generated Images) (images created as digital data)
3. Digital images (images recorded in digital form)
   digital stills camera
   digital video camera

Digital Nonlinear Editing Systems (Off-Line Editing)

Virtually all "off-line" digital editing systems incorporate some effects options as standard (*Flame, Fire, Jaleo, Film Composer,* etc.). The final output is normally at video resolution. Some of the systems can import files from digital film scanners, and others need a conversion utility. *Flame* can import Cineon files and supports resolution up to 2K × 1,558. In most cases it is possible to increase the output resolution by "rezing up" (increasing resolution) prior to recording to film.

Generally, when nonlinear digital editing systems are used in feature film production, an E.D.L. (Edit Decision List) is generated, which is used to conform (to match up all cuts) the cutting copy, or as a direct reference for negative cutting. The actual effects are done at film resolution using either a "film-to-film" or "film-to-digital-to-film" approach, and the final result is cut into the film. However, some of the less complicated opticals are often included in the editing process to serve as guides.

Increasing the Effective Telecine Resolution

A scene requiring pan-and-tilt camera movement inside the frame can benefit from the electronic "pan-and-scan" technique readily available in the telecine scanning approach. The extent of the "pan and scan" is limited because the digitized image has to be "blown up" with the resultant loss of resolution. However, using the "virtual frame" approach, the image can be divided into several segments; each segment is blown up optically during the telecine transfer and scanned separately at full resolution, resulting in the maximum number of pixels per line being used to sample each segment.

An extensive "pan and scan" move can be made across the frame using a video postproduction system like *Flame* without any loss in resolution, as long as the final output is video. A four-segment transfer effectively increases the resolution four times. The virtual frame is now effectively made up of 1,440 pixels per hori-

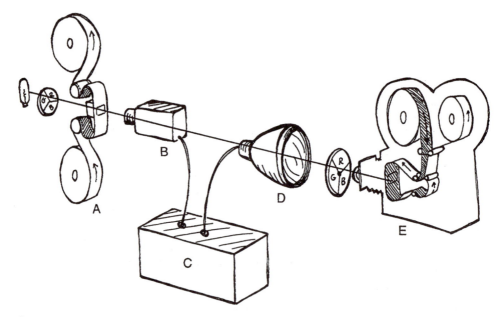

Figure 12.10 "Film-to-Digital-to-Film" duplicating method: (A) film projector; (B) digital camera; (C) electronic storage; (D) cathode ray tube; (E) film camera.

zontal line and the number of lines has doubled. An eight-segment transfer will result in 2,880 pixels per line (which is exactly identical to Quantel's "Domino" scanner) and four times as many lines as the standard telecine transfer at 1:1 ratio.

DIGITAL-TO-FILM TRANSFER

The final stage of the "film-to-digital-to-film" duplicating process involves the recording of the electronic image onto a film negative. This is done on a digital film recorder.

Preparation of Image Files

There are two basic approaches to recording an image onto film from a digital file: CRT (Cathode Ray Tube) and laser. In both cases, the image file has to be prepared to ensure correct color reproduction and to maximize the dynamic range. Often an image file may need to be transferred from one data format to another using software like Domino's *Quicksilver* before it can be outputted to film. It is also possible to increase the effective resolution sent to the recorder by multiplying the pixels, so that a scene digitally processed at a lower resolution can be outputted to film at a higher resolution. An important part of image preparation is to ensure that the digital image is broken up into three separate signals representing the three color-separation components: Red, Green, and Blue.

CRT Digital Film Recorder

The film recorder consists of a film camera and a lens photographing a black-and-white electronic image displayed on a Cathode Ray Tube (CRT). Each frame of film is exposed three times through R-G-B color-separation filters with the CRT tube displaying the corresponding R-G-B record of the image. The film is held in a pin-registered "shuttle" gate and advanced to the next frame at the end of the cycle. The R-G-B color-separation filters are mounted in a circular holder in front of the lens and moved into position sequentially.

Changing Formats

All standard 35mm aspect ratios can be accommodated with the same film gate. A certain amount of repositioning of the image is possible at this stage. Some digital recorders are equipped with cameras that have interchangeable film gates to handle VistaVision and 16mm formats. A change of format also requires repositioning of the camera relative to the CRT and the lens in order to match the

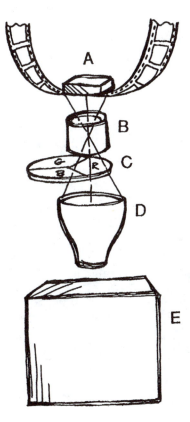

Figure 12.11   (A) Camera gate; (B) Camera lens; (C) R-G-B color wheel; (D) Cathode Ray Tube; (E) Electrical storage and processing.

image size to the appropriate format. Oxberry camera is used on a number of digital recorders including: Solitaire, Sleco, Agfa, and Autologic.

Film Stocks

Either color negative or color intermediate (5244) film stocks can be used to record the image. As this negative is going to be cut in with other nonduplicated material, it is very important that it matches the film stock used for the rest of the production. The sensitivity of the film stock affects the imaging time, which can vary from 15 seconds to 3 minutes per frame. It is also possible to use other film stocks, including the black-and-white panchromatic separation film 5235, to record each color-separation element without the need for R-G-B filters.

Control and Monitoring

The control station of the digital recorder provides exposure control as well as a certain amount of digital retouching before the image is recorded on film. The recorder incorporates an integrated disc-based memory that can store digital film images at full resolution. The image can be viewed at full resolution on a film-color-balanced monitor, which matches the color of the projected film print. Real time replays are possible at lower resolutions.

LASER RECORDERS

The three black-and-white color-separation components (R-G-B) of the image in digital form are used to modulate the light from three separate lasers. The light

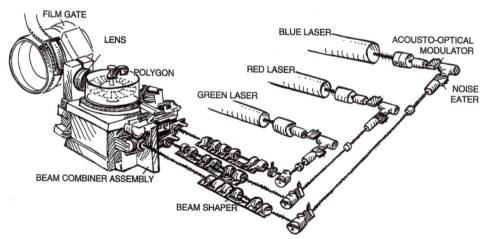

Figure 12.12   Light beams forming the Red, Green, and Blue lasers are modulated by electronic input of the digital information representing a Red, Green, and Blue record of the image. The laser beams are combined to form a full-color image on film.

beams of the Red, Green, and Blue lasers are recombined at the film gate to record a color image. This approach requires a custom-designed film gate. Kodak's "Lightning" film recorder employs the same type of cylindrical gate as the "Lightning" scanner (see Figure 12-6b). The lasers scan the film by means of a sixteen-facet polygon, and the film is advanced by the rotation of the cylindrical gate. The LUX Laser Cinema recorder employs a single-faceted mirror spinning at high speed to deflect the laser beam onto a curved film gate.

DIGITAL CAMERAS

The same digital cameras used to scan film to data can be used for animation and motion-control model cinematography. This is particularly useful when it involves shooting an element that will be composited digitally in any case. Fixed array CCD cameras are more suitable for this type of application. The same digital camera used on the Oxberry Cinescan 6400 scanner (OX6300) can be used on an animation stand or on a motion-control rig for stop-motion work. It has a $3K \times 2K$ chip with a total of 6,291,456 pixels.

Obviously, a digital camera is best suited for stop-frame work because each frame has to be exposed three times through the R-G-B filters. This can put some constraints on motion-control operations but makes no difference in regular animation work. The real drawback is the cost.

Digital Stills Cameras

Often in compositing, a background insert is required that can be a still. Instead of taking a still on film and then scanning it in for digital manipulation and insertion into the composite image, the insert can be shot on a digital camera and recorded directly as digital data. The resolution of even the best digital stills cameras does not approach even the 2K resolution, but bearing in mind that the insert is going to occupy only a proportion of the original frame, this may be sufficient.

Nikon's E3/E3s digital cameras (1,280 × 1,000 pixels) have a Reduction Optical System that enables Nikkor lenses to capture virtually identical full-frame pictures on a 2/3-inch chip as on a conventional 35mm film frame.

A major attraction of a digital camera like Agfa's ePhoto 1280 (1,280 × 960 pixels) is the two-inch LCD screen. A large print of the background image can be prepared with a cutout "window" for the LCD screen so that the image to be photographed can be viewed in its correct relationship to the final composite image. (See Chapter 3, "Visual Effects Compositing.")

Digital Video Camera

Digital video color cameras lack the resolution required for film work, although the resolution of 720 pixels per line is perfectly adequate for television and video recording. However, some of the newer models have increased pixel resolution.

Three video cameras in line would produce over 2K of digital information horizontally. It would take four digital video cameras side by side to cover the frame at 3K resolution horizontally and only 0.5K vertically. However, if the action occupies only a small area of the frame (one-third or one-fourth of the horizontal angle), a digital video camera can provide a live-action image at matching resolution (e.g., live-action inserts into windows of model sets, etc.). If the model shot involves a camera move, then image-tracking software can be used to lock these live-action inserts to specific points within the frame.

Model	Saneson	Pixels (HxV)	Pixel Size (HxVum)	Fill Facrot	Dynamic Range	Frames per Second
1.4i	KAF 1400	1,317 x 1,035	6.8 x 6.8	100%	8 bit	6.9
1.4/HF	KAF 1400	1,317 x 1,035	6.8 x 6.8	100%	8 bit	10.2
1.6i 1.6i/AB 1.6i/TEC	KAF 1600	1,534 x 1,024	9.0 x 9.0	100% 70% AB Models	10 bit	5.1
4.2i 4.2i/HF	KAF 4201	2,029 x 2,044	9.0 x 9.0	100%	8 bit/ 10 bit	2.1 (HF Model)
ES 1.0/ 8 bit ES 1.0/ 10bit ES 1.0/ TH	KAI-1001M	1,008 x 1,008	9.0 x 9.0	60%	8 bit/ 10 bit SC/TH 8 bit	15/30
ES 1.0/ 1215, 1230, 1260	TH-7887A	1,024 x 1,024	14.0 x 14.0	72%	8, 10, 12 bit	15 30 60
6.3i 6.3i/ 10 bit	KAF 6310	3,072 x 2,048	9.0 x 9.0	100% 70% AB Models	8-10 bit	1.2
ES 310	KAI-0 20M	648 x 484	9.0 x 9.0	60%	8 bit	Up to 85
16.8i	KAF 16800	4,096 x 4,096	9.0 x 9.0	100%	8 bit	.5

Figure 12.13 Kodak Megaplus series of digital cameras with performance characteristics.

INDEX